Searching For the Lady of the Dunes
Christopher Setterlund

Contents

Introduction

"Ruth Marie Terry," Victor said as he ran his gloved fingers over the engraved stone, "she finally has her name back." Christopher was crouched beside the stone placing a piece of sea glass he had found earlier alongside many other trinkets that had been left there. For nearly fifty years this had been the resting place of the Lady of the Dunes. Nearly two years earlier Victor had begun what he thought would be just another film project. He could not have been more wrong. Through persistence, perseverance, and causing good trouble where needed Victor had created conversation and helped push the Lady of the Dunes case back to the forefront of law enforcement's minds.

Victor had returned to Provincetown for closure. He had walked miles over the desolate dunes to visit an unremarkable spot among scrub pines where a body had been found in 1974. Christopher, who had become a reliable ally and the writer of the book chronicling Victor's documentary film, had accompanied him on the journey. He had never been to the actual crime scene and needed that closure himself.

As the pair left St. Peter's Cemetery, saying goodbyes to others that had been important to the story of the Lady of the Dunes, Victor felt as though a chapter of his life was over. How did he get there though?

To understand the resolution it is important to go back to the reason why he had been there in the first place. The beginning is long before Victor had heard of the case. It is even before the moment that Ruth Marie Terry ceased to exist and the Lady of the Dunes took her place. The beginning highlights another young woman, another restless soul, taken from this earth too soon. The beginning starts with Sydney.

Prologue

To Sydney -

Eighteen

Fifty-five years ago we were both eighteen, mentally and emotionally rushing to finish high school and begin our forever journey to whatever the future held for us.

That Senior Year, the 'Lunch Bunch' spent every noon across the table from each other, all talking at the same time, trading sandwiches, laughing over the latest joke, or at some girl's huge hair. No worries, no drama, and no way to know what monster was coming for you.

A lot of years have past, but not for you. I'm seventy-three and you'll forever be eighteen, as you are in that class picture I've carried in one handbag to the next for fifty-five years.

I wish we could have been seventy-three together. Rest In Peace, little one. You'll never be forgotten.

- Elaine

Sydney Monzon was murdered in 1968 by notorious Cape Cod serial killer Tony Costa. That is not her legacy. Her legacy is that she was a real person. She was a graduate of Nauset Regional High School in Eastham, full of life, with hopes and dreams, and friends like Elaine who still miss her and remember her.

The Lady of the Dunes was murdered in 1974 by an unknown assailant(s), and left to rot in the barren Provincetown seashore. That should not be her legacy. Like Sydney, the Lady was a real person, full of life, with hopes and dreams, and friends. Some of these friends might still be missing her to this day, wishing they could memorialize her in a beautiful way like Elaine did for Sydney.

Sydney Monzon has a grave where family and friends can at least visit and pay respects. The Lady of the Dunes has a grave, but for nearly five decades had no name, no identity. The overarching purpose of this book, and the film it is a companion to, is not so much to find the killer. It is not so much to ask why this case nears a half-century without a full resolution. No, the purpose of this book is to give the Lady of the Dunes her name back.

It will be stated repeatedly in the forthcoming pages, the Lady of the Dunes was a human, a real person, and at the very least as a human she deserved to have her birth name on her grave stone. For all that she had taken we at least could return that to her.

What follows is an in depth look into the battles fought to find resolution. What follows goes far beyond a behind the scenes look at a true crime documentary. What follows is a search for the truth. Whether that truth ruffled some feathers, was seen as inconvenient, or was welcomed by those feeling it was long overdue, it was a search for the truth nonetheless. What follows is the search for the Lady of the Dunes.

Chapter 1, The Story of the Lady of the Dunes

"Have you ever heard the story of the Lady of the Dunes?" Victor Franko asked of his wife Maura.

"No, I don't think I have. Who is she?"

Victor Franko knew the name, but knew nothing of the person behind one of New England's most enduring and somber unsolved murder mysteries. He was a young filmmaker with a wife and an infant son.

Only recently Victor had spent nearly five months researching and filming his latest project, a documentary about iconic author Henry David Thoreau. He had enjoyed *Walden* as a child in school and fell in love with the idea of Thoreau after coming across a copy of Cape Cod when on a trip to Salem years later.

The subject of the Lady of the Dunes had been brought up to Victor in several interviews during the Thoreau documentary. He thought that it would be wise to at least look into it. On the drive home from Provincetown to Norton, Massachusetts after wrapping up the filming of the Thoreau project Victor had made up his mind to begin searching for the Lady of the Dunes.

Cape Cod, Massachusetts is a sandy peninsula with no shortage of pristine beaches, quaint shops, and delicious restaurants. For nearly a century and a half people have flocked there in the summer in the hopes of creating lasting memories. It has seen more than its share of beautiful moments captured by countless visitors.

Victor was no novice when it came to Cape Cod. Despite growing up an hour from Cape Cod in the small town of South Attleboro on the Rhode Island state border Victor had frequented the Cape a lot during his childhood. Summering in Dennis from the mid-1980s through 1998 afforded him ample opportunity to discover why the peninsula was a vacation destination. Whether it was attending and being kicked out of summer camp in Brewster, dropping untold amounts of quarters into the machines at the Holiday Hill arcade, or simply walking to Sea Street Beach from his family's home on Shad Hole Road, Victor had Cape Cod sand in his shoes and the sea air in his lungs.

Much like in the 1980's when Victor first stepped foot on the Cape in the 1970's Cape Cod in the summer was blissful. There was a year-round population of only 96,656 in 1970. Though summers routinely saw that number more than double the Cape was seen as safe and friendly. It was common for the younger generation to hitchhike all over the peninsula and spend the night sleeping on the cool beach sand if a suitable room was not available.

The Hippie spirit of the 1960s was still alive and well, permeating every nook and cranny of the Cape. T-shirt and bell-bottom clad people filled the streets in their Volkswagens, Toyotas, Fords, and Datsuns. There were sunny days at the beach, dinner at Thompson's Clam Bar or Mildred's Chowder House, and maybe a few drinks and dancing at the Mill Hill Club.

For all of the fun and sun, there have been several notable and disturbing crimes on the peninsula. Truro, barely a town of 1,234 in 1970 saw Tony Costa murder at least four people there between 1968-69. American fashion writer Christa Worthington was brutally raped and murdered in 2002 in her home in Truro. Hadden Clark, currently in prison for two known murders, has claimed to have murdered others and buried some of the evidence on his grandparents' property in nearby Wellfleet.

Having little to no knowledge of the Lady of the Dunes gave Victor Franko a relatively clean slate as to where to start looking for information. General overviews of the story were one thing. To get the true feel of the murder Victor had to be in the moment. He began searching online newspaper archives. An in-depth article from a Boston-based newspaper from December 1974 began to give the basic facts Victor needed.

On the hot afternoon of Friday, July 26, 1974, a woman's body was found in the dunes roughly a mile east of the Race Point Ranger Station in Provincetown. A young girl had been chasing a dog when both dog and girl came upon the body among a cluster of scrub pines. After the young girl had alerted her mother both went to find someone in authority. They returned accompanied by park ranger James Hankins who was quoted in the article saying the scene was 'ghastly.'

Determined to be anywhere between 20-40 years old, 5' 6 1/2" and 145 pounds, the woman had long auburn or reddish-blonde hair tied in a ponytail with rubber elastic. Her nude body was lying face-down on half of a light-green heavy cotton beach blanket, with her head rested on a pair of folded blue jeans.

Upon closer inspection, the scene was quite gruesome. The woman's hands had been removed, with one arm removed at the elbow, presumably to preclude fingerprint identification or other distinguishing markings being found. Blunt force trauma had crushed the left side of her skull. In addition, the young woman's head was nearly severed with an instrument possibly similar to a military entrenching tool though no weapon was found at the scene.

Victor found it interesting when park ranger Hankins was quoted saying 'there was no sign of a struggle, even the sand hadn't been disturbed.'

Initial coroner's reports had her death occurring anywhere from ten days to three weeks before the discovery. Attempts to identify the woman were unsuccessful at the time. In the Boston newspaper article, nearly five months after the murder, there were few leads. Two sets of footprints had been nearby, as well as a set of tire tracks located fifty feet from the body, but no suspects were seen as case solvers.

Unable to be identified she was buried at St. Peter's Cemetery in Provincetown on October 19, 1974, with a simple granite marker stating:

Unidentified Female Body
Found Race Point Dunes
July 26, 1974

The woman's identity has remained unknown for decades. Extensive dental work had been done yet had revealed no definitive answer as to who the 'Lady of the Dunes' was.

For many years the theory was that the mysterious woman was Rory Gene Kesinger. Kesinger was a young criminal. She was part of a gun-running and drug-smuggling group that had been able to elude capture from authorities in Alaska, Texas, Kansas, and California.

In May 1973 Kesinger was finally caught in Pembroke, Massachusetts. She was able to procure an officer's gun during a scuffle but was unable to use it before being cuffed. Kesinger was taken to Plymouth County Jail. On May 26, 1973, while awaiting her trial, and likely a lengthy jail sentence, Kesinger used a smuggled hacksaw to saw through the bars of her cell. She repelled down the wall using bed sheets and escaped in a waiting car. Kesinger has never been seen again.

Kesinger was not connected to the Lady of the Dunes until 1990. Former Provincetown Detective Warren Tobias was of the belief that Kesinger was the unidentified female found in the dunes. She matches the body found in age range and most physical features. Tobias said in an interview with the Provincetown Banner in 1995 that he thought Kesinger was murdered by accomplices that feared she might turn 'snitch' and that her body was subsequently dumped in the dunes.

In 2000 the Lady of the Dunes' body was exhumed for a second time, the first being 1980, in the hopes of using DNA technology to identify her. A sample had been taken from Rory Kesinger's mother for comparison. The results seemed to rule out Kesinger as the Lady, at least according to those who did the testing and saw the results. The body was exhumed a third time in 2013 again with inconclusive results.

In May 2010 new facial recognition software allowed forensic experts from the National Center for Missing and Exploited Children and the Smithsonian Institution to create a composite of the woman's face again in the hopes of her being identified.

Victor spent hours scrolling through archival photos, news clips, and YouTube videos about the case. He was even able to find a black and white crime scene photo from the Provincetown Police Department in the public domain of Wikipedia. It was the most infamous unsolved murder on Cape Cod and one of the most well-known yet unknown crimes of the 20th century. Why was this case such a mystery?

Days were spent combing the internet for information. Victor began to form his own ideas and opinions. Despite it being a brutal and shocking crime the story of the Lady of the Dunes itself was not that uncommon.

According to the FBI's Uniformed Crime Report Data, as of 2020, there were currently 250,000 unsolved murders in the United States. That number is estimated to grow by roughly 6,000 each year. Some of the most infamous unsolved murders and murderers include the Black Dahlia, JonBenet Ramsey, Jack the Ripper, the Zodiac Killer, and others.

In the late 20th and early 21st century missing person data was far less structured and reliable. In a post from the International Commission on Missing Persons dated 2019 there are several reasons why this has been the case:

'There are few comprehensive and reliable statistics regarding the number of persons who go missing throughout the world as a result of trafficking, drug-related violence, and migration. Even the numbers of persons missing as a result of armed conflict and human rights abuses, which are more intensively monitored, are difficult to verify, given the reluctance of most states to deal honestly and effectively with this issue.'

Modern forensic testing and an increase in online databases have made it increasingly possible to find and identify missing persons. This is even the case for those missing for decades. DNA testing is far more prevalent today more than 35 years since British geneticist Sir Alec Jeffreys first discovered the technique of testing at the Department of Genetics at the University of Leicester in England in 1984.

According to Hopkins Medicine.org, a proper DNA test can be performed with as little as 15-25 micrograms of high-quality material. A microgram is one-millionth of a gram. In other terms less than a small grain of sand material is necessary.

So what of the Lady of the Dunes? Her skull resides in Boston. There is enough material, and enough reason, for another DNA test. As of August 2022, there were more than twenty million people in Ancestry's database and more than twelve million people in the 23&Me database. Could one of those people be a connection to the mysterious Lady of the Dunes?

Victor's mind went beyond the Lady herself. He thought of the family whose loved one met her end on Cape Cod in 1974. They deserved closure. What if Victor could be the one to give that closure? His mind got ahead of itself with visions of major media interviews about how he was the one to crack the seemingly impossible Lady of the Dunes case. Now he just had to find that first step.

Another surprising fact in his initial research was the lack of any sort of credible documentary films about the case. Anything Victor found was filled with speculation and sensationalized.

To create something worth spending considerable time and effort on Victor needed sources. He needed people he could speak to that were much more familiar with the Lady of the Dunes than he was. Not just any sources though, he wanted reputable ones. People who could give Victor's newfound project something it could not buy: credibility.

Reading through more news articles Victor quickly amassed a list of people he thought might be helpful. He would do a little background work on them and it would ultimately lead to a dead end. It became frustrating. If he could not find a credible source to begin with then no matter his intentions his project would be seen as nothing more than a retread of other past Lady of the Dunes pieces that he felt were sensationalized.

The list of potential names to interview became filled with lines crossing most of them out. One promising lead remained though his name was James Meads Jr. His father James Sr. had worked extensively on the Lady of the Dunes case while the Chief of the Provincetown Police Department. Victor had seen his name in the first newspaper article he had read from December 1974. It was worth a shot to reach out. The only roadblock was how to contact him.

James Meads Sr. sadly passed away in December 2011 at the age of seventy-eight. He had been the Chief of the Provincetown Police Department for twenty-two years ending his tenure in 1992. It was while reading his obituary through an online news website that Victor had seen Jimmy Jr.'s name. He wrote down all of the potential leads from the obituary, which felt a bit creepy to him, and hoped that one of them could be helpful.

In the day of everybody having caller identification on their telephones, it was not a big surprise that Victor, an unknown number to them, did not have his calls answered by many people. Victor tried them all, including calling a plumbing contractor business. He felt as though that roadblock might be insurmountable. That was until he found Nancy Meads.

Through fate or a stroke of sheer luck, Jimmy Sr.'s sister, Nancy, picked up the phone after only one ring. Being used to having his calls ignored or going to voicemail Victor was caught off guard by the gentle hushed voice that filled his ears.

She said hello in a kind manner. However, once Victor began to explain who he was and why he was calling her the tone changed.

"I'm terribly sorry to bother you," Victor said as humbly as he could, "I am working on a documentary about the Lady of the Dunes murder mystery. I know that Jimmy Meads was your brother and the former Chief of police in Provincetown." There was an audible sigh from Nancy that disheartened Victor.

"Yes he was my brother," she replied, "but I don't have any information that you haven't heard before. You might be better off contacting somebody else."

"I've been trying to find people with intimate knowledge of the story," Victor said quickly. He was speaking faster than he normally would as he knew Nancy was getting close to hanging up. "Please Ms. Meads," he continued, "I'm just trying to find out who she was and why this happened to her."

"Why me though?"

"Your brother was the closest connection to the case I have found thus far. I was hoping maybe he had shared some of his thoughts with you over the years."

"Jimmy was a great man," Nancy said firmly, "we don't want anyone coming around trying to sully his name or reputation."

Victor explained that his only goal with this project was to try his best to solve the Lady of the Dunes case. He told Nancy about Maura and their young son, about their home in Norton, Massachusetts. It was an attempt to build trust with someone who was justifiably protective of her own family's good name.

As the silence lingered on both ends of the phone line Victor began losing hope. Then as if by fate his son came tooling into the room adorably shouting gibberish. He heard a chuckle from Nancy.

"Why don't you give me a call in a few days," she said sweetly, "I think someone else needs your attention right now." The fact that she was willing to speak again was huge in Victor's mind, and his son deserved a little Daddy Time. He thanked her and set up a call for three days from then and the two parted ways.

Victor could hardly contain his excitement as he bounced his son on his knee. He had a good feeling that he had won over Nancy Meads thanks to his little boy.

Three days after their initial call Victor called Nancy Meads again. This time her tone was far more jovial. He explained a little more about his son, in an attempt perhaps to butter her up if that was necessary. It ended up not being the case.

Nancy almost immediately had a piece of important information to share.

"I think the best person for you to speak with is my nephew, Jimmy's son," she said. "His name is also Jimmy. If you give me your number I'll have him call you." Victor pumped his fist in celebration.

"Thank you so much, Ms. Meads," he replied.

"You can call me Nancy. I might have a few other people for you to reach out to." Victor's eyes widened and he smiled so widely that he thought Nancy might be able to hear it through the phone.

"I can't tell you how much I appreciate this Nancy," Victor said as the brief phone call ended. Although he knew a call from Jimmy Meads Jr. was likely not imminent he could not help but stare at his phone in anticipation.

Two days passed with no phone call. On the third day after speaking with Nancy, Victor began to think maybe Jimmy was not swayed by his aunt to give a chance to some strange filmmaker. The afternoon drifted on and Victor began helping Maura prepare dinner after she had gotten home from work. It was nearing 6 pm and he was in the midst of unevenly peeling several Russet potatoes to be boiled when from the living room he heard the familiar sound of his phone ringing. He dropped the potato in his hand and ran off.

The name on the Caller ID was unfamiliar but said Provincetown, Massachusetts. It was him! Victor answered, trying to stay as calm as he could.

"Is this Victor Franko?"

"Yes, it is."

"My Aunt Nancy told me I needed to call you," he said with a hint of hesitation. "My name is Jimmy Meads Jr."

"Thank you so much for speaking with me," Victor replied. He shook his head as he sounded overly wooden in his response.

"I apologize for not getting to you sooner, but I was working all day. When I got done and checked my phone there was a message from my aunt saying I needed to speak with a film director about my Dad. So what is this about?"

"I am in the beginning of a possible project about the Lady of the Dunes murder mystery and I know your father was an important person when it came to that case." Victor could hear Jimmy sigh loudly.

"There are plenty of resources you can find online about the case and my father's involvement in it."

"I've started looking into them but I thought it would be better to have those who actually knew him speak on it."

"You know, my father was a great cop, a credit to the force and to Ptown," Jimmy said sounding like he was ready for the phone call to end. "Yet after all of his years of service, the main thing people want to remember him for is the Lady of the Dunes. I'm sorry but I will not be part of something that points the finger at my father as to why it hasn't been solved."

"That's not my intention," Victor quickly replied. He was trying to stop the inevitable hanging up of the phone. "I want to try to solve it, to find out who she was. I don't want to blame law enforcement, and definitely not your father." The line was quiet. Had Jimmy hung up during Victor's explanation? He then heard another sigh from Jimmy and breathed his own in relief.

"So how exactly can I help you then, Mr. Franko?"

"I just want as much information as I can get about your father, about his connection to the case. I am just getting familiar with the Lady of the Dunes and am looking for people to help guide me in the right direction."

"How much time do you have?" Jimmy chuckled a bit and Victor grabbed a notebook and a pen.

"As much as you'll give me." What came next was the turning point for Victor as far as the Lady of the Dunes project went.

Jimmy started with the bad news. It was highly unlikely that any law enforcement, current or former, would be willing to speak on the record about the case. Much like Jimmy Meads Sr. many law enforcement associated with the case had previously been attacked by the media.

"It's a unique case, and a tough road if you go that way Victor," Jimmy admitted. "I'm not saying don't contact past and present members of the Ptown Police. Just don't expect much cooperation."

"I understand. I mean almost fifty years and no suspects, no real leads. There's not much positive that can come from people asking about that."

"There's a reason why my family has declined every chance to participate in any story surrounding this case. It's never a glowing portrait of law enforcement and we love my father too much to put our names behind any smear campaigns."

Jimmy told a story of how in 2006 a documentary television show came asking about the Lady of the Dunes and his father's involvement. The show centered around a psychic profiler, a medium, and a paranormal investigator as they tried to solve cold cases with their unorthodox methods. The Meads Family declined involvement when they were approached.

"They didn't solve a thing on that show," Jimmy said angrily. "So you can understand why I was naturally skeptical of you when my aunt mentioned you were a documentary filmmaker, right?"

"I can understand," Victor replied, "that's why I tried to explain my motives from the start. I figured after almost fifty years I was not the first weirdo to ever contact you about the Lady of the Dunes." Jimmy had a hearty laugh and from there the conversation became more of old friends catching up rather than strangers who had just met.

Victor spent copious time scribbling notes onto a few pages of his notebook, Jimmy rattled off several names of people that needed to be contacted next. There were also several minutes-long stretches where Victor simply listened to wonderful stories being told. Jimmy spoke of Provincetown in the 1970s and how different it was from present-day. He painted such a vivid picture. Fishermen were arriving with their catch, young people dancing the night away at the affectionately nicknamed Piggy's nightclub, and families lining up thirty-deep to grab lunch at the Lobster Pot. Victor could see it as he closed his eyes. It seemed impossible that such a horrific crime as what happened to the Lady of the Dunes could have happened during such a Utopian time.

After nearly an hour on the phone, and with the tantalizing scent of dinner coming from the kitchen, Victor knew he was needed by Maura. He began to wrap up what ended up being a delightful conversation with Jimmy Meads Jr.

"Thank you so much, Jimmy," Victor said. " I know I've taken up a lot of your time and I wanted you to know how much I appreciate it and the leads you have given me."

"You're very welcome," he responded, "if you need any more information just give me a call. Good luck with your story. My aunt said she had a good feeling about you and she was right." The two ended the conversation with the intention of connecting again somewhere down the road.

Victor entered the kitchen with Maura sitting at the table halfway done with her meal and their son with half his meal on himself.

"How did it go?" Maura asked curiously. "I heard you laughing a lot more than I expected."

"It went really well," Victor replied with a wide smile. "I think I've got something here."

Victor had no idea of the pull that the Meads Family had and what their support of his project would mean. Jimmy's leads were big and behind the scenes, Nancy Meads was making calls and endorsing Victor. Knowing how protective of their legacy the Meads family were the fact that they were actively working with Victor gave him and his project credibility that money could not buy.

For his part, Victor began with a man named Bob. He had been in local law enforcement and politics for decades. More than that, being a native of Provincetown Bob had some knowledge of the Lady of the Dunes case. However, it was through Bob that Victor became acquainted with another infamous Cape Cod criminal: Antone Charles Costa.

Bob gave Victor a crash course in all things Tony Costa. He explained that Costa had been a carpenter living in Provincetown during the late 1960s. Between 1968-1969 Tony had been accused of murdering anywhere from four to eight young women.

In March 1969 three bodies were found in a heavily wooded area of Truro. Those bodies belonged to Patricia Walsh, Mary Anne Wysocki, and Sydney Monzon. It was later revealed to be Costa's garden for growing marijuana and he was subsequently arrested. The bodies were viciously mutilated with three of them having their hearts removed. Those same three all had signs of necrophilia as well. A fourth body belonging to Susan Perry had been found a mile and a half from the site of the other three.

After being diagnosed with schizoid personality and despite his lawyers saying he was too into drugs to know what he was doing Tony Costa was convicted of two murders and sentenced to life in prison in May 1970. He died May 12, 1974, with the official report explaining his death as suicide by hanging via a leather belt.

Hearing of another grizzly crime in Truro began to chip away at Victor's pristine view he had of the outer shores of Cape Cod that he had during his filming of the Thoreau documentary. The fact that these two cases occurred in such proximity in both distance and time was shocking to Victor.

Bob seemed to labor with his words as he dove deeper into the horrors of Tony Costa. Victor, being an investigative filmmaker, tried to gently ask for more information as this was all new to him. He soon found out that for Bob, it was reliving a nightmare that he did not enjoy digging up.

"I'm sorry," Victor said with empathy, "Tony Costa is a new story to me. I don't mean to try to push you into reliving that case. It must have been a really shocking crime." Bob sighed and gave a quiet 'mmm hmm' sound in agreement. It sounded as if he was on the verge of tears.

"It's not your fault," Bob replied after clearing his throat, "even though it's been over fifty years those memories come flooding back in vivid color every time."

"I won't bring it up again," Victor said.

"The reason why it's such a tough subject is because Sydney Monzon was my girlfriend at one time." Victor let out a gasp and then felt bad for doing so.

"Oh my God, I'm so sorry."

"We had both moved on, she had been living with Tony in a place owned by a man named Staniford Sorrentino. They were into drugs and Sorrentino was into some bad things. She ended up getting caught up in all of it and..." Bob trailed off, the emotion had gotten the better of him.

"Would it be alright if I called you again sometime?" Victor wanted to leave Bob alone with his grief for the time being.

"Yes, that would be fine."

Victor hung up and took a deep breath. That conversation had been more intense than he had expected. He made it a point to write down in his notebook two names: Tony Costa and Sydney Monzon. They were both heavily underlined.

After speaking with Bob and learning about Tony Costa it began to paint a much more complicated picture of what Provincetown and the surrounding area were like during the late 1960s and early 1970s. Bob had mentioned drug use when it pertained to Costa. Could that also have played a part in the Lady of the Dunes? Drugs didn't necessarily lead to murder but it was something he could not eliminate.

Victor began searching for others who were around at the time to connect with. Nancy Meads had left a message on his phone the week prior and gave him several names, many of whom were former police officers in the town. He thought at the very least mentioning Nancy to them might get him a few minutes. It turned out that Bob was the anomaly.

What followed over the next several days was terribly disheartening and somewhat unnerving for Victor. On a sheet of paper, he listed four names of former Provincetown law enforcement. When he was done speaking with them all that he had was a torn-up paper and a feeling that there was much more to this project than had been presented in the past.

All four people Victor spoke with refused to give him any sort of interview for the prospective documentary. Three of the four people responded with a variation of 'No way in Hell!' when Victor asked them to be interviewed about the Lady of the Dunes.

When pressed for a reason one of the people replied that they 'didn't want to make any enemies.' They continued by explaining that Provincetown is a small community.

"Everybody knows everybody," the person said quickly and quietly. It was as if they feared even speaking the words aloud. "At some point, everybody who lives here is either an artist, a fisherman, a cop, or married to someone else who grew up in town."

"Is there anything you can give me? Anything at all?"

"We're a tight-knit community here," the person replied in a tone that conveyed the gravity of what he was about to say. "The people are aware of and protective of, the image of our town. That story(the Lady of the Dunes) is a part of history that should be left alone."

"I'm just trying to find some answers."

"If you want answers then stay where you are and look from there. Don't come up here sniffing around." Victor cold a cold chill from where the conversation was going. There was a long pause. "There are people here who don't want that case to be solved. Now you think about that."

The person hung up leaving Victor in stunned silence at his desk. The way that the person said for him to 'think about that' gave him pause briefly. Was it a warning, or a threat? This was the first time that he felt a sense of unease. Maybe the Lady of the Dunes was meant to remain a mystery?

The next evening while having dinner Maura could tell that something was weighing on Victor. He had not told her of the series of unsuccessful phone calls and had certainly not told her of the ominous tone of the last one with a former member of law enforcement.

"I'm not sure if this project is going to work," Victor said with disappointment.

"What happened?" Maura answered with surprise. "You had been doing well, getting the Meads Family to talk to you was huge you said."

"I've spoken with a few former cops the last few days. If they didn't immediately reject my interview request then they were telling me I would be wise to stay out of Provincetown and that some in the community don't want the case to be solved."

"That's strange," Maura replied, "it's been over forty years. Why are they so protective of this case?"

"I mean the town is very tight," Victor admitted, "I've heard that from basically everyone I've spoken to on and off the record."

"It just feels like there's way more going on here than just a girl found in the dunes."

"I agree, I just don't want to create a fluff piece that ends up in a pile with the other speculative pieces on the case that I've been seeing online."

While eating dinner the couple discussed the pros and cons of pressing on despite some initial resistance. Victor had a few more names Nancy Meads had given him. He decided that since she had been so hospitable to him and gone out of her way to vouch for him and find him contacts he owed it to her to at least use those contacts.

First was a local fisherman. He immediately refused to comment further once Victor explained why he was calling. He did not even get a chance to name-drop Nancy. The second number belonged to another former police officer. Victor dialed the number.

"Hello?"

"Hello sir, I don't want to take up much of your time, but Nancy Meads gave me your information. I am beginning a documentary about the Lady of the Dunes case and..." The voice on the other end cut Victor off.

"Oh yeah, Peter," he said, "I was expecting you. Didn't know you spoke to Nancy Meads."

"My name isn't Peter," Victor responded in confusion. "I'm Victor Franko."

"This isn't Peter Manso?"

"No sir, do you have a minute though to talk about the Lady of the Dunes?"

"You're doing a documentary about that case?"

"Yes, I've already spoken with Nancy and Jimmy Meads Jr."

"There's already a documentary being made by Peter Manso. Whatever it is that you're doing is pointless, it's already being done. Don't waste your time." The man on the line grew gruffer with each passing word before hanging up.

Victor pulled his phone from his ear and stared at it. There was already another documentary being made? Maybe it was a sign to cut his losses. He began mindlessly scrolling social media to wash away the disappointment. Curiosity got the better of him and Victor began searching for this Peter Manso on the internet and social media. He wanted to see who had beaten him to the punch.

Only after clicking on an artsy black and white profile photo did Victor realize who this man was. The man eighty years of age was a well-known and respected author and journalist with a Ph.D. in English from the University of California at Berkeley. Manso, a New York native who had relocated to Truro, had written seminal biographies of Norman Mailer and Marlon Brando. His most recent work had come in 2011. The book

Reasonable Doubt: The Fashion Writer, Cape Cod, and the Trial of Chris McCowen covered the murder of his Truro neighbor Christa Worthington in 2002 and the trial of her alleged killer Christopher McCowen.

It turned out that Manso was working on a Lady of the Dunes film of his own along with a few others. Manso certainly had name recognition and credibility as an author and journalist. Rather than being intimidated, or conceding defeat, Victor decided to reach out to Peter to compare notes. It surely could not be any worse than the law enforcement refusing interviews and hanging up. He sent him a direct message explaining what he was doing for the Lady of the Dunes and waited.

Much to Victor's surprise Peter Manso responded almost immediately as if he had been waiting for such a message. It was agreed upon to have a phone conversation the next day. It would be a call Victor would not soon forget.

Late in the morning on the next day, Victor called Peter Manso. He had spent a little time researching him and was now a little excited to speak with such an accomplished writer.

"This is Peter," a crusty voice answered.

"Peter, hi this is Victor Franko, I contacted you on Facebook the other day."

"Yes." There was a pause. Victor waited a moment for more and then continued.

"Is this a bad time?"

"Well that all depends on why you are calling." Victor's initial excitement over speaking with Manso was quickly being replaced with confusion.

"I understand you are producing a documentary on the Lady of the Dunes." There was another pause.

"Can you speak up? I'm having a little trouble hearing you."

"Of course. I said, I was told that you are producing a documentary on the Lady of the Dunes. I too am producing a documentary on the subject matter." There was yet another pause and Victor wondered if maybe he needed to speak even louder.

"And?"

"Would you like to talk about it?"

"Sure, I like to talk."

"What do you want to know?"

"You called me, I assume you have some things that you'd care to know."

"I do," Victor replied trying his best to remain friendly, "but the phone works both ways and I'm sure you want to know something about my production."

"Victor, you are going to need to speak louder if you want me to hear you."

"Maybe its a bad connection, do you want me to call you back?" Victor was already speaking louder than he wanted to with a napping son in the same house.

"There's no need for that," Manso said dismissively, "just speak louder." Victor walked as far from his son's room as he could while remaining in the house and let it rip.

"I have spoken to a few people in Provincetown that are encouraging me to produce the documentary. All of them recommended I reach out to you."

"Have you read my book?"

"Which one?" Manso aggressively cleared his throat.

"Well, it would be nice if you have read any of them, but more important to the topic at hand, the one entitled Ptown: Art, Sex, and Money on the Outer Cape."

"No I have not."

"You should. Unless you are familiar with some of the characters in this story, you are not going to come close to solving her identity or finding her murderer."

"Is this the HBO deal that you are working on?" Victor had done his own researching into Manso's Lady of the Dunes project.

"Maybe. I have worked with HBO before with the Roy Cohn documentary." Manso paused before taking a sarcastic jab at Victor. "Have you seen that at least?"

"Yes I have, I enjoyed it." Victor waited for some sort of positive response, there wasn't one. "Both Meads brothers have shown interest in being interviewed for my documentary."

"Really? I find that interesting."

"Are they working with you?"

"Not as of right now, but they will. I have all the major players locked in. We are all stocked up for the cast and crew."

"I spoke with a few of your players."

"Players?" Manso responded like he hadn't just said 'major players.'

"Freddie, Paulie, Warren."

"I wouldn't go as far as calling them players. They know a great deal about the story. I consider them experts on the topic."

"Good to hear." Victor was trying to find some common ground with Manso who seemed content with throwing water on Victor's project.

"Just so you know, very few people will speak with you. Especially law enforcement."

"Really?"

"Yup, good luck trying to get anyone in uniform to call you back."

"I hate to disagree with you." Victor was interrupted by a shouting Manso.

"Victor! Please speak louder and clearer!" Manso's tone during much of the call made what Victor said next even sweeter.

"I've already spoken to the DA's Office last week." There was a familiar long pause.

"You're full of shit." Victor laughed loud enough for Manso to hear clearly.

"No, not completely. But I left them a message last Monday." Manso was not impressed.

"I doubt you'll hear from them."

"Peter, if my little documentary can help you get what you want, so be it. I don't want to be part of any problem." Victor thought he was being rather amiable, however Manso saw him in a less favorable light.

"I don't see you as anything like that. You have such a small budget you're borderline irrelevant." Victor smirked and rolled his eyes.

"If you say so. Still, if I can help."

"Well first things first, you need to read my book. And when you call me back, I want your opinion on who you think was involved with her murder. And I do not want to hear about Whitey Bulger. You can sell that to the tourists on Commercial Street, cause I'm not buying."

"Ok, will do. It was a pleasure."

"Thank you Victor," Manso said with the phone hanging up immediately after. Victor set out to possibly find a cheap eBook version of Manso's *Ptown* book.

However before moving forward with the book assignment that was Manso's *Ptown* Victor decided to make a call to an old friend he had. This friend had produced one of Victor's earlier films that had been based in Rhode Island. After a brief chat they decided to get together and have coffee. Their meetup became another watershed moment for the Lady of the Dunes project.

Within a week this friend had put Victor in touch with a former officer with the Providence, Rhode Island Police Department. It was a shot in the dark but Victor asked the contact about anybody they might know who could help him gain access to information about the Lady of the Dunes.

This person asked Victor to give him a little time and they would see what they could do. Victor expected it to be days or maybe even weeks before he heard back. It ended up being by the end of the same day. What Victor received was more than he could have hoped for. It was a list of several names including former FBI agents who had worked on the Whitey Bulger case, other former Federal agents, former members of the Massachusetts State Police, and people that were connected with potential murder suspect and convicted serial killer Hadden Clark. It was an overwhelming litany of new and potentially game changing contacts. Victor was incredibly grateful. However just having the names did not assure these people would wish to be interviewed.

Over time, much to Victor's delight, all of the contacts would respond to him. However it was a pair of new contacts that came from the bunch that proved to be invaluable. Unbeknownst to him several of the new contacts Victor connected with had passed his information on to a pair of very important people when it came to the Lady of the Dunes case.

When an unlisted phone number came across Victor's Caller ID he did not hesitate to answer. During the past several weeks he had become accustomed to receiving unlisted calls pertaining to the Lady of the Dunes, although some ended up being spam telemarketers. This was not one of them.

The person on the other line had a faintly familiar voice. They asked if they were speaking to Victor Franko. When Victor identified himself the unknown person explained that they had been told by several people that they needed to get in touch with someone who was asking around about the Lady of the Dunes. Victor bluntly asked if they had spoken before. The person admitted that indeed they had a brief phone conversation a few weeks prior.

It all came back to Victor. A few weeks earlier this person, who had deep connections to Provincetown, had been connected to Victor through Jimmy Meads. When Victor told this person that he was indeed working on a project centering around the nearly fifty-year-old murder mystery he was met with resistance. He did not understand why at the time and the conversation ended rather uneventfully.

The dots became connected during this second phone conversation. The person confessed that they were friends with Peter Manso. They were quite frank when they said that they really shouldn't even be speaking to Victor since Manso was also working on a Lady of the Dunes project. When Victor pointed out that it was this person who reached out this time the phone call rapidly came to a close. Before hanging up Victor tried to leave a little opening for the future. He said if anything changed with Manso's project would it be all right for Victor to reach out. The mysterious voice relented. However with it came explicit instructions. He would be the one to reach out to Victor if it was appropriate. Victor agreed to the terms and the phone call ended. Much like the first time they had spoken Victor assumed that he would not be hearing from that person again. It felt like a dead end.

His luck would change shortly. The other one of the two important new contacts made through the Providence Police connection was going to enter the stage. Victor would soon be introduced to Agent X.

Chapter 4, Peggy Sue

Victor spent a few days after speaking with his connection in Providence sifting through the subsequent pile of new contacts. Despite the good fortune of some new contacts outside of Provincetown, inside the town's borders was a different story. Much as Peter Manso had said, and much like Victor had already repeatedly experienced, no former local police wanted to be interviewed for the documentary. His well of contacts from Nancy Meads had almost run dry. There was one phone number left though. It had no name, only a number with a note Victor jotted down that said 'Just Call Her.'

Nancy had been insistent that Victor trust her and call this woman. Victor had little to lose. He was staring down reading Manso's 335-page *Ptown* book and decided to put that off a little longer by making the phone call. What he got was far more than he could have expected.

After a few rings, a woman answered.

"Hello ma'am," Victor said in an overly polite manner, "my name is Victor. Nancy Meads recommended I call you for a film I am creating about the Lady of the Dunes murder."

"Ooh yes," she replied, "I have been expecting your call. What can I help you with?"

"I'm not sure actually. When Nancy gave me your number she didn't give me your name, or even what your connection might be to this case. She just insisted I call you."

"I asked her not to give my name. If we're going to speak I would rather not give my real name. Just call me Peggy Sue." This call was already becoming strange, but Victor decided to just go with it.

"Sure Peggy Sue it is. What do you know about the Lady of the Dunes? Were you around Provincetown when it happened?"

"Yes, I was. I lived in Provincetown at the time."

"Did you grow up there?"

"I'd rather not say. My father was a fisherman."

"Did he work out of Provincetown?"

"I'd rather not say." Victor started to think that Peggy Sue wanted to share her story with as few follow-up questions as possible. He decided to just listen and take notes.

"I was the youngest of five children. The murder happened in 1974, right?"

"Yes, July 1974."

"In the summer of 1974, I was seventeen years old. I spent many a night sitting at the bar of the Crown and Anchor. I would wait to be picked up."

"Picked up?" Peggy Sue giggled quietly.

"I wasn't there to drink. I needed to make some money and that was usually a quick and easy way. In the summer there are lots of rich men looking to throw their money around for pretty young girls." That line got Victor's antennae up but he kept quiet as Peggy Sue was just getting started.

"I worked as a waitress," Peggy Sue continued. "Don't get me wrong, I made good money doing that, but I made five times that during the summer by just sitting at the bar waiting for an older gentleman to buy me a drink."

"So you worked as a prostitute?" Victor asked, hoping he wouldn't offend her.

"If you want to call it that, yes."

"You were seventeen? Did your parents know what was going on?" Peggy Sue cackled.

"My mother knew, but my father was clueless. He was busy with his fishermen friends in Dennis and Yarmouth joking about how Provincetown was 'Down Cape.' Down like a toilet where you flushed your shit to. He said it was nothing but gays, weirdos, and Communists."

"How did your mother know about what you were up to?"

"Most people knew that there was way more going on behind the scenes. There were underage girls and boys everywhere in Provincetown, especially at the Crown. In fact, you couldn't go more than a few feet without seeing sex, drugs, or guns."

"And nobody said anything?"

"As long as the trash was taken out before sunrise it was all kept quiet. It was good for tourism. During the summer the tourists would come and exploit everything in sight, including underage girls and boys."

"I can't believe that the police never stepped in and did anything."

"Please, during that time a lot of the cops in town worked part-time in the summers at these same clubs as bouncers or doormen. The Crown and Anchor had an off-duty cop working the door who would let underage kids in all the time!"

It was mind-boggling to Victor the scene that Peggy Sue was setting. Sex workers, drugs, guns, it seemed like something out of a movie.

"So this was going on at most of the local clubs?" Victor asked, hesitant to hear about the further exploits of the Sodom and Gomorrah that Provincetown in the 1970s seemed to be.

"Absolutely. Clubs, hotels, and restaurants, so many of them were involved in the sex industry then. I can only tell you what I remember and what I saw. I can tell you someone that you should check into, a man named Staniford Sorrentino. He was running the Crown and Anchor at the time." Hearing that name for the third time was like a cold slap in the face.

"You are the third person to mention Sorrentino. What do you know about him?"

"I don't know how much he benefited from the sex industry," Peggy Sue said. "It could have just been supplying the booze, drugs, and rooms. It could have been more. That's why you're making this film." That reminded Victor of why he had called her in the first place.

"What do you remember about the Lady of the Dunes?"

"I remember reading about it in the newspaper. The first thing that popped into my mind was that she was another sex worker. She could have been killed by her client, or by her pimp. It's hard to say."

"Did you remember many of the clients you had during those days? Were any of them dangerous?"

"Oh God honey," Peggy Sue chuckled, "I think my best summer I screwed a typical football team during July and August. Hard to remember all of the faces and personalities."

"A football team?"

"That's nothing," she continued, doubling down, "my big tough boyfriend who hated the gays that came in during the summer would allow them the privilege of going down on him for $50 each. I think during that same summer he had been blown by more than eighty men. I was tame compared to him."

Victor didn't know how to respond. Peggy Sue spoke so jovially and freely about her adventures that it almost made it feel less taboo.

"Do you have any idea who the Lady of the Dunes might have been?"

"Based solely on the description it's hard to say. On many nights during the summer I'd be sitting at the bar waiting for an older man to buy me a drink and make me an offer. There would often be other pretty young girls seated around me. Some could have been sex workers, some could have been innocent tourists. During July 1974 I was there a lot and could have very easily been sitting only a few stools away from the poor girl on her last night. But I cannot say so with any certainty."

Victor glanced at his open laptop to see the time. He had been speaking with Peggy Sue for nearly three hours. It felt like he had just watched a movie. He needed to take a moment to regroup after having so much unbelievable information dumped into his lap.

"Thank you so much for speaking with me Peggy Sue," Victor said. "I am sorry I took up so much of your time."

"It was my pleasure, Mr. Franko. And no, thank you for doing this documentary. This story needs to be told. Beyond just the Lady of the Dunes, the story of the wild times in Provincetown needs to be told too. Please let me know if you need any more information."

Victor thanked her again and ended the conversation. He didn't know if he needed a cigarette or a shower after hearing all of that. First and foremost Victor knew he had a new top name to research and that was Staniford Sorrentino. He had popped up too often to not be someone very important to the case. It looked like Victor had a book to get to reading.

Chapter 5, Needle In A Haystack

Amid a global pandemic, and being that it was now late January in Massachusetts, Victor found that heading out of his home in Norton less than appealing. Thankfully in the age of technology, he was able to easily find and order a used copy of Peter Manso's *Ptown* book. By taking advantage of expedited shipping he received his package only two days later.

Feeling like he was a child doing a book report again Victor planned to binge-read the 335-page book in two days if possible. He survived on copious amounts of black coffee and took liberal amounts of notes. Of specific interest to Victor was the information in the book about Staniford Sorrentino.

Victor had tried basic searches online for Sorrentino. The main results were his federal tax evasion trial in 1983 and his stated friendship with noted Boston mobster James 'Whitey' Bulger. While on trial Sorrentino in his own words described Bulger as "a sensitive, intelligent, intuitive person." Victor made sure to make a note to look into Bulger later.

The trouble was finding much else in the way of information about Sorrentino away from the federal trial. Bob had suggested looking into Sorrentino, as had Peggy Sue. Her story of him supplying alcohol, drugs, and rooms for sex workers at the Crown and Anchor specifically got Victor's attention. This man seemed to be a huge presence in Provincetown in the 1970s, yet finding detailed information about the man himself was akin to trying to find the proverbial needle in the haystack. Victor hoped that Manso's book would help to shed light on the darkness that was Sorrentino.

The binging of *Ptown* took two and a half days as husband and father duties took precedence over reading. However, the reading was worth it as Victor was able to paint a much better picture of who Staniford Sorrentino was.

Manso's *Ptown* described Sorrentino as a "decadent, roly-poly Nero who presided over" the Crown and Anchor. A former waitress at the Crown named Carolyn Tacke remarked that she could not remember a time Sorrentino was not high on uppers or cocaine. However, she noticed that rather than him getting thinner due to drug use he gained weight.

Sorrentino had come to Cape Cod in the early 1950s. Then he was a penniless high school music teacher and a former Opera singer. He slowly clawed his way up the ranks in Provincetown in the late 1950s. The big break came when he entered a business partnership with Boston brothers Henry and Carmine Vara in 1961. Together they bought the Sea Horse Inn hotel and transformed it into an entertainment complex known as the Crown and Anchor.

His Crown and Anchor was engaged in a heated rivalry with the nearby A-House and its owner Reggie Cabral. The constant one-upping included innocuous things like their outdoor patios, to each needing an S&M bar. Over time the flamboyantly gay Sorrentino transformed the Crown and Anchor from a delightful mix of gay and straight, men and women, to almost entirely gay men. Staniford would claim that to be false as women were "allowed in the pool and bar area."

Sorrentino would brazenly skim money off the top of the cash cow that was the Crown and Anchor. He enjoyed the company of younger men and having a supply of disposable income helped to gain their attention better than his bald and overweight physical appearance.

Sorrentino had paid cash for his house in Truro. This coupled with his lavish white Rolls-Royce, impressive collection of antiques, and numerous trips to Europe became his downfall. In 1984 Sorrentino was convicted of eight counts of tax evasion and sentenced to three years in prison. He was also ordered to pay $40,000 in fines plus all of his back taxes.

While out on bail awaiting his appeal Sorrentino fled to the Bahamas with one of his boyfriends who quickly left him to go back home. Sorrentino spent the next five years on the run. There were a few close calls but Staniford slipped by. His luck ran out when he flew back into Logan Airport in Boston on a small plane. He was detained by Customs and subsequently sentenced to six years in prison. After being released Sorrentino fell ill and died during the summer of 1998.

Much like after chatting with Peggy Sue Victor felt the need to either light a cigarette or take a shower after reading the Ptown book. Despite the book painting a vivid picture of the sex, drugs, and overall debauchery that was happening around Provincetown during the early 1970s there was still something missing.

Victor remembered an emotional Bob remarking about his ex-girlfriend Sydney Monzon moving in with serial killer Tony Costa. The house was owned by Staniford Sorrentino. Costa was only mentioned briefly in passing in Peter Manso's book. Victor couldn't help but be curious about the connection between Sorrentino and Costa. He was curious about how Sorrentino fit in with Whitey Bulger and ultimately the Lady of the Dunes as well.

Provincetown in the late 1960s and early 1970s felt like an onion with many layers that washed over each other like salty ocean waves. Victor also likened it to a spider's web where everything was intertwined. The Lady of the Dunes was at the center of the web, at least in Victor's project, yet more and more names were ending up stuck in the web. These names were the center of their own story's spider web, names like Sorrentino, Costa, Bulger, and the like.

The main stage of the Provincetown scene in the 1970s seemed to center around Sorrentino and the Crown and Anchor. Victor reached out to the Crown and Anchor itself in the hopes that either people who worked there in the 1970s were still there, or that someone knew how to contact former employees.

It ended up all being for naught. A call placed to the owner of the establishment went unanswered. Victor was not discouraged though, he had the invaluable resources of the Meads Family. After being put in touch with Peggy Sue it was time to give another call to Nancy Meads to see if she had any other hot leads.

It turned out that she did. Although this again was a double-edged sword. Nancy had a contact with intimate knowledge of the Crown and Anchor, specifically people who worked there during the 1970s that would be willing to speak with Victor. The only issue was that much like with Peggy Sue this contact did not wish to be named. Nancy promised she would be worth it and Victor trusted her. He took down her number and prepared to make the call.

After a few rings, a woman picked up. Victor explained who he was and that he had been given her number from Nancy. The woman was happy to speak to him and wished to be identified only as 'Dolly.' Though she did not wish to give her real name she did end up giving Victor several names of former Crown and Anchor employees. Many of these still lived in the area and she believed they would be willing to talk about the 1970s and Sorrentino.

The conversation delved into what Victor had learned about Sorrentino from Manso's book and essentially fact-checking many things versus what Dolly recalled. She was feisty and enjoyed spilling dirt of what she knew. Victor appreciated her candor. Dolly would turn out to be far more valuable than he could have imagined.

The conversation drew to an end and Victor thanked Dolly for her time and the names she gave him. It was up to him to pursue them. Before they parted ways Dolly said she would do some work behind the scenes and get back in touch with Victor in a week or so. Nancy Meads had come through again.

Over the next few days, Victor reached out to people. The first was one that Dolly had deemed as the most important. Victor reached out to the DNA Doe Project. It was a non-profit organization created in 2017. Their mission statement was to identify John and Jane Does using genetic genealogy.

The organization solved its first case on March 5, 2018, when a John Doe previously known as Joseph Newton Chandler III was identified as Robert Ivan Nichols. They stepped onto the national stage on April 11, 2018, at a press conference in Troy, Ohio. When a Jane Doe known only as 'Buckskin Girl' was identified as Marcia L. King it was then that the world knew of the potential of genetic genealogy to solve cold case identifications. Since then they have helped solve hundreds of cold cases.

It made perfect sense to Victor. The Lady of the Dunes was one of the country's most well-known Jane Doe's. The idea of a non-profit with a track record of cracking cold cases working to help give a name to the Lady of the Dunes was exciting.

The name Dolly had given Victor specifically was Margaret Press, PhD. She had co-founded the DNA Doe Project with Dr. Colleen Fitzpatrick. After spending much of her life as a software designer Press had developed an affinity for mystery writing. She wrote essays, short stories, and novels including a true crime based on a murder in her own neighborhood. As DNA testing became more prevalent Press joined in the movement. It culminated with the creation of the DNA Doe Project.

Margaret Press was based in California, three hours behind in time from the East Coast. Seeing that it was 11am Victor thought that a phone call at 8am Pacific Time might go unanswered. He decided to email instead. Hoping to capture her attention he titled the email simply 'Lady of the Dunes.' After writing a short paragraph and sending it Victor got to fumbling around the internet. He had barely had time to open a new tab when he heard the sound of a new email received.

It was from Margaret Press. Her response? 'Can we talk?' By 8:10am Pacific Time Victor and Margaret were engaged in conversation.

Victor began as he did with all of the new people he connected with. He explained his project. He told Margaret how his wish was to solve the case, to give the Lady of the Dunes a name. Victor thought it would be a great opportunity to attempt to solve the case using genetic genealogy. Margaret's response shocked Victor.

"We've already tried that twice," she said.

"Twice?"

"In 2017 and 2019. 2017's attempt didn't get very far, but 2019 was different. I feel we were close to solving that case."

"What happened?"

"Things went dark, not on our end. We were in contact with the town detective, the local newspaper and the District Attorney's Office. I felt that we were making good progress. Then things went dark. Our communication attempts got no answers."

"Did you ever hear back from anybody?"

"Yes, I ended up receiving a call. I was basically told that there are people in the town that do not want the case solved. That's all I can say."

It sounded all too familiar to Victor. The haunting shadow that the Lady of the Dunes cast over Provincetown nearly fifty years later was tough to break through. Margaret and Victor continued talking. He told her of some of the roadblocks he had been running into during his time working on his project. She, for her part, once again offered the DNA Doe Project's services if they were desired. Victor told her he definitely wanted them aboard, unfortunately it was not all up to him.

Victor and Margaret Press spoke for an hour. He told her he was going to contact the Massachusetts State Police Crime Laboratory. One side was on board, it was now up to Victor to try to get access to the DNA necessary.

A phone call was placed. Victor did not beat around the bush. He explained who he was and that he was working on a project looking to solve the Lady of the Dunes murder mystery. The person on the other end did not immediately dismiss him or hang up giving Victor a little hope.

In order to seem more legitimate Victor name dropped Margaret Press and the DNA Doe Project. The person from the Crime Laboratory was familiar with Margaret and DNA Doe. Victor said he was looking for information on any DNA samples from the Lady of the Dunes that could potentially be sent to DNA Doe for Margaret to use. The person gave Victor the contact information for the man who ran the office. It was as good as he could have hoped for.

Victor called Margaret back to share the contact information. As he read off the man's name Margaret let out a laugh. It turned out that the man who ran the state forensic office had actually dated Margaret's daughter twenty years earlier.

Victor saw this as a great sign for things to come. He left it in Margaret's hands to contact him and see if the office had any DNA from the Lady of the Dunes they could share with DNA Doe.

Margaret would send Victor a quick email later in the week letting him know that she had a good talk with the man from the State Police Crime Laboratory. She did not elaborate on that but she did also say that the District Attorney's Office, who had the power to release any DNA of the Lady of the Dunes, had responded to a DNA request. They simply stated they had received the offer from DNA Doe. This marked the third time Margaret Press and the DNA Doe Project had offered their help in solving the mystery of who was the Lady of the Dunes using genetic genealogy.

The next phone call Victor made was to a name he was already familiar with. Carolyn Tacke had been a waitress at the Crown and Anchor for years, including during the wild times of the 1970's. She had also been interviewed by Peter Manso for his *Ptown* book.

In the book Manso had described her as a tall blonde who worked at the Back Room of the Crown and Anchor. She had very fond memories of working there and of Sorrentino. She made it a point to mention that Sorrentino definitely could not have been involved in the murder of the Lady of the Dunes. He was often terrified by drag queen fights on the premises.

One thing that Tacke mentioned in Manso's book was the fact that she could not remember a time that Sorrentino wasn't on some sort of drugs, whether cocaine or other. This tied back into the connection between Sorrentino and Tony Costa, the drugs, and Sydney Monzon getting tangled up in it.

Carolyn had a great contact for Victor to try next. This one shed a little more light onto Staniford Sorrentino's tastes. His name was Dicky and during the 1970's he was well acquainted with the former Crown and Anchor owner.

"Hello, is this Dicky?" Victor asked after a man answered the phone.

"Yes it is. Who is this that's calling?"

"Carolyn Tacke gave me your information. My name is Victor Franko. I'm working on a documentary about the Lady of the Dunes. Right now I'm looking into the crazy world that was Provincetown in the 1970's. Specifically the Crown and Anchor and Staniford Sorrentino. Carolyn said you could help me in those areas." Dicky let out a hearty laugh.

"Oh yeah I can definitely help you there. I used to hang out at the Crown when I was sixteen, and let's just say I knew how to catch Stan's eye." Dicky paused as if he was giving Victor time to prepare himself. "I was a hot piece of Portuguese ass and Stan gave me lots of attention. I'm not gay but I knew I could use Stan's attraction to me to get things I wanted."

"What kinds of things?"

"Coke, booze, young girls, and money, lots of all of those things."

"What did Sorrentino get in return from you?"

"Outside of a hand-job nothing but the privilege of checking me out I guess."

"It sounds like a pretty good deal."

"Oh yeah, over the course of three summers Stan gave me tens of thousands of dollars, lots of drugs, and lots of women. It was a fair trade as far as I was concerned."

The conversation with Dicky left Victor with a few important questions. He knew from Manso's book that Sorrentino was skimming profits from the Crown. What about the drugs though? Where was he getting so much cocaine that he could just give it out to a prospective hookup? Did Sorrentino have that kind of supply? Or was he in business with someone who did? Victor felt that so much of the Provincetown scene in the 1970's revolved around Sorrentino and his connections.

Victor took a step back in his mind from Sorrentino. He allowed for the full stage to come into focus. He was searching for the Lady of the Dunes and wished to discover her identity and what happened to her and why. Yet there were so many more players than just a young girl brutally murdered and those directly responsible for it. Victor saw so many players on that stage.

He closed his eyes and leaned back in his chair letting his thoughts unravel. He thought of Sydney Monzon, which led to Tony Costa who had lived with Monzon in a house owned by Sorrentino. What was the connection between Costa and Sorrentino? Was it more than landlord/tenant and drug use?

A quick online search of Costa directed Victor toward a pair of book assignments. He ordered used copies of *In His Garden* by Leo Damore and *The Babysitter: My Summers with a Serial Killer* by Jennifer Jordan and Liza Rodman. One-day shipping meant that by the next evening Victor was cracking open his next slice of Provincetown history.

Chapter 6, A Garden, A Babysitter, and A Bartender

In His Garden gave Victor a deeper look into Tony Costa beyond the crash course Bob had given him early on in his research. Jimmy Meads Sr. had been familiar with Costa as Meads was a Sergeant on the Provincetown Police Department during the late 1960s. He had known him since he was young, coming to Provincetown from Somerville, Massachusetts during the summers. Meads even recruited Costa as an informant. He had pushed for early parole when Costa was serving six months in the Barnstable House of Correction for nonsupport of his wife and three children as a reward for his help as an informant.

Meads had questioned Costa and his mother when Patricia Walsh and Mary Anne Wysocki had gone missing. There was a connection as the girls and Costa had all been staying at Patricia Morton's guesthouse on Standish Street. There was not enough evidence for Meads to intervene before Costa's third and fourth murders. Still it seemed as though Meads knew Costa was involved.

The connection between Costa and Sorrentino began with Costa working and living at the Crown and Anchor. It advanced to Costa working as a handyman for Sorrentino and eventually moving into his private home with Sydney Monzon. It was mere walking distance from Sorrentino's house that Costa buried three of his victims in the area of his marijuana garden.

The story of Tony Costa was fleshed out more in *The Babysitter*. This book was written by Liza Rodman a woman who was babysat by Tony Costa beginning in 1966 when she was a child summering in Provincetown with her family. In her book she tells the story of Costa's troubled youth after his father died during World War II. He was showing signs of sociopathy early however he was kind and gentle when it came to Liza and her sister Louisa.

What Victor found of particular interest was the stories from Costa's time at the Massachusetts Correctional Institute in Walpole. First was something that seemed to be akin to a crossover from a comic book. During his time in prison one of Costa's fellow inmates was famed Boston Strangler Albert DeSalvo. Given both of their pensions for crafting leather goods in prison it was likely that they knew each other. The thought of Costa and DeSalvo sitting making wallets together tickled Victor some.

Furthermore both DeSalvo and Costa were unpopular prisoners. DeSalvo met his end on November 25, 1973 at the hands of other inmates. For Costa his unpopularity did not stop him from somehow acquiring drugs while in prison. Victor could not help but wonder how he was getting these drugs. How could he afford them and who was supplying them if Costa was so disliked?

If Costa had a contact that allowed him to still get his share of drugs while in prison in Walpole what was their relationship? Did Costa have knowledge of something? Victor thought back to Costa's association with Sorrentino and his association with some high ranking underworld people. Despite his death in 1974 being ruled a suicide it had always been shrouded in mystery. It could have been fellow inmates acting on their own. Or could it have been something deeper? Victor wondered if Costa knew something about Sorrentino's business.

Could he have been thinking of sharing some possibly incriminating evidence against Sorrentino or someone else? Could Tony Costa have been murdered because of something he knew with it being made to look like a suicide?

After finishing both books Victor contemplated his next step. Reading *In His Garden* got Victor thinking more about Sydney Monzon. He felt this sadness for her, she was one of the tragic characters on the stage that was this Lady of the Dunes project. She got wrapped up in the drug culture of the late 1960s and ultimately it cost her life.

The next step came when Victor heard from Carolyn Tacke again. She had another former Crown and Anchor employee who wished to speak with Victor. This call would open up a new door.

The man called himself 'Score' and was a former bartender at the Crown and other places in Provincetown during the 1970s time period. He had worked hard, rolling quarters nightly, and having more sex than anyone, with men and women. Score began his conversation with a story about someone long thought to be a suspect: James 'Whitey' Bulger.

The famed Boston mobster was a frequent guest at the Crown and Anchor. He typically had a different beautiful woman on his arm each time he came in. However one night Bulger arrived with the same woman he had been in with the previous time. A female bartender perked up at seeing the woman. It prompted the bartender to say to the woman on Bulger's arm that it was nice to see her again. It seemed a fairly innocent and innocuous comment at the time. Later in the evening however Bulger cornered the bartender and said to her with a wicked smile that if she ever said that again he would kill her.

Victor was fixated on the name Whitey Bulger and the possibility of his involvement in the Lady of the Dunes murder. However, Score threw a curve ball into the equation when he announced he had four of his own potential suspects when it came to the case. All four were locals and according to Score all four had it in them to kill her because of there reputations and vicinity and connection to organized crime.

First was a man named Joe. He was, as Score put it, 'a crazy fuck' and a drug dealer. Joe was tied in with Sorrentino and Bulger while also being a regular at the Crown and Anchor. Score explained that he was also friendly with the family of some of the local police which could be a reason why he was never pursued further as a suspect.

This name immediately jumped out to Victor. During one of his exchanges with Peter Manso he had mentioned the same person. This 'Joe' was a smuggler with connections to organized crime in Boston and Vietnam. So bad was this man Joe that Manso told Victor: 'If something bad happened in Provincetown from the mid-70s to the early-80s he was definitely associated with it.'

The second potential killer was a "bad ass up on Bangs Street" nicknamed 'Zeke' Score said. He would have been eighteen at the time of the murder. Unfortunately Zeke was rumored to have died on a boat at sea when he was twenty-two. Not much else is known of him making Zeke a relatively tough one to nail down.

Third was a man named Maurice. It was his nephew who claimed he was the killer. Maurice had worked for a time at Race Point Lighthouse, in the vicinity of where the Lady of the Dunes was found. He also had a truck capable of driving over the sand as well as access to military tools like the one thought to be what was used to nearly sever the young woman's head. Victor noted the nephew's name just in case he needed to speak with him later.

The fourth potential suspect was a man named Richie. Score referred to him as a handsome but crazy killer with mafia ties. Richie died in a car accident in 1982 although his son was still alive so there was another potential lead for Victor.

As far as what happened to the Lady of the Dunes and why, Score had his opinion.

"I believe that she was a disposal job," Score said. "I believe it was Joe, and his brother Bobby helped him get rid of the evidence." He continued with a quote that Victor thought so important that he jotted it down verbatim. "All the answers to your questions are resting in St. Peter's Cemetery."

Score told Victor several other stories of drugs, sex, and debauchery from his days at the Crown and Anchor but nothing stuck with him more than the story of Bulger. It fanned the flames of suspicion Victor had from the start. When doing his initial research into the Lady of the Dunes to see if it was a worthwhile endeavor Victor ready many articles from major news organizations and watched several true crime videos online. Although never fully naming Whitey Bulger as a suspect in the murder of the Lady of the Dunes all of them went out of their way to note that he did like to frequent Provincetown during the summers at the time.

Victor could not find any hard evidence of Bulger's involvement with the Lady of the Dunes case. However the mere fact that he was a frequenter of the Crown and Anchor made him wonder about what sort of connection Bulger had with Staniford Sorrentino. Bulger was in Provincetown at that time. Could he have been supplying Sorrentino drugs? Could he have been profiting from the raunchy and wild nightlife of the Crown and Anchor?

This chat with Score got Victor to go back where he started all of his research. The public case file through Wikipedia was thorough. Jimmy Meads Sr. had done a lot of work for 1974. He read it in depth, specifically the connection of Whitey Bulger. Victor tried reading between the lines for some sort of hidden meaning. It was no use.

Throughout Victor's reading and researching Bulger as a potential suspect another name kept popping up that seemed almost as intriguing. That name was Hadden Clark. A convicted killer of two people, 23-year-old Laura Houghteling and 6-year-old Michelle Dorr, Clark was serving two thirty-year sentences at the Eastern Correctional Institution in Westover, Maryland. Clark, who suffered from paranoid schizophrenia, had claimed to have murdered as many as a dozen people from the mid-1970's up until his capture in 1992.

Clark was born in Pennsylvania yet routinely summered on Cape Cod in the early 1970s. This included working as a cook at The Moors in Provincetown. The biggest potential connection between Clark and the Lady of the Dunes was the fact that in 2000 he actually confessed to her murder. Clark had even been allowed to leave prison under police supervision to return to his grandfather's property on Pamet Point Road in Wellfleet to search for the graves of two more women he claimed to have murdered during the 1980s. Though no graves were found Clark did lead police to a bucket containing 230 pieces of women's jewelry, including Houghteling's high school class ring. Clark claimed these were his 'trophies.'

When it came to the Lady of the Dunes Clark later on would say that he intended on telling the police her name and about his involvement but he claimed they mistreated him and therefore he chose to remain quiet about it. Anything Victor read or watched mentioned Clark's paranoid schizophrenia bringing his confession into doubt. Bulger and Clark were the two main suspects in Victor's mind up until he spoke with Score. The inclusion of four new potential suspects gave Victor a lot of food for thought.

It was time for Victor to step up his research. The case was still considered active nearly fifty years after the fact. Surely, that meant that there must be someone working on it. Victor quickly figured out that anything to do with the Lady of the Dunes currently would certainly be taking place at the District Attorney's Office. It came full circle as Victor had indeed left a message for them as he had told Peter Manso. What he hadn't mentioned was that it was an email to the generic address on the contact page.

    This time Victor would take the time to actually call. However, it was late in the evening and the call would have to wait until the next day. Until then Victor wrote down some simple basic questions he hoped that the District Attorney's Office could answer including the names of Score's four potential suspects. That was if they responded at all.

Early on the morning of February 1st Victor dialed the number for the District Attorney's Office. He left a simple message stating who he was, what he was doing, and that he had a few questions for them that he hoped they could help with. After hanging up Victor had low expectations for a callback any time soon. He began to go about his daily routine. It was not until the next day that Victor would receive the call he had hoped for.

Victor was in the process of changing his son's diaper when saw his phone light up near him. He grabbed it and looked at the ID: Restricted. There was no name, no number, just Restricted. Victor was not one to answer potential spam callers. However with the amount of new people he had been introduced to over the last several weeks he decided to answer.

It was the District Attorney's Office.

Victor thanked them for returning his call. The voice on the other end was polite. They informed Victor that the Lady of the Dunes case was still open and ongoing. All of the DNA tests that were done on her remains came back negative as far as a match went. They finally stressed that they do not listen to any podcasts, YouTube videos, or any fictionalized accounts of the case.

It felt as though they were trying to make a statement and end the conversation with as little interaction as possible. Victor let them know that it was not his intention to attack law enforcement when it came to the case. They replied that would be good. Before Victor could ask about Whitey Bulger, or Score's list of four suspects, the voice on the other end courteously but abruptly ended the call.

It had lasted all of two minutes.

The call was so quick that Victor's son did not even have time to move off of the changing table. Victor went back to finishing putting on a fresh diaper. The call had been rather disappointing. He decided his next move would be to circle back to Jimmy Meads Jr. and chat with him about what he had been learning about Sorrentino, the Crown and Anchor, and Score's potential suspects.

A few days later Victor got in touch with Jimmy. He began by telling him about his rather uneventful phone call with the District Attorney's Office.

Jimmy was not surprised by their response. He said that people go missing all the time.

"Look Victor," he said bluntly, "you're doing as good a job as you can with the resources you have. But unfortunately you're going to be limited by your experience. You'll get brushed off by higher-ups more and more the deeper you get into this case." Victor felt a bit deflated as he knew that Jimmy was right. He had relative success with the average citizens that had been connected to the case. However when it came to those in charge it was mostly a brick wall.

"What can I do to break through?" Victor asked.

"Honestly, I would recommend hiring a private investigator."

"Really?" Victor had always prided himself on being able to find out what he needed to on his own. "Aren't there any people at the Ptown Police that might be willing to talk to me?" There was a long pause and a few heavy breaths on the other line.

"No," Jimmy said emphatically, "nobody that I can think of who would be willing to help with your project." Victor was a bit deflated. If local law enforcement was not going to be of help it definitely hindered his progress. He did however trust Jimmy

Meads' judgment and was willing to look into a private investigator.

"Okay, I'll look into a P.I."

"There's a few more things," Jimmy replied. "First there's a man named Dennis Minsky I think you should talk to. He grew up in the area and knew my Dad as well." Minsky was a name that Victor knew well. He had been interviewed by Victor for the Thoreau documentary. Minsky was a local author, writing for the Provincetown Independent newspaper. He was also a biologist and naturalist at the Provincetown Conservation Trust and Provincetown Center for Coastal Studies. It would be great to chat with Dennis again.

"He's a great contact," Victor happily replied, "I worked with him on my Thoreau doc so I'll definitely reach out."

"Now this last thing, you need to have an open mind for."

"What's that?"

"You might want to consider hiring a psychic." Victor couldn't help but roll his eyes upon hearing that.

"A psychic? Really?"

"Don't laugh, my Dad used a psychic in the 1980s on a case he was working on. I think it would at least be worth a shot." Victor decided to humor Jimmy but was not really giving serious thought to a psychic.

"Why did your father use a psychic?"

"He was a skeptic don't get me wrong, but he also wanted to try to solve the case by using any means he could."

The conversation rolled on for a few more minutes, focusing less on the details of the Lady of the Dunes and more on what it was like growing up in Provincetown. The two parted ways and Victor made a call to a familiar friend.

He scrolled through his phone and pulled up Dennis Minsky's number. It had been a few months since they had last spoken while Victor was beginning to wrap up his Thoreau documentary. Funnily enough when Dennis answered the phone he immediately asked how that project was progressing. Victor gave him a quick recap of what he had been up to. The tone quickly shifted when he asked Dennis if he knew anything about the Lady of the Dunes. Victor knew full well that he would.

Dennis was like an encyclopedia of knowledge when it came to Provincetown and its history. Quickly he began relaying information that Victor was familiar with. Dennis asked why he was asking about the Lady of the Dunes. When Victor revealed it was his latest project Dennis got excited. The two decided to get together in the near future when Victor made a return trip to Provincetown. After chatting for a few more minutes Victor revealed to Dennis his next step. It was time for him to begin looking for a private investigator.

Within only a few days Victor had complied a list of several locally based potential private investigators. He crafted an email to send to all of them. In it he told of who he was, a little about his past projects, and then got down to business. He explained how he was trying to solve the Lady of the Dunes murder mystery. Victor even went as far as to give a Cliffs Notes version of the case on the chance that one of these investigators wasn't familiar with it. It concluded with Victor asking for help with finding information and sources for this project as he had hit a wall as far as local law enforcement and the District Attorney's Office went.

Satisfied with his email Victor sent each potential investigator one and then played the waiting game. By the end of the same day he had a few hits. One of them stood out among the others due to his level of enthusiasm and intrigue about the Lady of the Dunes. His name was Frank.

Hailing from New Hampshire Frank impressed Victor with his qualifications. He was Vietnam Veteran Staff Sergeant with an honorable discharge, more pertinent to Victor was Frank's over forty years of service in criminal investigation. This included a twenty-four year civilian law enforcement career with a New Hampshire Police Department.

Frank was a perfect match for what Victor was looking for and he was immediately hopeful that his investigative skills would net him some important information. He shared with Frank what he had come up against as far as problems with researching the case as well as what he was hoping the P.I. could check into. After that Victor left Frank to get started.

Having a little more time to breathe knowing that an accomplished private investigator was on his team Victor thought it was time to give another call to Peter Manso and see if there was anything he could add to what Victor had found out since they last spoke.

Unsurprising to Victor, Peter Manso was just as gruff with him on their second phone call as the first.

"This is Peter."

"Peter, it's Victor. We spoke a few weeks ago."

"Oh yes, I remember," Manso answered sounding less than enthused. "How goes your investigation and more importantly, did you read my book?"

"I did, it was well written."

"Thank you. Thoughts?"

"Stan Sorrentino?"

"Yes?"

"He was involved."

"If you say so," Manso said coyly.

"I looked him up, there's very little online about him."

"So?"

"I find it interesting that someone like him has only six Googled leads and no images of him." Manso snickered.

"I hope you're not using Wikipedia as your main source of information."

"No, of course not."

"Because that would be nothing shy of an embarrassment and a waste of time." Victor skipped over Peter's not-so-subtle jab.

"The late night parties in his living room with his ingrown pool I find very interesting."

"Sure, what else?"

"I'm intrigued with Sorrentino, and the people he was associated with."

"Provincetown itself is one of the characters in this story," Manso began. "It's not just a murder in the dunes, you need to understand what was happening not just at the Crown and Anchor in the summer of '74 but all over town. Much like Romeo and Juliet with their setting."

"Fair Verona?"

"It's important to the story. That's why Shakespeare mentions it in the first paragraph before even talking about any of the central characters. Think about it."

"I will."

"Have you been to her grave?"

"Not yet."

"You should, all of your answers are buried in that cemetery."

"I am going to mention how the community did embrace her and found her a home at St. Peters. The idea of welcoming the drifter and giving her a home." Manso was not feeling Victor's narrative.

"That's a bunch of bullshit," Manso crudely replied. "They threw her in a grave on the outskirts of the cemetery."

"A better spot than Tony Costa." There was a pause before Manso gave Victor his due.

"That's true."

"I do want to help the case by bringing some new insight and hoping to conclude on some sort of positive."

"Maybe you can help raise us some funds?" Manso's demeanor seemed to be changing on someone he referred to as 'borderline irrelevant' during their first conversation.

"For the HBO deal?"

"Yeah, that wouldn't hurt. I looked you up and saw how you have raised money for other productions. Maybe you can work for me?"

"Peter, I am having a little bit of a bad connection, can you repeat that?"

"Can you hear me now?"

"Much better, thank you."

Manso said unequivocally that it was all connected to Sorrentino. Being a writer he summed it up by telling Victor that Sorrentino's Crown and Anchor was representative of the time. The location was the stage for all of the characters in the story.

In Victor's mind it came down to whether Sorrentino was the main character, or just another character in the greater story. Manso pushed Victor to look deeper into Sorrentino. However when Victor asked Manso for something in the way of specific places to look he insisted that Victor was moving in the right direction. Beside the point of having Victor do his own research Manso was between and rock and a hard place. During his own research into his Lady of the Dunes project Manso revealed that he had made quite a few enemies.

Manso thought there was some sort of conspiracy going on when it came to the Lady of the Dunes. When Victor pressed him further about his own issues with law enforcement and his Lady of the Dunes project he was surprisingly candid. Manso said that he saw his potential HBO project as a chance to shine the light on his conspiracy idea. He also saw the chance for a book deal, a television deal, and most importantly to Manso an opportunity to "piss off a lot of people in Ptown and the Lower Cape."

Victor smiled to himself as he listened to Manso expand on his thoughts on the case. Sure a book deal and an eventual distributor for his own project would be a suitable endgame, however Victor felt more and more compelled to find the answers that had eluded this case for nearly fifty years. The potential successes that came from that would be a bonus.

The conversation with Peter Manso went on for well over an hour before Manso suddenly made the decision that he had spoken enough.

"I wish you well in your little production. Invite me to the premiere and we can talk then."

"Will do."

"Thank you." Once again Manso hung up immediately after speaking his final words.

In a good sign, Victor received a check-in from P.I. Frank. It had only taken the veteran investigator twenty-four hours to come up with a laundry list of insight into the case. Frank had numerous members of law enforcement, local and federal, in addition to lawyers and more. Victor was thrilled to have someone on his same wavelength that he could bounce ideas off.

Victor had a lingering feeling that mistakes were made in the case, whether intentional or accidental. This was purely based on what he had been reading and his own conversations with people thus far. Talks with Jimmy Meads and Peter Manso along with his search for a private investigator had occupied most of his time when it came to the Lady of the Dunes. However, a new contact was about to make their presence known.

Victor's phone rang. He looked at the Caller ID. It said 'Unlisted.' Cautiously Victor answered.

"Hello?"

"Victor Franko?"

"Yes."

"It's not every day I get multiple calls from ghosts from the past telling me that I should call back someone from South Attleboro." Victor was confused as to who this stranger was.

"I'm sorry?" There was a faint chuckle on the other line.

"You made multiple calls and most of them called me. Now, I'm calling you." The person on the other line gave their first name to Victor. However, what followed underlined the seriousness of the situation. "This call is confidential. If you mention that you spoke with me, I will deny it and then destroy all of your credibility. Do you understand?" Victor struggled to catch his breath, his heart was pounding through his chest.

"Yes." The tone of the call lightened a little after Victor complied.

"Great, sorry for being a hard ass," the voice continued. "I just don't want my name brought up. I don't want anyone knowing that I spoke to you and especially having anyone know my motives. Good, bad, or indifferent."

The serious yet cryptic tone of this conversation soon made sense to Victor but at that point, he was unsure of what was happening.

"Ok?" That word was all Victor could muster in response.

"Maybe it would be appropriate to just call me 'Agent X' for that reason alone"

"I like that," Victor said while nodding. "It makes things more dramatic."

"Whatever that's worth. So let's get down to it. Tell me what you know about the Lady of the Dunes."

The conversation delved into whom Victor had spoken to thus far. He explained how Nancy and Jimmy Meads had given him an air of credibility that had helped him get in touch with others familiar with the Lady of the Dunes and Provincetown in the 1970s in general. He then added how law enforcement overall had not been willing to speak with him on the case.

Agent X was not surprised. They had been closely connected to the Lady of the Dunes case both as an insider and on the fringes for many years. It was reiterated to Victor by Agent X that Provincetown, for better or for worse, was the smallest town on the planet, akin to one big family. As far as the Lady of the Dunes case, local politics, the way Provincetown operated, and Victor's project went Agent X explained that it all boiled down to how many times he could hear the words 'don't go there' and keep going there.

Victor probed the idea of malfeasance. He asked Agent X if it was a possibility when it came to the investigation of the Lady of the Dunes. They brought up that they had heard a rumor about missing evidence but did not reveal any specifics. Instead, they gave Victor the name of someone they thought might be able to help. His name was Art.

Art was a retired United States Marshall. He had nearly forty years of experience in law enforcement including being a local police officer in Massachusetts. Art had spent twenty-five years as a U.S. Marshall so he had the pedigree. Nearly as important was the fact that he was also a native of Provincetown.

Agent X thought it wise for Victor to contact Art about potential malfeasance. Victor agreed and the hour-long conversation with Agent X ended with a promise that he would be contacting Art next.

An issue immediately popped up for Victor when it came to getting in touch with Art. His fame. Throughout his career, Art had appeared on such shows as America's Most Wanted and Unsolved Mysteries. He had also produced and starred in "Alcatraz; Search for the Truth" and its follow-up Special "Alcatraz; The Lost Evidence" on History Channel.

The connections to Travel Channel, Discovery Channel, National Geographic, and others meant that Art was not simply someone whose phone number was readily available. For Victor to reach him he first had to go through Art's agent. This man was in charge of setting up the telephone calls between Art and Victor.

Once Victor had Art on the phone though all of the maneuverings in dealing with his agent became worth it. Having grown up in Provincetown Art was very familiar with the community. He gave Victor a heads up much in the same way that Agent X had that many wanted the Lady of the Dunes to stay buried until she was forgotten.

Victor explained his project to Art. He included how he was looking to shine a new light on the case, not necessarily exploit it, or even place blame on law enforcement. Art was thrilled that Victor was doing a documentary and an investigation. Naturally, Victor asked him if he'd be interested in being involved in the project. Art was polite yet non-committal deferring to his agent.

It was time though for the million-dollar question. After a positive conversation up to that point, Victor bluntly asked Art if he thought there was any malfeasance on the part of law enforcement when it came to the Lady of the Dunes.

Art was a straight shooter and said he had heard of rumors of missing evidence when it came to the case. When Victor asked the obvious follow-up question of 'Why?' Art did not have a concrete answer. The Why and How of potential missing evidence were baffling. It brought Victor back to the first question he had asked himself when hearing about the case: Just who was the Lady of the Dunes?

Victor thanked Art for his time and asked if he could contact him again in the future to which Art agreed. Victor sat in silence holding his phone. He stared at the wall beside his desk asking himself 'Why?' Surely potentially missing evidence could be a coincidence. It could be accidental. However, he could not ignore the barrage of roadblocks that kept popping up when it came to his efforts of collecting information about the case. Some people didn't want to talk about it. Other people advised him to leave it alone. Who was the Lady of the Dunes and why did her murder illicit such a strong reaction from the tight-knit community of Provincetown?

A second call was placed to Agent X after Victor collected his thoughts. He told them that he had spoken to Art who had mentioned potential missing evidence in the case. Surprisingly Agent X was much more forthcoming during the second call. They had made some calls on their own looking into the possibility of missing evidence.

First Agent X prefaced their comments by admitting that missing evidence was far more common than Victor might think and that it also was not necessarily always nefarious. They then dropped a bombshell. After making some calls Agent X confirmed for Victor that evidence had indeed gone missing in the

Lady of the Dunes case. Victor gasped. Again he asked the question: 'Why?' Agent X did not have a definitive answer. They went back to the statement that not all lost evidence is done with malice. Victor had trouble believing that was the case this time.

Agent X brought up malfeasance. Victor had that word and its dictionary definition, 'wrongdoing or misconduct especially by a public official,' swirling around his mind for several days. The longtime former member of law enforcement doubled down by telling Victor that from what they had heard from their contacts this was malfeasance bordering on incompetence.

Agent X went on to also say that they did not see this as being some sort of conspiracy by those who investigated the case, thus why they leaned in toward the incompetence explanation.

Victor finally felt comfortable enough with Agent X to ask them about their thoughts on possible suspects like Whitey Bulger. Although they never outright said they thought Bulger was involved in the murder of the Lady of the Dunes Agent X brought to the forefront another potentially important piece of the puzzle.

"Have you ever heard of the Combat Zone?"

"No, should I have?"

"I think that to get a wider view of the landscape you might want to learn about the Combat Zone. Let's just say that it was the adult entertainment district of Boston in the 1960s and 70s. It might have a big influence on this case you're looking into."

Victor thanked Agent X and immediately did a deep dive into this Combat Zone they spoke of.

The Combat Zone was the seedy adult entertainment district of Boston. It extended along Washington Street between

Boylston Street and Kneeland Street. Home to strip clubs, adult movies, and peep shows, filled with sex workers and men willing to pay for it all, the Combat Zone existed in one form or another from the 1960s into the early-90s when it was finally closed down.

This notorious area of the city drew people from all walks of life. Legitimate businessmen shoulder to shoulder with organized criminals. Thus Victor immediately saw the reason Agent X had recommended doing the research.

Interestingly Victor found that some of the strippers and sex workers, allegedly, were earning enough money to put themselves through college. He had always thought that was a bit of a myth about stripping.

Then Victor came to something of particular interest. There was a connection between the Combat Zone and organized crime as many of the strip clubs were mafia owned. It was not much of a leap to think that strippers and sex workers could have had mafia bosses that loaned them out like property to wealthy customers.

His mind began to connect dots that might or might not exist. The Combat Zone, organized crime, sex workers, Provincetown, and the Lady of the Dunes, could they all be linked? Victor decided to keep this new lead front and center going forward.

Victor decided to spend the next week or so taking a breather. There had been mountains of information and numerous layers to the story behind the case that he felt he needed to push away from the table for a little while and let things settle.

Once he felt ready to dive back into the Lady of the Dunes near the end of February Victor reached back out to his hired private investigator Frank. He had been doing behind-the-scenes work with his sources and Victor was curious about his thoughts about how the case had been handled. Agent X and Art had both heavily implied malfeasance. What were Frank's thoughts?

The P.I. had been going through what public records there were for the Lady of the Dunes case. In his opinion, Frank felt the entire investigation was problematic from the get-go. He believed that more could have been done with the case both in the beginning and in the decades since. Frank believed that the malfeasance had taken place at the state level. Victor played dumb and when he asked him what led him to that conclusion Frank replied that he had heard some things through his contacts. However, he could not, and would not, name any names.

Malfeasance, the P.I. was the third different person to use that word. The fact that Frank's sources had given him the belief made Victor think that this was something that needed to be further probed. Victor and Frank began going back and forth about specifics. Frank knew things to look for and he gave Victor some important questions to be asked. These questions though would need to be answered by the District Attorney's Office.

After the conversation with Frank ended Victor had two major roads to follow when it came to the next steps in the Lady of the Dunes case. There was one before the murder and one after. How big of a part did Sorrentino play in the events leading to her death? Secondly, what, if any, malfeasance took place in the aftermath of the murder?

Victor was not a private detective and he was not a member of law enforcement. He was a simple filmmaker and at times felt out of his league when it came to piecing together what he was being told from his sources when it came to the Lady of the Dunes case. Still, while he felt like he was being a bit overwhelmed with information Victor knew he was just getting beneath the surface and had to press on. It was his opinion after speaking with Agent X, Art, and Frank that malfeasance had taken place during the investigation with potential evidence going missing. He knew he was going to have another conversation with the District Attorney's Office coming up.

Before February ended a second call was placed to Art. This was again done through his agent. It was far more of a cordial chat than the first. Victor explained how rough his initial conversation was with the District Attorney's Office. Art reiterated his opinion that evidence had gone missing. Victor mentioned his conversations with Frank the P.I. and Agent X, though not naming them specifically. When Victor asked Art to potentially participate in the documentary he again deferred to his agent.

Victor called Arnold after hanging up with Art to talk turkey about his client appearing in the project. The asking price for Art turned out to be far too much for Victor to afford. He thanked the agent and moved on with the project grateful to have at least had the pair of conversations with Art.

Interestingly in the moments after speaking with Art and his agent, Victor did an internet search for Art and came upon a June 2020 appearance on the Crawlspace Podcast. Having a little time to kill Victor watched the video on YouTube. Of particular interest was the story put forth in 2018 by Joe Hill, son of legendary author Stephen King.

The story centered around an unnamed extra from the 1975 movie Jaws which was filmed mainly on the island of Martha's Vineyard only a few miles off of Cape Cod. Despite being released in 1975 the movie was shot beginning in May 1974. In a scene where a ferry is arriving at the dock the unnamed extra walks into the frame for a fleeting moment and she appears to bear a striking resemblance to the police sketches of the Lady of the Dunes. No records of extras were kept for the film leaving the young woman nameless.

Speculation was rabid that this extra could be the elusive Lady of the Dunes in the flesh. However, on the podcast, Art had to pour cold water on the theory. It turned out that the unnamed extra in Jaws was alive and well. She was a Martha's Vineyard native, living there for sixty years. The woman was a private person who wanted her identity to remain as such. She had called law enforcement not too long after the Joe Hill story came out to let them know that she was the unnamed extra and was not dead.

The podcast was a fun distraction for a little while. In short order though Victor had a lot to give his attention to. Victor looked at his copious piles of notes and contacts. He knew he already had in his eyes an interesting story to be shared. How was that story to be presented though? The through lines of Sorrentino, the dark underbelly of 1970s Provincetown, and potential malfeasance during the investigation of the Lady of the Dunes' murder were all compelling. As the calendar turned to March Victor decided to work with what he had thus far. He wanted to begin to cultivate his search for the Lady of the Dunes into a cohesive documentary.

There was another important step he wanted to take in his journey of discovery. Actually, it was thousands of steps. Victor knew he needed to have his feet on the ground where the murder took place. He began to make plans to visit not just Provincetown, but the dunes where the infamous Jane Doe met her demise.

Chapter 8, Like A Grain of Sand

To take a few steps forward sometimes one must take a step back. That was Victor's thinking as the calendar turned to March. He had spent the better part of two months researching the Lady of the Dunes case. In that time Victor had compiled dozens of interviewees, some he had spoken to and some not yet approached. The worldwide pandemic had made virtual meetings and telephone calls preferable. However, Victor knew that to get to the true meat of the story he needed boots on the ground and face-to-face interaction. At some point, Victor was going to need to make the drive out to Provincetown.

Before that would be attempted he first had to plan for the bigger picture. What exactly was his plan for the Lady of the Dunes project? How was it going to look? The beginning of March proved to be the time for Victor to collect all of his work. His heavily scribbled notebook pages, saved emails, notes from his smartphone, bookmarked websites, and everything else he had accumulated during his research, get them all out on the kitchen table and see exactly what he had.

Victor had a lot of basic information about the murder itself with cited bits from Wikipedia and Buzzfeed Unsolved. He had the seedy backstory of Provincetown in the 1970s and how that might have been a factor in the murder. Victor thought of those who could have been involved. He thought of Sorrentino, Bulger, Score's list of four suspects, Hadden Clark, and wanted to dig further into each before making any sort of claims.

Throughout all of the grizzly details of the murder, the sex and drugs, and the somber story of an unknown family whose loved one was left dead in the dunes, one beacon of light kept shining through. That beacon was Jimmy Meads Sr. Victor thought back to Nancy Meads and Jimmy Jr. and all of the leads they had given him. Beyond that he thought about the fact that they had not wished to work with anyone else who had done projects about the Lady of the Dunes. Yet for some reason the Meads Family saw something in Victor that allowed him into their lives. He felt a sense of duty to honor their efforts and trust.

Victor's initial idea for a Lady of the Dunes documentary would focus closely on Jimmy Meads, his character, and his hard work on the initial investigation. With all of the talk of malfeasance and missing evidence during the investigation by Agent X, Art, and Frank Victor thought it would be a good move to also focus on a member of law enforcement who went above and beyond trying to solve the case. He thought a tight thirty-minute piece would work out great.

Having a rough idea of what the documentary would focus on Victor went to his list of people to speak with. Calls were made and emails were sent. When all was said and done twenty-six people in total were on board to be interviewed for the documentary. There were more people Victor wanted to speak with, however for every 'yes' he received there were just as many 'no's.' The issue with those who said no was the same narrative that Victor had been running into from the beginning. People knew something yet were either uninterested or unwilling to speak on the record about it.

Over the course of the first half of March Victor ended up with nineteen interviewees and was satisfied with it. Some of his closest contacts during the process of research were on board beginning with Nancy and Jimmy Meads. Frank the P.I. was a natural due to his current work on the project alongside Victor. Carolyn Tacke formerly of the Crown & Anchor also agreed to be a part of the film itself. Former Provincetown Police Chief Jeff Jaran was brought into the fold as well. Jaran had reopened the Lady of the Dunes case early in his career. He had also brought her skull to Washington D.C. which allowed for the most recent composite to be rendered.

Dennis Minsky was a given to be a part of it as well. Victor was particularly interested in getting Minsky's wife to join in due to a story he had heard. The story being that at some point in the past where she was working she had refused a tip from controversial lawyer Roy Cohn.

Victor made it a point to let these people know what he was going to ask them when the cameras were rolling so that they would be prepared and know it wasn't some sort of ambush.

From there it was networking and research that gained Victor access to his other subjects. Nancy Meads reached out to Michael Meads, Jimmy's brother, to bring him on board. Nancy also got ninety-year-old Provincetown resident Mildred Champlin involved. She was an important contact because she owned a shack out in the dunes near Race Point. Victor hoped that she would at some point allow him access to it but was not going to overstep his bounds.

The local connection was strong. Victor reached out to Stephen Desroches upon recommendation. Desroches had been a journalist for the Cape Codder newspaper and Provincetown Magazine. He had also done his own research into the Lady of the Dunes case some twenty years earlier.

After Desroches Victor found local author Jeannette de Beauvoir from Provincetown. She had written the Sydney Riley mystery series set in Provincetown. Just as important to Victor though was the fact that she had written an historical fiction book about the Lady of the Dunes. Jeannette was one who knew the enigmatic power of the Province Lands dunes.

Thinking ahead Victor reached out to Provincetown's 92.1 WOMR. A radio personality there agreed to help with the eventual narration of the documentary.

In the age of instant connection and technology Victor was pleasantly surprised by the fact that he was able to connect online with Father Hugh 'Mick' McCullough. He was Pastor of the St. Peter the Apostle Church in Provincetown. It was here that the unidentified body of the Lady of the Dunes was buried.

Victor's online detective work allowed him to connect with Alyssa Metcalfe. She was integral since it was Alyssa's sister, Leslie, who had discovered the mutilated body of the Lady of the Dunes when she was twelve years old. Leslie sadly passed away in 1996.

Heeding the words of Jimmy Meads Jr. Victor also reached out to a few psychics. In total five psychic mediums would end up being a part of the documentary process in varying degrees.

Victor befriended Charlie Worroll, the Host of the Crimelines True Crime podcast. She had published a Lady of the Dunes episode in March 2020 and felt like a good person to bounce theories off of.

In a bit of luck Jessica Harper, actress from such films as Minority Report, Pennies From Heaven, Love and Death, and others, agreed to be a part of Victor's production at no cost to him. She had a connection to Cape Cod through family vacations.

Much like Peter Manso had said to him about Provincetown in the 1970s being akin to a grand stage Victor through his time and research had created his own stage. It was filled with players he felt would lend expertise and credibility to his documentary.

Happy with the connections he had made Victor was ready to move forward. However the mood surrounding the Lady of the Dunes documentary had changed. Victor's idea of a short, concise piece about the efforts of Jimmy Meads' investigation had gone out the window. The more he spoke with people and set up interviews, the more he sifted through information, Victor kept coming back to the same question. Why had this case not been solved?

Sure that question had popped in his head from time to time over the last few months but now as he gazed upon his list of participants in the project the question was screaming loudly in his ears. There were piles of papers with notes he had scribbled. There were many theories and lots of speculation. Yet for nearly half a century the names of both the killer and victim remained in the dark. Victor's desire to showcase a hard working lawman was replaced with a need to solve a mystery.

Spring had arrived in New England and Victor felt it was time to get boots on the ground. He had spent much time on the Outer Cape during the Thoreau documentary yet this would be different. There would be no meditative walk along the beach hearkening back to Henry David Thoreau. This would be more akin to a morbid tourist trip. Victor needed to be where the Lady of the Dunes took her last breath. The only questions were where was the location and how to get there?

Victor knew of an approximate location of where the body was found. It was deep in the isolated dunes east of Race Point Beach in Provincetown. He had seen reports of the location being anywhere from a mile to two-miles east of the Race Point Ranger Station. That vague information left Victor was looking at an area of roughly 200 acres to find a spot of a few square feet. In the end he decided to go and get a feel for what the terrain was like.

Knowing what a sensitive subject the Lady of the Dunes was to the Provincetown community as a whole Victor was not sure how much of his plan he should broadcast. There was a very popular dune tour company that took people around the Province Lands area. He contacted them to get a feel for what the area was like east of Race Point. Surprisingly the company offered to take

him out there. Though he debated it, Victor thought it best if he
went out on his own and soaked in the atmosphere.

Not wanting to wander for the sake of wandering Victor
chose the venerable C-Scape Dune Shack as a sort of endgame for
the eventual trip across the dunes. The time was right to act. The
next clear day Victor had on his schedule was Friday, March 26th.
He decided that would be when he made his journey out into the
dunes.

That morning Victor prepared to hike the soft sand and be
exposed to the elements. Outside of his home in Norton it was
foggy and seasonably warm, however it was due to be misty, with
temperatures in the fifties and winds gusting to nearly twenty
miles per hour in Provincetown. He made sure to dress
accordingly.

One hundred miles of road lay between Norton and
Provincetown. Victor spent the first half hour psyching himself up
about the wind and drizzle he would be facing. The longer he
drove along the highway the more he began feeling a sense of
uncertainty. What would he see? What would he feel?

The finish line for the drive was the Province Lands
Visitors Center. It had a beautiful observation deck with views of
the surrounding dunes. On a cool, drizzly, March morning the
parking lot was barren. Victor stepped out of his car. The closing
of the door echoed across the emptiness. He walked across the
asphalt, shuffling his feet a bit as his mind wandered. Where to
start?

Cape Cod was home to more than one hundred miles of
paved recreational bicycle paths. Provincetown had its own trail
that looped around the Province Lands, its dunes, forests, and
cranberry bogs. It passed nearby the visitors center amphitheater.
Victor began to follow the trail east. The hissing wind through the

surrounding trees gave the illusion that Victor was not alone. When it would stop the true measure of the solitude was apparent. Even the birds seemed to absent.

Following a rough pin-drop from his smartphone's GPS Victor continued east along the trail until he seemed to be nearly straight south of what was the vicinity of the Lady of the Dunes' discovery site. Unfortunately there was a cover of relatively thick, spiny, brush along the trail. Not wanting to miss his mark Victor threw caution to the wind and made a dash through the brush.

Several hundred feet of brush, Scotch pine, and well-placed stones, needed to be crossed before Victor found a clearing to regain his bearings. His heart was pounding. Naturally as beads of sweat began forming on his forehead the wind that had been incessantly blowing grew still.

From this point on it was a straight shot north. The damp sand made quick progress impossible. Victor looked for clumps of moss to step on for traction. He felt like he had gone many miles yet when he checked his phone it had barely been another few hundred feet. The silence was deafening for much of Victor's journey. At times he would stop and simply look around. It was nothing but hulking sand dunes and diminutive pine tress as far as he could see. It gave of the sense of a living breathing graveyard that Victor was surrounded by.

Victor had made the trek along Cape Cod's outer beach for the Thoreau documentary. It had been a peaceful journey bordering on walking meditation. Stumbling and sinking into the rolling dunes on this day felt more like a somber chore. A half-mile or so from the bike trail Victor knew he was at least in the right area. Even if it wasn't the exact spot the surrounding acres all had similar topography.

It was gray, breezy, and above all cold. The entire atmosphere felt different in the expanse of nothing. It was as if

Victor had been dropped into a different world. He felt a sense of unease. It was not so much fear as it was a sense of loneliness. Victor looked around and after surveying the scene he wondered to himself: How did she get out here? Walking hundreds of yards through barren dunes certainly did not seem like an ideal sort of rendezvous.

Off in the distance Victor could made out the shape of the C-Scape Dune Shack. People often hiked the sand to lay eyes upon the historic buildings that dotted the landscape. That was typically in the light of day though. Those that inhabited the shacks during the season were more often driving in properly equipped vehicles over makeshift sandy roads. There was one not far from where Victor stood. It led to C-Scape, passing by where the shack had stood before being moved to its present location in 1978.

Being driven to the area where the Lady of the Dunes was found would have been an easier way for someone to get out there. Was that a possibility? Did someone drive her out there, murder her, and drive away? Victor decided to file that speculation away for his future interviewees. However after more than an hour wandering the cold, empty Province Lands Victor decided to make his way back to his car to warm up. It had been surreal with shades of sadness during the entirety of his time out there. Those feelings subsided only briefly when the heat from inside his car struck his skin.

Walking among the dunes in the area where the unknown woman had been found made it all feel real. Before that day and that hike there was always a slight disconnect, like looking through a window pane. Knowing that the Lady of the Dunes had perished in the area surrounding where he had walked made her into a real person to Victor for the first time. Sure, he had felt a sense of duty and determination to possibly solve a decades old mystery. Now as he sat in his car with the heat washing over his face things felt different.

Victor sat in the empty parking lot of the Province Lands Visitors Center. He stared off into the distance toward where he had just been. This had become more than just his newest project. This had become deeper and personal to him. The Lady of the Dunes was more than an unsolved murder. She was more than a story slowly fading with time. No, she was a real person who met a horrifying end.

The drive back to Norton was filled with quiet reflection. Victor kept the radio off leaving his mind to wander freely to the sound of his heater. When he got home he and Maura sat in the living room. Victor unloaded all that he was thinking and feeling. The Lady of the Dunes had become a real person with family, a history, hopes, dreams, and the like.

The couple's weekly chats about Victor's progress with the documentary typically were filled with facts and statistics and quotes from people Maura was not familiar with. During this conversation the tone had changed. Gone was the filmmaker looking to complete a compelling project. He was replaced with a reflective and somber father, son, and human being. Victor was still determined to create a worthy documentary. However just as important now was shining a light on the fact that the case had not been solved in nearly half a century. This was time that the family and friends of the Lady of the Dunes had suffered not knowing what had happened to her. In Victor's mind that was the harshest reality.

Chapter 9, I Don't Care What You Say

April began with Victor nailing down the interview schedules for his return to Cape Cod. It was surprisingly easy setting up the interviews. This came in large part due to the involvement of Jimmy Meads Jr. and the Meads Family. They gave Victor a sense of legitimacy that brokered a lot of deals.

The plan for the actual shooting of the documentary was for Victor to head to Provincetown on Friday April 9th. It would be a three-day trip and nearly nonstop shoot. Victor wanted to get as much film in the can as he could during that weekend.

The initial plan for April 9th was to start the day early at the St. Peter's Cemetery where the Lady of the Dunes was buried. There he would speak with Father McCullough. Next were four interviews to be conducted at the Provincetown Theater on Bradford Street. Victor was intrigued by the interview he had scheduled after with Dolly. She had been a great help in connecting Victor with former Crown and Anchor employees and other locals. He had high hopes that she might have something else up her sleeve. Finally the first day's shooting was to end with the New York psychic sitting down with the Meads Family. Perhaps if he had an extra moment Victor might grab lunch or remember to breathe.

There was so much coming up with the film. Victor knew that he was on the verge of creating something important. He wanted to get the word out. The Lady of the Dunes was an enduring mystery. Surely Victor's hard work on trying to get to the bottom of the who and the why was newsworthy. He decided that he would contact several local newspapers with essentially a press release about what he was doing. What Victor was hoping for was to get some publicity for the upcoming film and perhaps even get some new information about the Lady of the Dunes from potential readers.

Four newspapers were decided upon to contact. Two were on Cape Cod while the other two were larger Boston-based outlets. Victor crafted a concise narrative about who he was, what he was doing, and what he hoped to accomplish with the documentary. The pair of Cape Cod newspapers listened to Victor's pitch and seemed to be intrigued. The Boston newspapers did as well and requested followup calls. The ball was at least rolling.

There was another branch to the tree that Victor needed to get back to tending to. That was the District Attorney's Office and the possibility of missing evidence. Victor's panel of experts: Agent X, Art, and Frank the P.I. all believed that malfeasance had led to evidence going missing. Earning his 'private investigator' title Frank reached out to Victor with an important question that he said needed to be asked to those at the office.

Victor decided the best route was to send an email. The question was simple yet slightly obscure. 'Who was the head custodian that was in charge of evidence between 1985-1995?' This question came from reports that evidence had been 'accidentally' tossed from a locker sometime in the 1990's. He was hoping by some stroke of luck that he could get confirmation on this story from the District Attorney's Office.

Fatherly duties called and Victor attended to his son. He did not expect to hear anything back from the District Attorney's Office on that day if at all. A small bit of surprise came over him when he heard the email chime altering him that he had received something. It was in fact a reply to his email. The response gave Victor the name of the head custodian he was looking for. Feeling a little more confident Victor responded. He asked if it was alright to speak with someone from the District Attorney's Office before he potentially did an interview with both Boston-based newspapers. The response he got would change everything about the Lady of the Dunes in Victor's mind.

Mere minutes later his phone was ringing. The Called ID showed 'Restricted.' Putting two and two together Victor knew this was the District Attorney's Office as he had asked for. He picked up and was greeted by booming anger.

"Why are you contacting us again?!" The voice growled. "We already answered your questions." Victor was taken aback by the level of vitriol he was being met with and was not sure how to proceed.

"I was just looking for the name of the head custodian." The response was swift as if they knew where Victor's line of questioning was leading.

"There is no missing evidence! Her skull is in Boston, it is not lost."

"I wanted to try to speak with you before I go talking to the newspapers. Just so you'd know what I was potentially going to say."

"I don't care what you say to any newspapers. There is no missing evidence." Victor wanted to press them about the reported locker of thrown away evidence, but he was stunned by the agitation coming through the phone. "I am so tired of people like you and people like Peter Manso going around exploiting this case for profit."

"Hey, don't put me in that category," Victor snapped back, "I'm not trying to exploit the case." This response actually got a laugh from the other end of the line.

"Yeah, right." Victor was all set with this conversation.

"Okay, great, well if you have any questions for me be sure to give me a call." His sarcastic tone was picked up. The phone call was ended swiftly by the voice on the other end.

His raised voice had drawn the attention of Maura who had been trying to get their son to nap. Victor was furiously running his fingers through his hair and shaking his head. When Maura sat down next to him at the kitchen table he began to explain what had just happened.

The head custodian question had proven to light an angry fire under the District Attorney's Office. It was at this point that Maura said what Victor was already thinking.

"This has to do with way more than just a random girl in the dunes."

"I feel the same way," Victor replied. "I keep coming back to why. Why hasn't this been solved in almost fifty years?" Maura felt there was suspicion everywhere.

"The victim herself is like the tip of the iceberg. The only thing for certain is someone was murdered, everything else is shrouded in suspicion. Who she was. Who killed her. Why she was killed. Where she was killed. Why there has been no resolution. Why the community has been so quiet about it. There's all of these questions and no answers."

"I hope I can find some."

Victor always felt more centered after chatting with Maura about his projects but especially with the Lady of the Dunes. He had gone from barely knowing anything about the case at the beginning of January to being overwhelmed with facts, stories, quotes, and rumors three months later. It always felt good to talk about it and get a fresh set of eyes on what he was dealing with. Victor felt a sense of calm and a sense of purpose when it came to the documentary.

In what was perhaps the most positive surprise yet for Victor the Provincetown community came together in support of the documentary. This was seen by the fact that fourteen rooms in various hotels were put aside for Victor, his crew of four camera operators and a line producer, as well as several people coming into town to be interviewed for the film. This type of warmth had not been the typical case and Victor knew that. He felt that a bit of luck was on his side. That and again the credibility given to his project by the Meads Family.

Though he knew it was still an uphill climb the outpouring of support from the people in Provincetown made Victor feel good. It made him believe that, although some were adamant that Victor stay away and leave the case alone, many people who had lived there for a long time wanted to see some sort of resolution when it came to the Lady of the Dunes.

In a moment of what he thought was serendipity as Victor was thinking about Jimmy Meads Jr. and the Meads Family his phone began to ring. It was Jimmy himself. Victor had a big smile when he picked up. That was quickly wiped away.

"I had to call you, just pulled over," Jimmy said sounding startled.

"What's going on?"

"I just saw Peter Manso being taken out of his house on a stretcher and being loaded into an ambulance." Victor's eyes grew wide.

"Do you know what happened? Is he going to be all right?"

"I have no idea. I literally just saw it a few minutes ago and pulled over to call you and let you know."

"Wow, just wow," Victor couldn't think of anything constructive to say and he felt badly about that. Jimmy explained that he had somewhere to be otherwise he might be tempted to follow the ambulance and find out Manso's condition on his own. They parted with Victor simply asking Jimmy to let him know if he heard anything later.

Victor walked around the house in a haze wondering about the fate of Peter Manso. The answer came quickly. His phone rang and it was Warren Tobias. Although they had only spoken briefly before Victor knew Tobias as a close friend of Peter Manso. Tobias had been a member of local law enforcement for thirty-five years, including a time as Police Chief. Tobias had long thought that the Lady of the Dunes had been wanted fugitive Rory Gene Kesinger, although DNA tests later seemed to dismiss her as a match. He was Manso's 'ace in the hole' when it came to his Lady of the Dunes project.

"Victor, it's Warren Tobias."

"Hi Warren, how is everything?" Victor had a feeling as to the nature of the phone call, yet felt the need to play dumb.

"I wanted to reach out and let you know that Peter Manso just died." There was a quiver in Warren's voice as he let those words of his friend's death come out. Victor sighed.

"Oh my God," he replied, "I'm sorry."

"It was very sudden. I know that you had been in touch with him a few times about your films you're both doing. I thought you'd like to know."

"Jimmy Meads had actually called me to tell me he had seen an ambulance at the house."

"Please don't say anything," Warren continued, "the press doesn't even know yet."

"I won't, I really appreciate you letting me know. I'm sorry again about Peter."

Sure he had been a bit rough around the edges when it came to his conversations with Victor but Manso had been a wealth of information. He had given Victor some great leads and the idea of Provincetown in the 1970s being a big stage was a concept that had stuck with him. Peter Manso had helped to push the direction of Victor's story. Plus the District Attorney's Office disliked Manso, this gave he and Victor a unique kinship.

He had fully intended to call Peter a third time and possibly look him up during his shoot in Provincetown. At the very least Manso would have gotten the invite to the premiere of the documentary whenever that would be. Victor spent some time out for a walk in his neighborhood processing Peter Manso's death.

Later in the evening Victor felt like diving back into preparation for the trip to Provincetown. He thought he had another easy interview to setup when he reached back out to Bob. Bob's connection with Sydney Monzon, and thus Tony Costa and the whole stage that was Provincetown at that time, made him an invaluable connection. Plus they had previously spoken and Bob had seemed amiable to being a part of the documentary.

It caught Victor off guard when Bob flat out refused to be a part of the film going forward. He stated that he had no interest in being in front of a camera, or speaking any more about Costa, Sydney, the Lady of the Dunes, any of it. When Victor gently pressed him for more details why Bob ended the conversation by telling Victor he already had gotten more from him than anyone before and that should be enough.

He was angry at first after Bob hung up. Victor needed eyewitnesses to that time period in Provincetown to make the documentary mean more than other rumor and innuendo pieces that permeated the internet. He stewed for a few minutes before it dawned on him. Victor could not imagine the anguish Bob had gone through living with the fact that someone he had cared deeply for had been coldly murdered. Victor had at times been looking at the Lady of the Dunes case as if he was watching a play from the audience. He was a part of it though. He was on the stage. Bob's desire to not relive the past anymore began to make sense to Victor. All he could do was respect Bob's wishes and leave him alone.

Thumbing through his contacts for the film Victor came across the person that had been working with Peter Manso on his Lady of the Dunes project. Knowing their connection Victor called their number and left a brief message simply sharing his condolences on Manso's death. He did not give it a second thought until a short while later when he received a response. After exchanging a few pleasantries and condolences about Manso the person who had been working on Manso's Lady of the Dunes project asked a rather blunt question.

"So you're trying to solve who the murderer was, and who was murdered, right?"

"Yep."

"See, that's where you're wrong."

"Why?"

"The problem is that you should be looking at the investigation as much as the crime itself."

"Why? What are you getting at?"

"You should be asking yourself why after nearly fifty years law enforcement still has no clue."

"Conspiracy?"

"That's what many would assume. If you ask me, I say incompetence."

"Why? What makes you say that?"

"How does state evidence get thrown out by mistake? Think about it."

This marked the fourth important person to lean into incompetence as a prevailing issue with the Lady of the Dunes case. Victor asked if they could perhaps catch up in a few weeks and talk more as he was getting prepared to head to Provincetown to shoot for the documentary. They agreed and wished Victor good luck in his filming.

After the two parted ways Victor returned to his contacts for the film. The name he had given the person he had just spoken to was simply 'Manso's Guy.' Victor deleted it and with a cheeky smile replaced it with 'Agent Y.' The conversation they had just had was peppered with Victor asking 'Why?' He also couldn't help but ask himself why this person was helping with the Lady of the Dunes case, first with Manso and now possibly with Victor. Their next conversation in a few weeks would be be interesting.

In the meantime the hours were ticking down to Victor and his crew heading to Provincetown. He planned on it being one long shoot, getting as much film and audio as possible. However as had been the case throughout his three months working on his Lady of the Dunes project Victor knew to be ready for anything that might come his way.

Chapter 10, The Shoot Day One

Thursday April 8th was a mix of nervous energy and confident stillness. As a producer of several other films Victor knew what went into the preparation before the shooting began. He had been there before and felt quite confident in his research and the interviews he had set up.

That being said there was also this feeling that he was doing something more meaningful than simply a documentary about an old murder case. The people he had spoken with close connection to the case, those that had lived in the community and experienced the fallout, their stories and emotions gave this project more weight in Victor's mind.

After dinner he made one last walk through of his equipment. He needed to go to bed early as the next morning was to start at 4am. Victor laid out his clothes for the morning and had everything he needed close by. His plan was to give himself as much time as he could to sleep. Then when morning came he could essentially sleepwalk out of the house to his car. The tossing and turning lasted for what felt like hours but eventually Victor fell asleep. He periodically woke up during the night feeling the anticipation usually reserved for children on Christmas Eve. Victor was surprisingly spry for 4am when his alarm went off. He had kept his phone close to his side of the bed to allow him to shut the alarm off before waking Maura.

The sun was not due to rise in Provincetown until about ten minutes after six. This meant Victor's entire drive would be appropriately cloaked in darkness. His setting up the night before paid off allowing Victor to slip out the front door within half an hour of waking up.

It was dark and chilly with a temperature barely above forty degrees. Victor had finished packing up his car and took a moment to stare at his darkened home before leaving Norton bound for Provincetown.

I-495 was barren and empty. Victor kept his speed reasonable not wanting to get a ticket at the start of the trip. Seeing the signs for Cape Cod got him energized. It began to feel real. It began to feel important. This film mattered.

Victor managed to cross over the Bourne Bridge and keep his energy up all the way into Orleans. He knew it was about time to grab a coffee to help fight off the darkness around him. First though he had something he needed to do.

The gravel crunched under the tires of Victor's car. When he stopped and opened the door he made it a point to close it quietly. The sky was a faint orange and purple as the act of sunrise was beginning. It was 6am and Victor walked softly through rows of headstones. He had arrived at Evergreen Cemetery in Eastham.

It took a few minutes to find the exact spot he had jotted down on his phone. Then Victor stopped. He passed a triangular shaped rock with a plaque on it that read: 'Monzon.' There at his feet was the marker for Sydney Monzon. He took in a deep breath after reading the inscription: 'Lived Each Second To Its Fullest.'

Sydney Monzon's connection to Tony Costa and Staniford Sorrentino had initially fascinated Victor. He was looking at the story from a filmmaker's perspective, seeing her as a character on the stage. As time passed though he began to feel a connection, a deeper sadness, for this young girl that got mixed up with less than reputable people and ultimately lost her life because of it.

Victor's had not initially planned to visit Sydney's grave. The dark drive onto Cape Cod had changed his mind. Now as the sun's rays began to tickle the tops of surrounding trees he was glad he was there. Sydney Monzon finally felt like a real person.

He bowed his head and said a little prayer. Route 6 behind him was quiet. The only sounds breaking the sad and eerie silence were birds welcoming the new morning with song. Victor stood at Sydney Monzon's grave and looked around, soaking in the atmosphere. Again in his mind Victor thought of the importance of what he was doing. It mattered.

The sun was now present in the sky. The Outer Cape was slowly waking up on the chilly Friday morning. Victor stopped near the Evergreen Cemetery and bought a coffee. He took another moment to stand outside of his car, the cup of coffee resting on the roof, to gaze at his surroundings. The hallowed sandy grounds of Henry David Thoreau's walks were less than two miles to Victor's east from where he stood. They felt like a million miles in distance and time for him now.

It was still more than a half hour to get into Provincetown. Despite making good time up to that point Victor did not want to simply wait around. His crew of four camera operators and a line producer would be arriving later in the morning along with the New York psychic who was driving all night to get there. This left a few hours of time to kill for Victor before the actual filming could get started. He decided to get moving and head toward what was to be the first filming location: St. Peter the Apostle Church Cemetery in Provincetown. It was the burial site of the Lady of the Dunes.

St. Peter's Cemetery was located on Alden Street. It was far enough from the bustling center of Commercial Street that when Victor slowly pulled into the cemetery he felt like he was the only person on Earth at that time. He knew that the burial site of the Lady of the Dunes was at the bottom of a hill next to the chapel on the cemetery grounds. Victor drove toward the chapel and parked at the end of a driveway leading to a garage to its right.

He stepped from out of his car, closing the door as quietly as possible. It was so quiet that Victor felt that even the slightest sounds from his car door could shatter the scenery like a fragile pane of glass. He took a deep breath of the cool early-spring air. Though it bordered the community the cemetery at St. Peter's felt like its own world. It felt like it didn't belong where it was. Victor began walking toward a row of small rectangular headstones lined up at the bottom of that hill.

The search for the grave was quick and unspectacular. It was in fact the first stone in the line Victor walked toward. Upon seeing the actual stone Victor took in a long breath and let out a sigh. Below his feet was the resting place of the Lady of the Dunes.

"I've been looking for you," Victor whispered. He stared at her stone absorbing in all of its mundane details. The words carved into the stone were quite prophetic for Victor and his entire purpose for being there. "Unidentified Female Body. Found Race Point Dunes. July 26, 1974." Victor read the words aloud. They made it all feel real. She was there, yet she was not there. Again it gave importance to what Victor was doing. He wanted to give her a name. If Victor could not solve the case he at least wanted this 'unidentified female body' to have a name. She was a human being, she was someone's daughter, the Lady of the Dunes deserved to at least have a name.

Much like he had done at Sydney Monzon's grave Victor said a quiet prayer as he stood over the marker for the Lady of the Dunes. He raised his head and began to wander. Victor was immediately struck by the enormity of the St. Peter's cemetery. The grounds encompassed approximately twenty-five acres of land with six different roads abutting the cemetery.

Victor walked up the hill toward the chapel and stood next to a tall white cross in a grassy area. From there he surveyed the scene. There were thousands of stones stretching off into the distance. The silence was broken by a voice calling out to Victor from near the garage. A man approached cordially asking Victor what he was doing there.

"My name is Victor," he said in a quiet voice, thinking he might wake the neighbors so early, "I'm a documentary filmmaker. I'm here to begin a shoot for a film about the Lady of the Dunes."

"Ah, I see," the man replied. "I'm the head groundskeeper. I try to get my morning duties done as soon as the sun comes up. Not used seeing anyone else out here so early. I actually thought my eyes were playing tricks on me."

"Do they often play tricks on you out here?" The groundskeeper laughed a bit.

"It's a pretty big cemetery, you're bound to see or hear things every now and then."

"What do you know about her?" Victor pointed toward the stone of the Lady of the Dunes.

"I know she's been dug up a bunch," he answered. "Poor Mo, he was the one that had to do it each time."

"Mo?"

"Yeah, Mo was the old groundskeeper."

"Is he around? I'd love to speak with him." The man shook his head.

"Unfortunately Mo is no longer with us."

"Oh, I'm sorry."

"It was a real shame, he died after falling off of the lawnmower here." The man beckoned Victor to follow him. After walking for a minute, several steps behind him, the groundskeeper came to a spot and stopped.

"What's here?" Victor asked confused as the man pointed a finger.

"This is where Mo died." Victor was not sure how to react to that morbid fact.

"Wow," he then had a thought pop into his head. "Did Mo ever say anything about what it was like digging her body up?"

"He said he was told she was like soup."

"Soup?"

"Yeah, like her remains were soupy." Victor tried his best not to picture exactly what 'soupy' remains would look like, especially on an empty stomach, but it was no use. "She is headless, and handless, in a body bag. The casket I believe is metal and black. That's about all there is to it."

"Do you know where Tony Costa is buried in here?"

"Oh yeah, of course." There was another brief field trip leading Victor further from his car and further into the creepy stillness of St. Peter's cemetery with the stranger he had only just met. "He's right here." The groundskeeper pointed to a rectangular stone near a split-rail fence.

"That stone says 'Cecilia Bent Bonaviri.'"

"That's Tony's mother," the groundskeeper explained. "He's buried here." The man took a few steps over and stomped his foot on a patch of grass.

"Oh, no headstone?"

"They didn't want people coming out and possibly doing damage to the grounds."

As Victor stood on top of Tony Costa's unmarked grave he and the groundskeeper continued on in conversation. They spoke of the lay of the land of St. Peter's and how wonderfully odd it was. Even this creepy area of Tony Chop Chop's grave was juxtaposed by residential homes direct across Winslow Street which abutted the cemetery. The conversation lasted closed to an hour when a pair of vehicles pulled onto the property. Victor's crew had arrived.

Victor excused himself from the groundskeeper, who had never given his name, and went to get the first day's shoot underway. The unloading of equipment took close to ten minutes. Victor dispatched all four camera operators to begin getting B-Roll footage. This was footage supplementary to the main project. The camera people went in different directions to get shots of the graves, chapel, nearby homes and buildings, and anything else that could be interesting.

In addition to B-Roll the crew got some photos and video of the cemetery specifically the areas around the Lady of the Dunes' grave as well as Tony Costa's. This included a personal favorite shot of the 252-foot-tall Pilgrim Monument in the background with the Lady of the Dunes' marker in the foreground.

The New York psychic arrived at the St. Peter's cemetery nearly two hours into Victor's time there. They apologized for not getting there sooner. Victor joked that they should have just flown and landed at the airport nearby. After exchanging a few pleasantries with Victor the New York psychic turned their head and looked into the direction of the Lady of the Dunes' grave.

They politely excused themselves and walked slowly over toward it. It looked like they were wading through a haze of bad vibes in order to reach it. They bowed their head and exhaled long and loud several times. They then raised their head and let out one long exhale while looking into the pale blue early-April sky. Later on the New York psychic would tell Victor of how overwhelmed with all sorts of emotions they were while standing above the final resting place of the Lady of the Dunes.

While Victor waited for the arrival of Father Hugh 'Mick' McCullough he walked the New York psychic over to the grave of Jimmy Meads Sr. Once there Victor and the psychic asked the former Police Chief for permission to speak with his sons for the documentary. The psychic felt the presence of Chief Meads and remarked to Victor that he felt the spirit was present to help solve the case. Victor headed back to where his car was parked to await Father McCullough.

The final piece of the puzzle for Victor at St. Peter's was meeting and interviewing Father McCullough. Once he arrived Victor gave him time to gather himself before attempting to ask him any questions. Father Mick was a straight shooter as Victor found out immediately. He had entered the Seminary in 1968 and had seen and heard nearly everything imaginable in the more than half century since. Victor chatted with him off camera with Father Mick revealing that he did not want to be interviewed for the documentary.

Victor was disappointed but the stoic man of the cloth compromised. He allowed the crew to shoot him standing in silent prayer over the grave of the Lady of the Dunes. It was an impactful scene for the film. The beautifully somber piece of footage did not come without a catch. Father Mick told Victor he did not want that footage or the church itself distorted in any way. Although that was never something the crossed his mind Victor still made it a point to promise compliance with the longtime pastor's wishes.

Before leaving to explore Provincetown a little, the New York psychic did say something simple and yet so deeply reassuring to Victor.

"I am overwhelmed with the importance of what you are trying to do," they said with an unflappable sincerity. It was the same sentiment Victor had been feeling since leaving his home. From their coat pocket the psychic produced a simple sheet of white-lined paper, folded several times, and handed it to Victor.

"What's this?"

"Words from the Lady of the Dunes," they replied.

"What do you mean?"

"I was a little later than expected because I had to pull over about a half-mile down the road. A voice was coming to me, telling me things. It was her. Please read it when you have the chance."

"This is amazing," Victor replied. He wanted to take a longer time to read it and study it but his day was full. "I promise I will take the time to really study it tonight."

"I know you will. I just had one thing to ask. Do you know what 'RAD' means?"

"RAD?"

"Yes, most of what the Lady said makes sense for her life and circumstances of her death as you'll read. The very last thing she said to me were the letters R-A-D. I wondered if it made any sense to you?"

"No, not really." The sheet of paper was potentially a glimpse into the mind of the Lady of the Dunes. Victor was very appreciative and thanked the psychic for being a part of the documentary. The two would meet up again later in the day.

It was mid-morning. Time for Victor and his crew to move on to the next filming location, the Provincetown Theater on Bradford Street. Victor thanked Father Mick while the crew loaded the cameras and other miscellaneous equipment into their vehicles. During this final parting of ways Victor had hoped there might be some sage words of wisdom from the pastor when it came to the documentary. There were none. It was simple and cordial.

As Victor walked back to his car Father Mick stood watching. He had not specifically said it however Victor could not help but feel that Father Mick and the church in general wanted the Lady of the Dunes and her story to rest. Victor waved as he was the final vehicle to exit St. Peter's cemetery. He turned the corner and lost sight of Father Mick.

The Provincetown Theater was only a mile and a half from the cemetery, a rather short drive. Victor had four interviews for the documentary lined up inside the theater on that day. It would be his home for at least the next several hours.

For a theater company with a rich history dating back to 1963 the building itself was rather unassuming. Barely larger than a typical convenience store from the outside Victor and his crew took up much of the dirt parking area behind it upon arrival.

The pandemic had stopped in-person performances at the Provincetown Theater. The company however was making full use of technology and offering online streaming of new shows. The interior of the theater therefore was still active and gave off a slight sense of normalcy for Victor upon walking in.

Three staff members were on duty that day when Victor entered. He explained who he was and why he was there before ushering in his crew. For their part the staff knew about Victor and his documentary and were very supportive. Each of them told Victor how they wanted the story of the Lady of the Dunes to be told. They also said they represented a good portion of the Provincetown community in that sentiment.

There was a little bit of time for Victor to wander the theater after setting up. He had the first of his four interviews coming in less than half an hour so Victor could not go far. Instead he walked the theater trying to soak in the atmosphere. The Provincetown Theater was small and humble. In Victor's mind it spoke true of what the town and community as a whole was.

What Victor could not shake was how the theater itself gave off a Twin Peaks vibe in his mind. There was a dark red curtain that reminded Victor of the extradimensional Black Lodge location from the vaunted television series. The black grand piano hearkened back to old smokey jazz clubs from the 1940s. Victor allowed himself to get lost in the moment briefly. His daydream was broken as one of the staff members of the theater let him know that his first interview subject was there.

The initial interview subject at the Provincetown Theater was local dentist Dr. Gerard J. Kinahan. Serving the Lower Cape since 1982 Dr. Kinahan was highly regarded and deeply respected in the field of dentistry. It was through Victor's conversations with Dolly that he learned that Police Chief Meads' dentist was still alive. This fact was particularly random at the time however it paid dividends when it came time to work on the filming for the documentary.

When compiling his list of potential names to interview Victor reached out to Dr. Kinahan. The first thing the longtime dentist said when returning Victor's call was "What took you so long?" Dr. Kinahan had been waiting a long time for someone to come around looking to interview him in connection with the Lady of the Dunes case.

Dr. Kinahan spoke of Jimmy Meads Sr. being a patient of his and developing a trust over the years.

"At first the Chief was quite intimidating, by his imposing size and somewhat stoic demeanor. Once I got to know him and he let his guard down he ended up being a really good guy, with a good sense of humor."

Victor left it open-ended when asking Dr. Kinahan about the dental records of the Lady of the Dunes.

The rapport built with the Chief allowed Dr. Kinahan access to a highly confidential piece of evidence. Sometime during the 1980s Chief Meads was having a routine teeth cleaning at Kinahan's office. When it was done the Chief asked Kinahan if it would be possible for him to come down to the police station that weekend as he had something he wanted his opinion on.

That weekend came and after arriving at the station Meads beckoned Kinahan to a private room. In there the police chief produced a cardboard box which he gently placed on a long table. He carefully opened the box and reached in. Meads produced a skull.

"This is the skull of the Lady of the Dunes," Meads explained. Dr. Kinahan was caught off guard to see the skull in general at first. The Chief asked his friend if he could examine the skull for anything unusual. Kinahan obliged and noticed several loose teeth rolling around in the bottom of the box. One by one he began to pick up the teeth and put them in the appropriate sockets. Kinahan thought the skull had a complete, or nearly complete, set of teeth.

The reason this was shocking, Kinahan told Victor, was due to the fact that when the autopsy was done on the body the dentist who examined her recorded that she had teeth missing as well as extensive dental work.

"Did they forge the autopsy report?" Victor asked Kinahan.

Dr. Kinahan would not go that far. He did say that he knew those dentists that had worked on the autopsy and that he held them in high regard.

"I have seen estimates of her having in the neighborhood of three to four thousand dollars worth of dental work done. What I saw contradicts that. She had a series of silver fillings, the ones common for the time. There were also a few gold inlays which seemed out of sync with the rest of the teeth."

"Why is that?"

"Those types of gold inlays are relatively cheap and are something that would usually be done at a dental school like Tufts where I went."

"Where is Tufts?"

"Kneeland Street in Boston, right on the corner where the Combat Zone ended. In fact I remember that some of the working girls from the Combat Zone would sometimes come into Tufts for inexpensive dental work." Victor did not know it at the time but that last statement by Dr. Kinahan would turn out to be a very important piece of information.

"So what do you think about the reports of her expensive dental work on the internet?"

"Untrue. She had at most $1,200 worth of work done," Kinahan said. "I believe that most of the information online, Wikipedia, YouTube, podcasts, news articles, and the like are complete fabrications."

Victor thanked Dr. Kinahan and took a moment to digest what he had just heard. It was only the first interview and already the idea of malfeasance had crept back into his mind. If it was true and much of the information readily available online was false the question came back to: Why? Was it simply a lack of due diligence by amateur sleuths with web pages, or something more sinister? Could it be that people intentionally had put false information out there to muddy the waters and make solving the case more difficult?

There was little time to think as Dennis Minsky strode into the theater. Victor was already acquainted with him from the Thoreau documentary. Due in no small part to the pandemic restrictions Minsky showed up to the interview looking rather shaggy. He had not been to a barber in a year and resembled the love-child of Walt Whitman and Kurt Vonnegut. His very long hair and beard made Minsky look like a fictional character from a fantasy novel, but he was an absolutely real and authentic person.

Minsky was an invaluable resource. He had come to Provincetown as a young man. Being there in the late 1960's Minsky knew not only Jimmy Meads Sr., but also Tony Costa and Staniford Sorrentino. He had spent a summer working directly with Tony Costa as handymen. Minsky was a living, breathing encyclopedia of Provincetown history, the good and the bad.

"Long ago Provincetown was dominated by the Portuguese," Minsky began as if starting a dissertation on the history of Provincetown. "Then in the 60s the younger generation, hippies I guess you'd call them, came in. I was one of them. There was initially friction between the old guard and new generation, but nothing overly serious."

"So it was kind of a melting pot where everybody for better or for worse got along?"

"Sort of. The hippies were more transient. They'd come in and then leave. It was around this time that Provincetown became a public haven for the gay community."

"Do you think the Lady of the Dunes could have been a part of that transient community?"

"Possibly, a lot of faces were there one day and gone the next and nobody batted an eye. It's just the way Provincetown was then."

Minsky went on to tell stories of Chief Meads and his dedication to law enforcement. He was seen as ahead of his time as far as compassion and understanding. This was on full display on one particular night.

"There was a night when a guy I knew was messed up on something, maybe acid or heroin. He thought he was in the Viet Cong. Painted his face up and everything. He crawled on his hands and knees into the Chief's yard and slashed his tires.

Eventually the Chief apprehended him and held him until the police arrived."

Third for the interviewing process was Jimmy Meads Jr. and his brother Michael. Jimmy Jr. was by this point more of an old friend for Victor having spoken with him numerous times during the process of beginning the documentary. Michael was a new face.

Victor had a blast looking over some old family photos of Police Chief Meads. He felt like he had been invited into the Meads Family's world. In a place where it was 50/50 that people would want to talk about the Lady of the Dunes the Meads Family had been shining beacons of the good in town.

Jimmy Jr. and Michael spoke in reverent terms about Provincetown as they remembered it growing up. It sounded much more like a slice of 'Olde Cape Cod' than the darker stories Victor had become used to hearing from the 1970s. It could not have hurt that for Jimmy Jr. and Michael Meads their father was the Chief of Police. To them that Provincetown is the one that they liked to remember and that Provincetown was the one that their father presided over.

More so the Chief was a good father. He took his boys fishing, hunting, and more. The adoration and respect for Chief Meads extended beyond the family. He was seen as tough but fair and by many the best police chief Provincetown had ever seen.

The brothers also confirmed what Dennis Minsky had said earlier about knowing someone who had attacked Chief Meads in his driveway. Jimmy Jr. and Michael added some more details to the story. It was while Chief Meads was walking home from work. Meads noticed the slashed tires. His senses were heightened which allowed him to feel the man's presence as he swung the knife. The Chief ducked and the blade went into one of the already slashed tires. Despite having just finished his day's work Chief Meads brought the agitated man down and held him until backup arrived.

Before ending the session with Jimmy Jr. and Michael Meads Victor made plans with them for later. Once the interviews had wrapped up Victor and the New York psychic were going to meet them at their old house to talk some more.

Victor might have been biased toward the Meads Family already but it seemed clear to him that although there could have been malfeasance in the Lady of the Dunes case it was nothing that involved Chief Meads and his work.

Last but not least for the day's interviews at the Provincetown Theater was a fire lieutenant from a small town in Central Massachusetts. As the pair chatted Victor produced a black and white photo of the Lady of the Dunes' body as it was found at the crime scene. This photo was easily accessible on the internet. Although it did not show her face the lieutenant made a startling revelation after gazing at it only briefly.

"She didn't die there," he said, "that's a drop site." Victor's eyes got wide.

"What do you mean drop site?" The lieutenant pointed to a specific part of the photo.

"Look at her ankles, they look crossed over. When you pick up a dead body, you cross the ankles, or if you drag the body you drag them by the legs crossed over."

Victor's mind was racing. Could it be true? Could the Lady of the Dunes have been murdered somewhere else and then brought out to the remote Race Point highlands and dropped there? If so, where?

Each of the four interviews at the Provincetown Theater had been a home run for different reasons. Still, Victor had more questions than when he started and little time to reflect on them. He had to have a quick bite to eat after packing up and then head to the Meads house for a more intimate interview. Knowing that they'd be back for a second round of interviews the following day Victor told the crew to leave whatever they could at the theater. The theater's stage and the piano that sat upon it was covered with papers and equipment.

Less than an hour after concluding his interview with the fire lieutenant Victor was sitting at the kitchen table inside the Meads family home. He was flanked by a camera operator as well as the New York psychic who had enjoyed their time wandering Provincetown's Commercial Street earlier.

Jimmy Jr., Michael, and Nancy Meads were gracious hosts. They were however slightly skeptical of the guest Victor brought. Not only were they psychic but they also were from Upstate New York. It was a double whammy that might have been hard to overcome. However the psychic intended to prove they were indeed the real deal. Police Chief Meads was channeled through them. However it took a lot for the family to believe that their relative was in fact there with them in the kitchen.

For nearly half and hour the New York psychic relayed words from beyond. The spirit of Chief Meads repeatedly gave assurance and confirmation that he was the person speaking through the psychic. It was only when things were said that Jimmy Jr. and Michael would know that the family was convinced that it was all real.

Police Chief Meads mentioned how proud he was of his children and his granddaughter. He spoke through the psychic about so many good times through the years that brought tears to the eyes of his family. The conversation moved into things Chief Meads had always wanted to say to his family. Victor sat in the background partially in amazement of the things that the psychic was revealing through Chief Meads and partially overjoyed that the Meads Family was getting to hear them.

The communication between Chief Meads and his family shifted to what it was like at the moment of crossing over. The Chief revealed that there were multiple family members there to greet him. However one person that greeted him caused a shock wave through the kitchen. Chief Meads said that the Lady of the Dunes herself met him. He was thrilled to say that she had her hands unlike what had happened to her at the time of her death. Although he never said the name of the Lady of the Dunes Chief Meads said that she personally thanked him for all of the years he had spent trying to solve her murder. The pair embraced in the afterlife with the Chief saying that it was his validation for all of his hard work he had done on the case.

Victor's camera operator filmed the entirety of the intensely personal ninety minute conversation between the Meads Family at their departed Jimmy Sr. through the psychic. It was emotionally draining and yet satisfying at the same time. When the communication ended and the camera stopped rolling Victor decided that the footage was far too personal. Out of respect for the Meads Family he decided not to use any of it for the documentary.

Victor and his crew left the Meads house and went their separate ways for the night. For Victor his home base was the Stowaway bed and breakfast establishment on Bradford Street. The house itself felt like home and the guests were urged to treat it as such. There were seven guest rooms on two floors allowing for some privacy.

It was at this point, after shooting wrapped for the day, and before dinner that Victor remembered the folded white-lined paper that the New York psychic had handed him at St. Peter's. He pulled it from his jacket pocket and sat in the comfortable armchair to read it. Victor unfolded it and began to read.

There was a lot to digest in the full page, front and back, of writing. The psychic had channeled the Lady of the Dunes who spoke of her life. She said she was from the mid-Atlantic area, was an only child, and was estranged from her mother.

Victor noted that in the writing the Lady of the Dunes mentioned that she might have been killed because she saw something she shouldn't have. There may have been blueprints or sketches of a place that her lover at the time had plans to rob.

It might have been a potential pregnancy that caused an issue as the lover accused the Lady of the Dunes of sleeping around.

Her death itself was meant to be an overdose but she refused the pills her lover offered. Thus she was struck in the head and never regained consciousness.

The Lady of the Dunes said her lover was mentally ill and had assistance in carrying out, and covering up, the murder, and also help keeping it unsolved.

Victor raised an eyebrow when in the psychic's writing the Lady of the Dunes noted her lover, and likely murderer, had a name starting with a J or a G.

She was appreciative of the altruistic intentions the documentary had, and even noted that in the afterlife she now had her hands.

The psychic's letter ended with the strange letters RAD.

Victor folded the white-lined paper back up and finally was able to exhale. He could see every description, he could hear her voice. There were many clues to ponder, the mid-Atlantic, the mentally unstable lover with the J or G first name. Still Victor's eyes lingered on RAD. What did it mean? He needed more time to sit and think but hunger got the best of him.

Dinner was relatively quick. A few of the crew ventured two towns south to Wellfleet to have some sandwiches knowing that there would be another early morning ahead of them. Victor enjoyed the dumplings he ordered at Kung Fu Dumplings on Commercial Street with the rest of the crew. After sunset Victor had a far less formal meeting. This was for a few drinks with Dolly. He could not wait to pick her brain about Provincetown gossip in person.

It was very fitting that the pair met at what was seen at the epicenter of the debauchery of 1970s Provincetown, the Crown and Anchor. Victor was in the belly of the beast so to say. Despite being told by those who would speak to him that Provincetown was different now Victor couldn't help but look around with a skeptical eye.

A few hours of drinks and laughs did wonders for Victor. Dolly picked up the tab for the drinks which included copious white wine for her and Dark and Stormy's for Victor. He appreciated that. Dolly also made it a point to tell him that no matter what Victor's documentary was already a success. The fact that he was able to pull off the project in Dolly's eyes was nothing short of miraculous. An actual documentary on the Lady of the Dunes complete with in depth contributions from those who had up until that point refused to work with other projects was amazing to her.

Much of their time chatting was filled with Dolly unloading several unbelievable but true stories of the Provincetown that she knew. These were things that Victor knew would not be possible to include in the documentary yet were still fun to hear. He would share some of them with the crew though.

Dolly did bring the mood in the room down a little when she gave Victor an ominous warning wrapped in between slugs from the wine glass. She lowered her voice slightly and stared dead in his eyes.

"You're the talk of the town."

"What do you mean?"

"Everybody is buzzing about your project. We just had American Horror Story here so some people are on high alert. It's not necessarily a bad thing. Just a heads up. If you think you're being paranoid, seeing people giving longer stares than usual. Those won't be coincidence. They know who you are and why you're here."

For his part Victor played it off like it was nothing and gave a sheepish smile. Those skeptical eyes he had upon entering Crown and Anchor now felt totally justified. Victor sipped his Dark and Stormy and scanned the room. Anyone who happened to meet his glance was immediately scrutinized.

'What are you hiding?' Victor would think to himself.

The idea of an early night was not to be for Victor. After several hours and several more drinks he graciously thanked Dolly for all of her help with the project. They parted ways and Victor stumbled his way back to the Stowaway. He had a great first day of shooting and a great night of eating, drinking, and juicy gossip. His body might hate him in the morning but at that point Victor was satisfied.

Upon returning to his room Victor found a note on the table. It was an invite from the Stowaway's owner to come downstairs around midnight for a cocktail. They wanted to talk all about the Lady of the Dunes.

"Sorry, not tonight," Victor said to himself as he crumbled the note in his hand. He was too tired and nearly drunk. Besides that he had another early morning rendezvous planned. Victor was returning to the Lady of the Dunes' grave at 6am.

Chapter 11, The Shoot Day Two

The predawn hours of Saturday April 10th were chilly. Victor's alarm went off and he debated simply rolling back over and returning to his hungover sleep. However he remembered that he was in Provincetown for an important reason. Victor sat on the edge of the bed with his head in his hands trying to will himself to stand. It was 5:30am and still dark outside. He rocked himself forward and back like a car stuck in the mud and slowly rose to his feet with a muted groan.

Why was he up so early? Why was he paying another visit to the grave of the Lady of the Dunes? She was the reason why he was there but it was deeper. Victor felt like he was being pulled there. He didn't want to go, he needed to go.

Slowly Victor got himself dressed. He shuffled as quietly as possible out the front door of the Stowaway. It was a quick five-minute drive back to St. Peter's cemetery.

As Victor drove onto the cemetery grounds he turned his heater off in the car and rolled his window down. He breathed in the silence and the chilly morning air. It was 6 am and he was again standing in the presence of the Lady of the Dunes.

Crickets chirped in the distance as robins, chickadees, and blue jays started serenading the day. The sun began rising behind the cemetery's chapel on the hill surrounding the building in a colorful orange hue. Victor stared down at the grave. His mind kept thinking: 'Who are you?' There were no answers at that point.

Victor bowed his head and closed his eyes. He felt the cold but also felt the overwhelming sense of sadness that permeated the Lady of the Dunes' final resting place. He whispered asking her to show him the way. Again there were no answers.

St. Peter's cemetery was far more somber and desolate than it was the previous morning. Then there was Father Mick, the groundskeeper, and his entire crew. This morning it was only Victor and the Lady of the Dunes.

Once the cemetery was bathed in the full early morning sun Victor decided to grab a coffee and get ready for the day. He had four more interviews to conduct at the Provincetown Theater. Luckily in anticipation, Victor had left as much of his material as he could there. This was beneficial as with his slight hangover from the previous night's drinking with Dolly he would have very likely forgotten something important.

The second morning of interviews at the Provincetown Theater was old hat for Victor. There were four interviews lined up just as there were the previous day. He had high hopes for each of them. The first to arrive was Dr. Claire Glynn. Originally from Dublin, Ireland Glynn achieved her PhD in Molecular Medicine. She now taught in the Forensic Science Department at the University of New Haven in Connecticut. Glynn came with a highly regarded reputation as the best in the area when it came to forensic DNA.

Dr. Glynn's main talking point had to do with the extraction of DNA. She explained to Victor about the 23andMe and Ancestry.com direct-to-consumer DNA testing sites. It was a crash course in DNA 101 for Victor. Dr. Glynn stated that it was virtually impossible that the Lady of the Dunes did not have some sort of familial connection on either of those DNA databases.

Victor brought up the argument that it would be difficult to get usable DNA from the Lady of the Dunes' remains since they were nearly fifty years old. Dr. Glynn shot this idea down.

"In order to get the DNA," she began, "we do not swab a bone. We drill into it. So the idea that something from 1974 would not yield usable DNA is a lie."

Following the interview with Dr. Glynn Victor welcomed in local journalist Stephen Desroches. Having worked for the Cape Codder newspaper and Provincetown Magazine and being a well respected journalist Desroches was privy to things the public at large was not.

"The Lady of the Dunes is more akin to a ghost story. Things down here tend to get romanticized and the mythology part can take over. Remember the famous quote from (Edgar Allan) Poe: Believe half of what you see and none of what you hear." Desroches lingered on that phrase as if trying to let it sink in to Victor's mind about his own work.

"What's your experiences with the Lady of the Dunes case?"

"When I first got started in this business I did my own investigation into the murder. I was privy to some inside stuff including viewing the police case file."

"What did you see?"

"There were a lot of photos. She had been dead anywhere from ten days to three weeks. In the hot July sun you can imagine what damage was done. Her skin was black, like a rotten banana peel. You know about the hands, the near-decapitation, but for me it was the maggots. They were everywhere. In the wounds, on the body, it was as if I could hear them through the photos."

"What do you think her murder says about Provincetown at the time?"

"That time, the 1970s, was the last gasp of lawlessness, and it had been lawless for decades."

"How so?"

"The transient, seasonal, nature of life here, it lends itself to anonymity. It would have been a great place for a criminal, or criminals, to come to get away with whatever business they were into."

Victor took a few minutes for a breather after the somber and disturbing chat with Desroches about the details of the police case file. Victor thought he'd like to see the photos, but did he really? Desroches descriptions had given him goosebumps several times. Luckily the Lady of the Dunes case file was not something that would just fall into his hands.

Award-winning local author Jeannette de Beauvoir offered a much more gentle presence when she walked into the theater and sat on stage for her interview. Her deep red hair and dimples combined with her soft-spoken nature helped Victor temporarily erase the graphic images that Stephen Desroches had described.

Jeanette explained the culture of Provincetown from back then, some of which still resonated to the present day.

"It was the place to go if you wanted to try something you'd always wanted to do. Art, music, or if you just wanted to be in the presence of those chasing their dreams. There was, and in some ways still is, a rebellious spirit here. It was in your face. Oh, you don't like it? Too bad, we're going to live the way we want."

In her own writing career de Beauvoir had taken on the task of telling the story of the Lady of the Dunes. Her 2017 historical fiction book Our Lady of the Dunes was what brought Jeannette to Victor's attention. Though it was fiction she had noticed something wonderful when it came to the Lady of the Dunes herself. Jeannette told Victor how she had seen the beauty that shone through such an awful act. After her murder the Lady of the Dunes was embraced by Provincetown. Despite not knowing who she was or where she was from the community gave her a home.

"She is a part of Provincetown now." That sentiment brought a smile to Victor's face.

Wrapping up the series of interviews was Victor's own private investigator Frank and his business partner Sue. Victor shared some of what he had heard during the previous interviews before asking any new questions to Frank and Sue. He handed them the crime scene photo.

"One thing I notice," Frank began, "is the lack of blood anywhere in this photo. Not on the body, or surrounding area. That leads me to believe that she wasn't killed there."

"You're the second person to say that," Victor added.

"The other question I'd ask is was the removal of her teeth through blunt force trauma, or was it more strategic?"

"They were sloppy," Sue chimed in, "the removal of teeth, and nearly her head, but they left her where she would eventually be found."

"Why do you think nobody has ever come forward to claim her?" Victor asked.

"She could have been from another state or even another country," Sue replied. "In Provincetown everyone knows everyone."

"I agree," Frank added, "word of mouth had to have gotten out fast about a dead girl in the dunes. The fact that nobody in town knew her leads me to think she was not local. It is the transient nature of Provincetown in the summer. One other thing is why did they take one hand and the other forearm? Was there something on her forearm that could have identified her? Or worse, linked her to whoever killed her?"

"The bottom line is that this case is solvable," Sue stated. "We just need to get all of the departments that have been working on it together and pool our resources. After nearly fifty years the fact that she still has no identity is ridiculous."

The idea of malfeasance was at the forefront of the conversation. Both Frank and Sue were aggravated that the investigation of the Lady of the Dunes murder was not done up to their own standards. Frank was of the opinion that full reconnaissance was not done by the authorities. Frank and Sue reiterated something that Victor had been hearing since he got there. Provincetown in the 1970s was simply a different world than today.

Much like the previous day Victor was thrilled with the set of interviews that he had conducted. Dr. Glynn, Stephen Desroches, Jeannette de Beauvoir, and Frank and Sue had all added their own layers of information and opinion on the case. There was much to process. The real possibility that DNA could be used to reveal the Lady of the Dunes' identity and the reaffirming that she likely did not die where she was found, those were the biggest talking points in Victor's mind.

Pressed for time Victor again left all of his material on top of the piano on the theater's stage. He had a second meeting at the Meads Family home. This time it was a different medium who was doing the interviewing. Interestingly this medium also came from far away to be a part of the project as they lived in Southern Maine.

Their time at the house was quite similar to the New York psychic's the day before. They felt the energy from Jimmy Meads Sr. all through the house. When connecting with the departed former Chief the medium cut to the chase and asked him what the Lady of the Dunes' name was. There was a long silence.

"He(Chief Meads) calls her 'Lulu' as a nickname." The medium began. "It's actually a bit funny."

"Why is that funny?" Victor asked confused.

"I call my best friend Lulu when her name is Lindsay."

"Does he know who killed her?"

"Who killed Lulu?" The medium from Maine asked out loud. There was a pause. "He won't say because they are still alive. He can say that she was not murdered in the dunes, she was dropped there."

This was the third time the idea of a separate murder site came up. Where was she murdered? More curious was how did she get to the remote area of the Race Point dunes? Did people carry her lifeless body over the sand? It seemed like a lot of work, but then again Victor had never killed anyone and needed to dispose of a body.

The second visit to the Meads House would have been a perfect high point for the second day of shooting in Provincetown. However for Victor it was the calm before the storm. Before wrapping for the day Victor returned to the Provincetown Theater to retrieve all of the belongings he had left. While he was on the stage attempting to corral all of the papers off of the piano Victor noticed something out of the ordinary.

Off to one side of the piano, away from the rest of the papers was a worn looking manila folder. Not sure if perhaps someone from the crew had left it Victor went over and picked it up. It was tied with twine which made it all the more curious. At that moment one of the staff at the theater walked into the room.

"Oh good Mr. Franko," they said, "I wanted to make sure that you got that folder."

"What is it?"

"I have no idea. It was left for you by someone at the front desk quite a while ago. I left it with the rest of the stuff on the piano." Victor was suspicious. Dolly had told him that people knew who he was and why he was there. Who could know of his whereabouts during the shoot? Still, it wasn't ticking, so Victor untied the twine and looked inside.

The first thing he spotted was a black and white photo. He pulled it free of the folder and let out an audible gasp that caught the attention of the staffer. It was a horrifically graphic photo of the Lady of the Dunes' body at the murder scene. Victor had never seen this photo before but it seemed oddly familiar. He quickly thumbed through the remainder of the folder's contents when it dawned on him: This was the actual Lady of the Dunes case file that Stephen Desroches had earlier described!

"Do you remember who left this folder?" The staffer simply shrugged their shoulders. Victor was a bit rattled by the photo. He was also a bit paranoid at the thought that he might now have access to something he shouldn't.

After packing everything up Victor began making the rounds of the theater. He questioned each of the staff about the folder and the person who left it. Nobody had seen anyone leave it. According to those inside the theater it was as if the folder just appeared. The only thing they knew was that the person likely left the folder during a time that Victor was there and in the process of doing his interviews.

The staff did not have the answers Victor needed as far as who dropped off the case file. Worrying about the mere fact that he was in possession of a possibly authentic police case file Victor made a call to his lawyer. He left a message and made it a point to explain that the file had been left for him and that nobody had a clue who had dropped it off. It was a complete mystery.

As Victor was packing up his car and thinking of potential names behind the drop off of the file Victor's phone began to ring. The man on the line revealed that he had been given Victor's number through the Meads Family and that they had suggested that he call. He feigned continuing to pack his car but in reality Victor was scanning the sidewalks up and down Bradford Street and the windows in the houses surrounding him. The man on the line wanted to meet for a drink later in the evening.

Despite his paranoia running high Victor agreed as at the very least they'd be in a public place. Before hanging up the only information Victor was given was that the man was a former Provincetown cop and that he wanted to meet Victor at the Old Colony Tap on Commercial Street.

The combination of the police case file and the strange phone call had Victor slightly unnerved. There were few people visible at that moment. Just because he couldn't see them didn't mean he wasn't being watched. Victor tried to shake off the distraction by doing something nice for his crew.

A call was placed to the iconic Spiritus Pizza on Commercial Street. They were as much a part of the fabric of Provincetown as any restaurant having been established in 1971. Victor placed his order. He drove around to the entrance to Commercial Street and looked every bit the tourist he was as he drove slowly looking for a safe place to park near Spiritus. Victor found a place just off of Commercial Street to park.

He stepped out of the car with the golden hour setting in. The rays of light that poked through bathed the building facades in orange. There was a sign reading 'Residential Parking.' It gave Victor pause for a moment. He did not want to get towed. However, it was not a long walk to get the pizza which was certainly ready by that point. Victor took the risk and started walking.

Only a few steps from the parking lot Victor heard the sound of a car slowly approaching. He briefly turned his head but did not stop to stare. It maintained its distance, roughly a car length behind him. Surely they were also looking for a safe place to park, Victor thought to himself.

The vehicle slowed to a crawl as Victor slowed down in front of Spiritus. He paused, reaching for the front door but not grabbing it. Victor listened. The car's engine rumbled directly behind him and he waited for something, a voice, a slamming of a door, but there was nothing.

'They know who you are and why you are here.' Victor heard Dolly's voice in his head again.

'This is stupid,' Victor thought. He whirled around to prove to himself that it was simply his own mind playing tricks on him. Victor saw a figure in the driver's seat. The position of the car and the sun silhouetted the figure enough that Victor couldn't tell if it was a man or a woman. However once Victor took a few steps toward the vehicle it pulled away.

A few minutes later Victor reemerged from Spiritus with a stack of pizza boxes held tightly in both hands. He froze. Slowly coming down Commercial Street was the same car that had just been stalking him. Again the lighting made it near-impossible to make out the driver's face. Again it slowed down when it got close to Victor. The passenger side window was halfway rolled down.

"Can I help you?" Victor called out over the boxes of pizza. There was no reply. It crept passed without stopping this time. Victor thought about trying to get the license plate but decided to just leave it alone as the vehicle turned a slow corner and faded away.

It could have been only a coincidence. It could have been somebody who was lost and needed directions. It could have been someone looking for a good time. Or it could have been someone that was not happy about some interloper coming into town and digging up the bones of a dark past. Victor hurried back to his car, feverishly looking over his shoulder as he loaded the pizzas inside. He stared down Commercial Street expecting the strange to come back around. It did not.

Victor dropped the pizzas off to his grateful staff. He did not mention the strange car, nor the case file that had been dropped off. It was time to meet the mystery caller at Old Colony Tap. Although Victor did not fear for his safety he was a little on edge about the meet up.

Old Colony Tap was a dive bar in the most endearing sense. It had been serving locals and visitors alike since 1937 when it was opened by Manuel Cook. Norman Mailer frequented the establishment which was dingy, dimly lit, and covered with nautical paraphernalia. Victor arrived long after dark and the lighting inside was not much better than Commercial Street itself. After the strange car incident only a short time earlier he was feeling a little vulnerable walking into a crowded bar. As Victor looked around at a room full of unknown faces he began to scan them all, much like he had been doing while out on the street. He wondered who knew what. Part of him wanted to simply shout out his name and why he was there and break the tension. Then a frail arm at a dark corner table waved.

Victor took a deep breath, walked over, and sat down. After making sure that this was his man they struck up a brief conversation about the weather before ordering a drink. They both got a can of Narragansett beer. There was a low hum of people talking around them yet the stereo popping open of the cans echoed off of the pine walls.

Now in his eighties this former cop regaled Victor with stories of Provincetown in the 1950s. He had a wistful tone and a gleam in his eyes as he spoke of that bygone era.

Victor snarkily interjected saying that it sounded like a far different place than it was in the late 1960s and into the 1970s. The elderly Portuguese man's gleam vanished and he furrowed his brown before taking a loud swig of his beer. He looked from side to side as if he was making sure that no prying eyes or ears were on them.

"Do you know why they call it the Lower Cape?" He asked in a gravelly whisper. "Or even worse, 'Down Cape?'"

"No, I haven't got a clue."

"It's because that's where you flush your garbage." Victor picked up on the former cop's subtle tone.

"Garbage?"

"When it comes to getting rid of your shit, you do it Down Cape, understand?"

"It's easier to make problems disappear around here, right?" The former cop nodded.

"At least that was the word on the street from the 60s through the 80s."

"What do you think they'd find if they did a thorough reconnaissance out there?"

"Oh, there's definitely bodies waiting to be found. More than a few out in the Truro woods and the dunes right out here in Ptown. That's just my opinion though." He felt it necessary to stick that disclaimer at the end of his statement. However, Victor agreed.

"I'm with you," Victor replied, "from the people I've talked to during this whole process I find it very easy to believe that those dunes and woods have been used as a dumping ground for decades."

"You're on the right track. St. Peter's holds all of the clues."

The two men chatted a little longer. The former officer was old school Portuguese and did not hide his disdain for the Lower Cape. There were points where Victor was certain someone was going to come over and say something, but nobody did. The man also told Victor that in his opinion those responsible for the murder of the Lady of the Dunes were all dead and gone.

"Do you know who did it?" Victor asked, throwing a Hail Mary pass.

"I have my suspicions, but nothing I'd like to put on the record."

"What was the buzz around here back when it happened?"

"At first when people heard about a dead girl in the dunes a lot of them thought it could have been another victim of Tony Chop Chop. That was quickly debunked since A. this was a fresh kill, and B. Costa had met his end a few months earlier in jail."

"Costa sounds a bit like a boogeyman," Victor said sucking in the last bit of foam from the bottom of his glass.

"Well it's like I said, there's bodies still to be found, they could be part of his spree. The thing is that once Costa was ruled out as the girl's killer people quickly began to assume it was a rogue fisherman that did it."

"Why a fisherman?"

"Who better to filet a fish than a fisherman?"

"And the location in the dunes?" The former cop gave a halfhearted chuckle.

"It was a perfect spot to get rid of a body."

"How so?"

"South of it was a campground, to the east was a parking lot and access to the beach. To the west, near Race Point, there were fishermen and some shady dealings. To the north was access only for those that owned the dune shacks."

"So it was not random?"

"Oh God no, whoever was involved in getting the body out there knew about the location. They knew finding the body would take time, but that it would eventually be found."

When it came time for another round of drinks Victor politely declined. He had learned his lesson from Dolly the night before. Plus he had some reading material back in his room at the Stowaway.

"Well I'm going to have another," the elderly former cop said with a smile, "thanks for meeting with me. The Meads' were right about you." Victor smiled.

"Thanks, I'd normally have another drink but I got something interesting I need to read back at my room." Part of Victor wondered if this former local police officer could have been the one with such access as to drop off the Lady of the Dunes case file to him. Though he did not come out and ask him Victor had intentionally mentioned it just to see if there might be some sort of reaction. There wasn't. The man simply nodded and motioned over to the server to bring him another Narragansett.

Victor found himself both excited and worried when he sat in an armchair with the weathered case file for the Lady of the Dunes on his lap. It was well past 10 pm, and the rest of the Stowaway was quiet. Victor was glad that there had been no invitation to chat on this night as he would have felt bad to have to turn down the owner again.

The folder was cracked open. It had a slightly earthy and musty smell like it had been packed away for quite a while and only recently was rediscovered. This was a treasure trove Victor could not have imagined having access to.

First he noticed numerous pencil scratched notes all over many pages including multiple question marks. It immediately came back around to what Victor's original plan for the documentary was going to be. He had wanted to showcase all of the hard work that Jimmy Meads Sr. had done on the case. Now Victor was seeing it first hand.

Meads left no stone unturned. He pondered whether someone who owned or was staying at one of the Province Lands dune shacks might have had something to do with the murder. The Lady of the Dunes' body was found a few hundred yards from the original location of the C-Scape shack after all.

There was in-depth research into every jeep rental and dune shack rental around the dates of the murder. Meads also combed local motel and hotel records looking for people who left in the middle of the night. Finally, there was the attempt to connect any possible civil or domestic disputes to the murder. Those also apparently led nowhere.

Victor flipped through the handwritten pages until he came to the black and white photo that had caught his attention back at the theater. He took in a deep breath and held it. There she was in the flesh, the Lady of the Dunes. The black and white film gave the photo an air of timelessness.

Slowly Victor exhaled as he studied the image before him. He could almost smell the death coming off of the paper. All of the descriptions of how the body was found were staring him in the face now in a gruesome reality. This photo had been taken after the body was discovered, however, the body had been lying in the summer sun for up to three weeks.

The Lady of the Dunes had been brutally murdered. Yet there wasn't much blood at the photographed site. Her head was nearly severed from her neck with the left side of her skull having been crushed. As had been reported her hands were missing. There were several crime scene photos. The closeup of her face caused Victor to wince and turn his head away momentarily. He forced himself to keep looking though as Victor felt she was owed his full attention to see what had been done to her. The original wounds of the murder itself were horrific. The trauma inflicted by weeks in the sun made it worse. Gone were her eyes, likely removed by birds. Maggots were strewn all over her body.

Hours went by. Victor sat by the light of a single table lamp repeatedly going over the pages of the case file. Each pass-through gave him something new to ponder. The big question he felt needed to be answered was who exactly had dropped this file off to him? Victor had a few suspects and had to find a way to ask without asking. This was due to the recurring fact that Victor was not sure if he was supposed to have the file.

The time was after 2am when Victor closed the case file and placed it underneath his folded-up jacket. He was not tired. Without the distraction of the horrific photos and sordid details of the murder, Victor's mind wandered back. As he gazed out to the dark and quiet Provincetown night he wondered if someone was staring back from the shadows. Victor turned off the table lamp. He stood beside the window scanning the area again. Minutes passed without a sound inside or outside. Knowing that he wasn't accomplishing anything by staring out the window Victor reluctantly retreated to his bed.

There would once again be a night of little sleep. He hadn't planned on it. Dolly's haunting words, the graphic case file, the strange car near Spiritus Pizza, the meeting at Old Colony Tap, it all was rolling around Victor's mind. Seeing the gruesome crime scene photos convinced Victor to pay another sunrise visit to the grave of the Lady of the Dunes. That was why he was there.

He wanted badly to help her gain a name. Victor hoped that possibly she might want to talk to him.

Chapter 12, The Shoot Day Three

Victor had slept for barely three hours when his alarm went off. It was 5am on Sunday. Luckily his fatigue was not alcohol related this time. He looked out of one of his windows into the darkness of the early morning. There was a chill around the glass and a noticeable fog in the air. It made his third trip to the Lady of the Dunes' grave feel even eerier than the others. Slowly Victor crept into St. Peter's cemetery. Even with the high beams on his car, it was difficult to see more than a few dozen feet in front of him.

By this point, Victor was as familiar with the lay of the cemetery as he was with any location in Provincetown. This morning was slightly different though. Victor knew that in a few short hours he would be out among the dunes with a medium named Amanda. The plan was to let her lead the way and see if she could pinpoint the site where the Lady of the Dunes was found. While still in the faint predawn light Victor had a few words to say to the subject of his documentary.

"I want to help you," Victor said in a voice barely above a whisper. "You have to do me just one favor. Tell me your name. I have several psychics that have been working with me. Tell one of them your name so we can help you. I know you want to be found, but I can't help you unless you say your name."

A cool breeze trickled through the foggy landscape as dawn arrived. There was no name said in Victor's presence. He had to leave and meet with Amanda for their walk out into the dunes. Victor hoped perhaps Amanda might have received a message from the Lady of the Dunes during her time in Provincetown. He sat in his car for a moment staring at the grave and listening.

Victor drove out to the Province Lands Visitors Center where he had last been on March 26th. Amanda met Victor in the parking lot shortly after he arrived. Although they had briefly bumped into each other the day before she had been working on her own most of the time since the crew arrived in Provincetown. Victor was excited to hear of anything unusual from Amanda.

The two walked up to the observation deck and looked out through the fog toward the area where the body of the Lady of the Dunes was found. They waited for two members of Victor's documentary crew to arrive. Victor planned to take Amanda on a walk out toward the crime scene, letting her instincts take over, and see what happened.

While leaning against the railing of the observation deck Amanda started off by telling Victor that she too had visited the grave of the Lady of the Dunes. She had visited on Saturday alone and had a deep sadness surrounding her during her time there. Amanda said she had wanted to bring flowers to the grave but wasn't sure of what color. Amanda told Victor that the Lady of the Dunes had mentioned that pink was her favorite color.

Later on Saturday evening, Amanda went for dinner at the Crown and Anchor. She said the food was great and the atmosphere was friendly. However, the back room kept calling to her. Amanda did take a walk around and felt a lot in the area but nothing concrete to the Lady of the Dunes.

Within ten minutes of Victor's arrival the crew pulled into the barren parking lot. It was devoid of any cars besides their own which only added to the dreamlike atmosphere. Victor wanted to get started on the long walk out among the sand. He gave Amanda and the crew a heads up about the sprint through the brush that was necessary. Amanda, for her part, was as passionate about getting some sort of resolution for the Lady of the Dunes and was not worried about getting dirty, literally.

In the back of his mind, Victor wondered how close he should bring Amanda before letting her find her own way. It had been about twenty minutes of trudging through the soft, damp sand with only a superficial conversation between the parties. Amanda finally stopped walking and pointed down.

"Wow, do you see those?" She asked Victor with an excitement that wasn't registering with him.

"The flowers?"

"They're pink! Just like she told me at the grave. She loved the color pink and pink flowers."

"Do you think it's a sign?"

"Honestly, this is the fifth or sixth bunch of pink flowers I've seen just along our route. The first couple could have been coincidence, but so many of them leading out to where she was found? Come on."

The foggy weather complicated things, it forced Victor to periodically check his phone for the notes he made when he made the walk out a few weeks prior.

A final check of the maps app on his phone told Victor it was showtime. The pair were roughly 400 yards from the crime scene which felt like much further on account of the fog and the topography. Victor turned to Amanda and simply asked her what she was feeling. The medium said 'so much,' and slowly began to move forward.

The camera focused on Amanda and where she was being guided. Victor hung back and watched. He did not want to interfere or sway Amanda in any way. She moved cautiously over the rolling sandscape wrought with patches of beach grass and moss. Victor's heart pounded as he watched the medium close the gap between herself and the Lady of the Dunes' crime scene. His doubt over the legitimacy of the medium faded away with each of her steps.

Amanda closed in on the area where Victor had walked a few weeks earlier. She stopped and stared at the ground before turning her head back to the rest of them. Amanda had a somber look on her face.

"It was here," she said quietly, "she was found here." Victor nodded. Amanda had found the spot. She mentioned feeling a spirit while there. It was a playful one, Amanda thought it could be a child. She mentioned the initials L and M. Victor looked around while he thought. Then it popped into his head.

"Oh, I bet it's Leslie Metcalfe," Victor blurted out. "She was the little girl that found the body." Amanda, for her part, looked disappointed.

"Well you spoiled it a bit for me, but that's all right."

"Sorry about that."

Part one of the dune excursion was over. Victor and Amanda along with the two camera operators returned to the parking lot of the Province Lands Visitors Center. He thanked Amanda for her hard work and dedication before she left to go back into town.

Victor's busy Sunday included meeting with ninety-year old Mildred Champlin. She owned a dune shack located roughly 800 yards east of the C-Scape shack.

There was barely enough time to grab a snack and coffee at the nearest convenience store before Victor was on call again. This time he drove to the parking lot at Race Point Beach. The only way to get out to Mildred Champlin's shack was by off-road vehicle. Luckily Mildred and her daughter were there to meet Victor and two members of his crew.

Though they had briefly spoken before to set up the time at the shack Victor was hoping to get to know Mildred a bit more as the day went on. His wish was granted as Mildred's daughter was behind the wheel of their four-wheel-drive Jeep while the other four people crammed into the backseat. Following the over-sand route it was just over two miles from the parking lot to the steps of the shack leaving ample time for small talk.

Mildred Champlin was something of a throwback, as was her dune shack. She and her husband Nathaniel had owned the property since 1953. Nathaniel had died in 2015 while Mildred was now ninety years old. The largest of the shacks located among the Peaked Hill Bars district it was originally built in 1936 by two Coast Guardsmen, Jake Loring, and Dominic Avila, using mostly materials salvaged from an old Provincetown barn. The shack had the nickname 'Mission Bell' due to its easily spotted bell just west of the shack.

Victor was able to take a few minutes while on the drive out to Mission Bell to take in the scenery surrounding him. The sound of the ocean's waves would get louder and then fade as the road weaved around like the Jeep was a boat floating down a river of sand. The route passed close to C-Scape and then continued. Mission Bell had a rustic beauty and charm about it as they pulled up in front of it.

When standing out only a few yards from the shack Victor was again taken aback by how isolated things were. It would be a perfect scenario for vacationing away from crowds, but it would also be a perfect area to leave a body behind without the risk of being spotted by nosy neighbors.

Mildred and her daughter went inside the shack first as if they were trying to make it presentable for their guests. A few minutes later Mildred came out of the shack and beckoned Victor up onto the deck. The morning fog had lifted some, leaving the day cool and overcast. Despite the less than perfect weather it was still possible to see the beach from the deck. This was because it was so close.

"You've got quite the view from here," Victor said with a smile.

"I do," Mildred replied, "unfortunately that view gets closer every day. We're the only shack that hasn't yet been moved back from the bluffs."

"The bell is a nice touch."

"My husband Nathaniel rescued that from an old schoolhouse in Michigan. He taught at Wayne State University in Detroit."

"You have owned this place since the 50s, right?"

"Oh yes."

"Has there ever been any pressure to sell from the government?"

"Not really, we've got an agreement with them that is in effect through the lives of our children." Victor found it very endearing how Mildred still spoke in terms of 'we' when mentioning her late husband.

"What was it like living out here back then?"

"Paradise. It was absolute paradise."

"Do you remember the Lady of the Dunes case?"

"Of course, such a horrible event."

"What do you remember about it?"

"That nothing like it had ever happened out here before, at least as far as I've known. We had gone into town for groceries. When we were coming back on Race Road there was another family speeding the other way, frantically waving their arms. They said they were headed into town to tell the police they had found a body in the dunes."

"Did anyone question you about if you had seen anything?"

"All I knew was that the little Metcalfe girl found the body while chasing after a dog. Her father went to the police. Chief

Meads and his crew came out and did their investigation. You saw how much of a chore it is getting out here, plus we don't have beach access from up on the bluff, so I've always wondered how she ended up way out here. It's not by accident."

"How did you get involved in the case?"

"The Chief brought us in, the owners of the five shacks in this area. We were interrogated for a bit to make sure we were in the clear."

"What did Chief Meads say to you?" Mildred was quiet for a moment. She looked as if she was going to speak but held back a few times. It appeared to Victor as if she had something important to say but wasn't sure if she should.

"He told us not to share the real location of where the body was found."

"Why not?"

"From what I remember the Chief told the press, and even wrote in the case file, a fake location. He wanted to weed out phony tips. So basically anybody who called in with tips saying they knew of the body in the fake location was obviously lying."

"Do you know if there were any real tips that were received?"

"As far as I remember Meads never received a tip about a location besides the fake one he had put out there. I have never, and will never share the real location of where her body was found, just so you know, Mr. Franko."

"I completely understand and respect that."

Victor hated to cut short the meeting out at Mission Bell but he had yet another pressing engagement. He was due back in town to meet with a local radio personality at 2pm. She worked for WOMR in Provincetown and had been hired by Victor to read voice over narration for the chapters of the documentary. Despite feeling like he was being pulled in a million different directions Victor was excited as his project grew closer to being a reality.

The ride back through the rolling sand in the back of the Jeep was fun and filled with casual conversation with Mildred about life out among the dunes. Victor tried to avoid serious subjects on the way back as he could tell that speaking of the Lady of the Dunes and the aftermath with Chief Meads was something that Mildred did not enjoy. The fact that she did speak to him about it though was something Victor did appreciate.

Victor and his crew parted ways with Mildred and her daughter in the Race Point Beach parking lot. It was less than ten minutes to drive back into town to the studio at WOMR.

Located in the former Eastern School building on Commercial Street the radio station felt more like visiting someone's home than a place of business. It was another example of the unique charm of Provincetown, a charm that seem to go against the dark shadows of which the Lady of the Dunes mystery resided. For Victor it was difficult to figure out which was the true Provincetown.

The voice over narrations went smoothly. Victor was thrilled with the job she had done. The plan was to use as many different types of mediums on the documentary. From the radio voice overs, doing the interviews at the Provincetown Theater, using podcasts, telephone calls, graphics, and obviously film Victor was covering his bases with all the possible ways to communicate.

Quick and painless was the best way to describe the narrations at WOMR. However as Victor stood on the corner of 494 Commercial Street in front of the radio station he felt eyes on him. He had noticed his paranoia increasing seemingly every hour that he had been on the shoot in Provincetown. He had played it off as a joke when Dolly had told him that people knew why he was here, but it had really gotten to him. Even at that moment as Victor looked around, although nobody was staring back at him he felt as though many of them were focused in on him.

Perhaps it was Victor's own imagination blowing things out of proportion? Dolly could have simply been playing with Victor's mind. Still, his presence there was coming fresh off the heels of another major project that had been filmed in town.

The hit television show American Horror Story had been filming part of their tenth season only a few scant weeks before Victor arrived. In fact they had been wrapping up when Victor had taken his trek out to the Lady of the Dunes site in late-March.

Much of the 'Red Tide' story arc had been filmed at 103 Commercial Street, just over a mile west of where he was standing. A few people had mentioned the show having been there, but nobody seemed to be against it. What made Victor's project different? Why was he receiving mixed signals with some people being willing to speak on record while others had politely told him to go pound sand?

Victor scanned the various faces within sight. When it came to older faces, ones that could have been there when the Lady of the Dunes murder occurred, he stopped and stared.

'What are you hiding?' He thought. It dawned on him that perhaps the reason American Horror Story had garnered praise was the fact that it was a fictional show. What Victor was doing was investigating real events involving real people. These events and people exposed a side of the town that some people wanted to leave in the past.

Plus Victor wasn't 'one of them.' He was an outsider despite many blissful summer adventures on Cape Cod. In the eyes of many in Provincetown Victor was an intruder, an interloper, a shit-disturber, and would be no matter what he did. In many ways it reminded him of things he had heard from a few of his interviewees for the documentary. They had said they knew the Lady of the Dunes wasn't a local based on how tightly-knit the community was. Victor felt that same sort of detachment. Provincetown was an intriguing and beautiful town, but Victor could not wait to get out of there.

Before the crew departed Victor decided to have a quick meeting with everyone. With production wrapping up in Provincetown he wanted to get an idea of where the storyline of the Lady of the Dunes was going.

A member of the crew brought up an interesting point. There was to end up being countless hours of footage left on the cutting room floor when it came to making the actual film. In those hours of footage was to certainly be important information pertaining to the Lady of the Dunes and Provincetown as a whole. It would be a shame for it not to be used.

Victor was not looking to make a three-hour film, or a second film all together. It was quickly suggested that the entire project would make a fascinating book. In that book all of the information gathered up to that point, and all that could be gathered afterward would be able to be put to use. Victor liked the idea and so it was decided that in addition to the documentary film itself there would also be a book written about it.

Despite the overall excitement of a second form of media for his project Victor did not have the slightest idea where to start when it came to finding an author. Two things were of the utmost importance to him though. The writer had to be reputable and had to be local. He wanted someone who would give the same amount of care and attention to the project as he had. He wanted someone deeply connected to the Cape like the Meads Family was to Provincetown to give the project legitimacy. The search for that particular person would have to wait until Victor got home to Norton.

It appeared that Sunday in Provincetown would wrap up rather quietly and uneventfully. He should have known better. It was close to 4pm when Victor's phone began to ring. He was packing up things at the Stowaway ready to return home to Maura and his son. Victor had been waiting for a return call from his lawyer concerning the Lady of the Dunes case file that was now in his possession. This is who he figured was calling. When he pulled his phone from his pocket however he saw it was another of the five mediums who Victor had been consulting with.

Shockingly the phone call was frantic as the medium tried to express what was going on. They exclaimed that they had found the actual site where the Lady of the Dunes had met her end. Victor had warmed to the idea of the dunes simply being a drop site so he was intrigued.

The breathless medium explained that they had been driving aimlessly around the Outer Cape in a sort of 'Jesus take the wheel' way. They had been drawn to a spot in Truro called Lombard Hollow Road. Needing to finish collecting his notes and packing Victor decided to send one of the cameramen out ahead of him to scope out the scene.

About a half hour later his phone rang again. This time it was the cameraman. All he said was that Victor needed to get out there as soon as he could. It sounded serious so Victor quickly crammed everything he had brought into his car. He barely had enough time for a quick thank you and goodbye to the owners of the Stowaway.

The GPS said fourteen minutes but Victor made it in ten. Lombard Hollow Road was on the western side of Route 6, little more than a mile from the Tony Costa murder site. It was as rural and isolated as one could get on Cape Cod in the 21st century. In fact without his GPS Victor likely would have driven past it as there were no road signs or anything denoting Lombard Hollow.

When he pulled up to where the medium and the cameraman stood Victor immediately felt a sense of unease bubbling under the surface. The first thing he noticed that gave him pause was the strikingly large amount of pink flowers near where the medium stood. These were the same that had dotted the dunes on the walk out to the drop site with Amanda the medium that morning.

The medium was adamant that they were standing at the actual murder site. Victor looked at the surroundings. They were more than one hundred yards from Route 6 and passing cars were barely audible. There were long periods of silence broken only by passing birds and chirping crickets. It felt like it could be a murder site. Still Victor needed something tangible.

"What is the connection from the Lady of the Dunes to this spot?" Victor bluntly asked.

The medium shocked Victor by proclaiming that there was evidence of the murder in that area in the form of a discarded tooth belonging to the Lady of the Dunes.

"One of her teeth?" Victor's eyes lit up. If that piece of evidence was in that area it would be a game changer.

Victor asked how it ended up in that general area. The medium sensed that it could have been taken out as a sort of trophy. Whoever were the perpetrators thought she was dead and pulled one of her teeth as proof. The Lady of the Dunes could have awakened as a result of the tooth being pulled and they panicked and dropped the tooth in the brush.

He had come this far and done things through the proper channels, still Victor was tempted to just start digging. It was in the front of his mind though that they were all standing on Cape Cod National Seashore property and he needed to get permission before undertaking such a task. Victor did not want to have his film potentially tarnished by getting in trouble with the law. The best he could do then was to drop a GPS pin on his phone to remember exactly where they were and reach out to the Seashore the following day.

Victor thanked the medium and his cameraman for coming out and more so for all of the hard work over the weekend in Provincetown. They both left leaving Victor standing alone on Lombard Hollow Road in the woods of South Truro.

"Are you here?" He quietly asked.

The proximity to Tony Costa's stomping grounds got Victor to wondering just what else could be around him in those woods. If the Lady of the Dunes had been taken to this area it couldn't have been by accident. Lombard Hollow was little more than an overgrown pathway that extended west seemingly into infinity. It was far too secluded and hidden to be stumbled upon. Why this area though? What was it about the South Truro woods that lent itself to such darkness and mystery?

Above all else Victor wanted it to be true. He wanted the tooth to be there in this area well over ten miles from where the actual body was found. It would be something new to the case, such a monumental piece of the puzzle, and go a long way to prove that Victor's efforts had meant something. As excited as he was for that potential victory Victor knew he had to do it the right way. He got back into his car, taking one last look at the expanse of pink flowers where the tooth might be, before slowly driving away.

Victor's mind raced as he tried to concentrate on the highway. It had been exciting doing three days of filming. All in all there was fifty-two hours of footage shot while on location. There had been a far greater outpouring of support from the Provincetown community as a whole. It was more than Victor had expected. He knew that it had not been the case over the last forty to fifty years and that fact gave Victor a feeling of pride in what he was doing.

Despite that an overwhelming solemn sense hung with him. Victor knew he was doing something good yet he still didn't have the answers he wanted. Foolishly he had hoped to have some sort of resolution in his three days in Provincetown. It would be great to get home and to share with Maura all that he had seen and heard. The random texts when reception was good just didn't cut it.

Not long after crossing over the Bourne Bridge and officially leaving Cape Cod behind, Victor's phone rang. This time it was his lawyer. The message was simple: keep your mouth shut about the case file. However Victor's lawyer did go on to say that he was safe from any sort of repercussions since the file was left for him and he did not take it. It gave Victor a sigh of relief.

He pulled into his driveway for the first time in three days just as the darkness filled the sky. It was good to be home. His phone rang as he turned the car off. Victor did not answer. It could wait. He just wanted to hug his family.

Victor awoke the next morning refreshed. The three previous days in Provincetown that consisted of nonstop interviews had yielded more than fifty hours of footage. He knew that his team of editors would be coming to him with questions very soon. There was also a plethora of notes from the five mediums which Victor knew he had to check. However he decided to take a little extra time to lay in bed and stare at the ceiling.

The previous evening had been a fun reintroduction to family life. Walking in the door he was met with hugs from Maura and the privilege of changing his son's full diaper. It was a lot of catching up while also helping to clean up the house and Victor loved every moment of it.

Only when he had done all of the father and husband duties that he could in the morning did Victor begin to check his messages. There were several including one from one of the mediums stating that the Lady of the Dunes had implored Victor and the entire crew of the project not to forget about her.

Victor had every intention of returning to Provincetown at some point. He had several loose ends he needed to tie up first though, and those could be done from home. There was Agent X that needed to be contacted again soon. There was Victor's attempts to get a newspaper article written about the documentary. On top of that he was getting ready for another project. This new film was to be shot up in the Catskill Mountains in New York and center around Rip van Winkle. In fact Victor was going to have to leave to begin that new project sometime in May.

In another message there was a long story about a connection one of the mediums had made with Sydney Monzon. Victor had seen Sydney as a sidetrack at first but over time she had become a far more important part of the project. When it came down to the big stage that was Provincetown at the time Victor felt Sydney Monzon and Staniford Sorrentino were as important of players as the Lady of the Dunes. She still was the center of his spiderweb.

Sydney told the medium that she had been hooked on drugs while living with Tony Costa and Staniford Sorrentino. When asked if she knew where Costa was getting the drugs Sydney said that she thought it could be Whitey Bulger.

Victor was wary of tossing Bulger's name out there as far as suspects in the Lady of the Dunes murder went. He wondered if there was any connection to Hadden Clark. Victor kept flipping back and forth between Bulger and Clark as his main suspects.

This extremely long message ended with a rather ominous request from the medium. There was a person that they felt could be involved in the murder of the Lady of the Dunes. This person was very much alive and the medium asked Victor if he might consider reaching out to them. There was a caveat in the fact that this person could be involved in organized crime. Victor feared he was tempting fate once too often.

He researched the person first and found they had a publicist which Victor chuckled about. He jotted their information down and sent a brief but friendly email. Surprisingly he heard back in short order. The publicist gave Victor contact information for their client. This was unexpected and a little unnerving as Victor had hoped for no reply, or a rejection, so he could at least say he tried. With the contact information right in front of him Victor felt obligated. Before doing anything though he made a quick call to Agent X.

Much like Victor, when Agent X heard the potential organized crime connection they were leery. It could be a potential important lead, but it could be a dangerous path to go down. For their part Agent X did not tell Victor to not reach out. Quite the opposite, Agent X thought it was worth a shot.

They recommended tossing some softball questions to this person. Agent X wanted to see if they might comment on Whitey Bulger, or Provincetown during that time period. Agent X told Victor explicitly to not ask if this person had killed the Lady of the Dunes, knew who killed her, or anything about the murder at all. It all sounded very ominous. Victor had to take his time deciding whether or not to contact this person no matter the potential connection to the Lady of the Dunes.

In the end the possibility of finding a new lead overruled his apprehension. Victor made the call. A voice picked up the phone and Victor was immediately rattled. He tried to explain who he was and what he was doing. He mentioned working on a Lady of the Dunes documentary which he wasn't sure if he should even say, but then why would he be calling in the first place? Before getting the chance to ask any of the softball questions the person stated forcefully yet calmly that they did not want anything to do with the documentary.

That was it. The phone call ended. Victor waited until his heart slowed back to normal. In a sense he was grateful that the entire conversation only lasted thirty seconds. Being naturally curious however, Victor made a few calls. He reached out to some contacts that might have inside information about this person. One of Victor's contacts in particular came right out and warned him to stay away. Victor was told this person was bad news and that he needed to lose their information.

Victor trusted the opinion of that contact and immediately threw the phone number into the trash. After the rat in a cage vibes Victor got at times during the shoot in Provincetown he was not looking to go after someone that could possibly put himself and his family in danger, no matter what it could mean for the Lady of the Dunes. He would never revisit that lead.

In order to move as far as he could from that dangerous lead Victor began searching for an author to write the companion book to the film. Simply typing in 'Cape Cod Author' he was bombarded with hits for one particular name. This man was well-known locally and nationally thanks to two of his books becoming major motion pictures. Victor could not find a website for him and took a shot in the dark by sending him a message through his business profile.

It was not exactly the first impression Victor had desired. He explained who he was and the documentary he had been working on. Knowing the stature of this author he found himself going overboard with his sell job of the project even though he knew the idea of potentially giving the Lady of the Dunes her name back should have spoken for itself. Victor did not know what to expect but he sent the message and hoped for the best.

To Victor's surprise the author responded the next day. Any hope quickly faded though in the first line of the reply. He told Victor that he was unfortunately booked up for the next few years with other projects. Despite that sad statement he did make sure to tell Victor that he thought the project was a great idea and that he wished he could have been the one to bring it to life in a literary sense. He wished Victor luck and that was the end of the message. It was back to the drawing board.

It felt like things were turning a corner in terms of publicity for the project a week or so after returning from Provincetown. Victor had two very productive talks with a pair of newspapers, one smaller local paper and one much larger. The people he chatted with were interested in the Lady of the Dunes subject and wanted to set up times to do in depth interviews some time in early May.

He found it interesting the difference in questions between the smaller and larger newspapers. The smaller one seemed far more interested in the story itself and Victor's work on the project. The larger paper asked some rather probing questions including wanting specific names of people he had spoken to at the State Police as well as the District Attorney's Office. Although it seemed like a lot of information to give during an introductory chat Victor was just happy that he would be able to get some press for his documentary.

Victor was being pulled in two different directions now, between continuing the work on the Lady of the Dunes documentary and getting prepared for his trip up to the Catskills. Despite that he worked hard to continue the momentum that had been gained from the Provincetown shoot.

There was constant conversation between Victor and people with the DNA Doe Project. They were still extremely interested in helping to solve the case. For his part Victor relayed that interest to anyone and everyone that he could think of. On that front though it felt like he was trudging through mud trying to make any headway.

Feeling frustrated with the lack of movement on the DNA front Victor decided to cut bait with that line for the moment. He also picked up the Lady of the Dunes case file for the first time in many days. It had been simply collecting dust in a box. Sure, his lawyer had told him he was safe from any prosecution since Victor had not stolen the file. That being said Victor was looking to get that important piece of evidence out of his possession. It came back to the original question of who had sent it to him.

He had thought everyone he had been in contact with during the filming process could have been the one that dropped it off at the Provincetown Theater. Once he actually sat down and gave it his full attention though Victor's mind came back to one person: Agent Y.

They ticked all of the boxes of someone that could have access to decades old police evidence. Victor had asked and they had denied it, but of course they would. He decided to call Agent Y's bluff. Victor had their mailing address and discretely sent the entire case file in a large flat rate envelope from the post office.

Even when standing in line at the post office holding the case file inside an innocuous envelope Victor felt as if there were eyes on him. He felt like he was getting away with something. When the post office clerk asked if the contents of the envelope were liquid, fragile, perishable, and the like, Victor slyly smiled and said 'no.'

Once the envelope was out of his hands Victor still had lingering paranoia. What if someone accidentally, or intentionally, opened the envelope and saw the case file? Even after Victor returned home and sat down in the living room he felt the need to keep his phone on the table in front of him. Nobody from the post office ever contacted him.

Over the coming days Victor expected Agent Y to reach out to question why he had sent them the case file. No contact was made. This cemented Victor's belief that in fact Agent Y was the person who left the Lady of the Dunes case file at the theater.

The case file out of his possession Victor felt it was time to resume his search for a local author to work on his Lady of the Dunes book. 'Cape Cod Author' was again searched. After Victor weeded out the hits for the author that had spurned him he found another potential match.

This one, although not nearly as well known as the other, had a half a dozen books connected to Cape Cod. He also came up many times with articles connected to Cape Cod history. These included stories about both Tony Costa and the Lady of the Dunes. His name was Christopher Setterlund.

Victor skimmed over Setterlund's previous works. The more he read the more he was intrigued. He took a shot in the dark and sent a message to him through his Facebook page asking him if he had time to speak about the Lady of the Dunes. Much like his previous author choice Setterlund responded rather quickly. However his response was less than enthusiastic. Setterlund wondered if he was the right person to talk to about the subject. Victor was persistent and his passion for the work he had been so diligently doing came shining through even through printed text.

Setterlund told Victor that he considered himself less than an expert on Cape Cod and its history. He tried to defer Victor to speaking with the police. Victor had to laugh out loud when reading that response. If Setterlund only knew the amount of roadblocks law enforcement had given him. It took some cajoling and some charm but Victor set up a phone meeting with Setterlund for the following week. He was cautiously optimistic.

The conversation with Setterlund the next week was jovial if not slightly one-sided. Victor loved sharing what he had learned throughout the months of interviews on the case. Having a fresh set of ears made the conversation at times it more of a lecture. Setterlund told Victor that he had grown up knowing the Lady of the Dunes story and that he found learning new bits of information about the case fascinating. Victor was already gauging Christopher's potential interest in becoming his writer though not overtly so. The two left things open-ended, deciding to have another phone conversation the following week.

Next on Victor's post-production checklist was contacting Alyssa Metcalfe. Her sister Leslie had been the one who had originally discovered the body of the Lady of the Dunes that fateful day in July 1974. Leslie also could have been the 'L.M.' Amanda had connected with while out in the dunes in Provincetown. Victor had assumed so.

Alyssa was prominent in literary arts on Cape Cod. She was happy to lend her knowledge to the project although her schedule did not allow her to do an in person interview. Speaking on the telephone worked out just fine.

She remembered that her family was from New York City but began visiting Cape Cod in 1966. There was a freedom, a family vibe between those who visited the rolling dunes of Provincetown during that time.

On the day in question Alyssa mentioned that she was not there. She had chosen to visit Nelson's Riding Stables on Race Point Road instead of hanging out in the dunes. Her sister Leslie, however, recounted the story to her.

According to Alyssa there was a dog owned by one of the other people out there. The dog was following them back to town for a while when it suddenly veered off the path and began barking at something. Leslie followed and what she saw would end up changing her life forever.

The dog was barking at something laying in front of a small patch of scrub pines. It was slightly obscured and with the changing light of the day the object was shadowed. Leslie thought it was a dead deer. The coloration of the carcass coupled by the shadows from the trees played tricks on her eyes.

It was only when she crept closer that Leslie realized that this was no deer, this was a human. It was a female, badly mutilated and decomposing in the hot July sun. Her skin was as dark as deer hide.

The dog's barking alerted others in the group who came and also laid eyes on the horrific scene by the scrub pine. It was at that point that they headed into town to get the police.
Victor was breathless as she listened to Alyssa's recounting of what Leslie saw. The visuals were so clear, hauntingly clear. He asked Alyssa how finding the body affected Leslie.

Alyssa said it did affect her sister. Leslie wondered what had happened to her and why. Although it was scarring to be twelve-years-old and witness such a horrific sight it came with an unexpected twist. There was a certain level of fame that came with being the one to find the body of the Lady of the Dunes. In a way it was intoxicating.

Sadly Leslie died at the young age of thirty-four in 1996. In a final note Leslie was buried in St. Peter's Cemetery, the same place as the Lady of the Dunes.

Near the end of April the project got another big break thanks to Agent X. Before the shoot in Provincetown Agent X had been only passively involved. They were very helpful with tidbits of information but stayed away from becoming fully invested in Victor's work. Once the shoot was finished and Victor was back at home Agent X became more interested in the nuts and bolts of the project. One specific point that they wanted to know more about was the elusive Agent Y. They were curious about what Agent Y's story was and their connection to the case.

Victor, not wanting to blow their cover, dealt only in vagueries when it came to Agent Y. He certainly did not share that he believed that Agent Y somehow had gained possession of the Lady of the Dunes case file.

It was during one of the conversations with Agent X that they gave Victor a lead that ended up changing the entire trajectory of the film. Agent X shared a lead from Rhode Island that they thought might prove to be helpful to Victor. It was an understatement.

Victor got in touch with Agent X's Rhode Island lead almost immediately. They had several intriguing contacts however one in particular was deemed as the most important for Victor to reach out to. His name was Theodore.

Theodore had been a detective in Montgomery County Maryland. More importantly he had worked on the case against Hadden Clark for several years in the 1990s. Theodore's prior experience with Clark sparked Victor's attention. From early on in the Lady of the Dunes project Victor had been zeroing in on his two potential lead suspects, one being Whitey Bulger, the other being Hadden Clark.

When it came to the 'stage' that Provincetown was in the late-1960s and early-1970s Hadden Clark was as big a part as anyone. Clark's grandfather, Silas, owned a home on Pamet Point Road in Wellfleet. It was part of a larger 7.3-acre plot of land. Hadden Clark grew up in Pennsylvania but spent many summers on Cape Cod at that home. He also worked in local restaurants during those summers.

Clark was convicted in Maryland of two murders in 1999 and sentenced to two consecutive thirty-year sentences, plus another ten years for robbery. The victims, twenty-three year-old Laura Houghteling and six-year-old Michelle Dorr, are the only definitive names Clark had been connected to. That being said it has on numerous occasions been theorized that he may have begun killing while a teenager with his body count being as high as eleven in six states.

In January 2000 Clark returned to Cape Cod from Maryland to lead local police on a search for two alleged bodies buried somewhere on his grandfather's former property. An investigation on the property a month earlier had turned up a bucket of jewelry including two rings belonging to Houghteling. This prompted police to allow for Clark to be their guide on the January journey.

Hadden Clark was diagnosed as paranoid schizophrenic in 1985 after being discharged from the Navy where he worked as a cook. He also enjoyed cross-dressing. For the search in January 2000 Clark demanded a skirt, panties, and a bra which the police bought from the K-Mart in Hyannis. He also demanded another prison inmate who closely resembled Jesus Christ be allowed to tag along. This was also agreed upon as the inmate was alleged to be the only one who could calm Clark down during his routine psychotic breakdowns.

It was reported that the only reason that the police acquiesced to Clark's demands was the fact that he had led law enforcement to the body of Michelle Dorr only a few weeks earlier. That, coupled with the finding of the jewelry bucket on his grandfather's property, gave him enough credibility for police to indulge his latest prison confession. Clark was widely known to enjoy sending police on pointless treasure hunts for his own amusement.

The January 2000 search was no different. The police were serenaded by long drawn out church hymns from Clark as they scoured the frigid Wellfleet woods. The search on Cape Cod was fruitless. Between January and April 2000 Clark and his Jesus-looking friend were shuttled between Massachusetts, Connecticut, New Jersey, and Pennsylvania looking for the remains of other suspected victims. Each time the search came up empty. Clark remains incarcerated in the Eastern Correctional Institute in Westover, Maryland.

Victor hoped that Theodore would be willing to talk about Hadden Clark when he first called him. He hoped that the Rhode Island connection had put in a good word for him. Victor had no idea what that first call would open up.

Theodore was enjoying some time fishing when Victor called him up. He was not sure if this would get them off on the wrong foot but Theodore was more than eager to chat. Victor started off by explaining who he was and what he was doing as far the Lady of the Dunes documentary.

Theodore's familiarity with Hadden Clark was evident from the beginning. He had worked on his case and handled him for over twenty years. Victor was blunt and told the former detective about how he had suspicions about Clark potentially being the killer of the Lady of the Dunes. Theodore's response to that was to ask Victor where were the bra and panties of the Lady of the Dunes. He particularly was interested in the panties.

Victor responded that both items were missing. The former detective immediately made a case that Clark could in fact have been her killer due to the fact that he was a cross-dresser who had an affinity for women's underwear. Theodore went on to give Victor some of Hadden Clark's backstory, specifically his connection to Cape Cod during the time surrounding the Lady of the Dunes case.

Theodore mentioned Clark's summers skulking around his grandfather's property. He also connected him to Provincetown restaurants. Although not sure if he ever worked at the Crown & Anchor the former detective was fairly certain that Clark had worked in the kitchen at The Moors Restaurant. The Moors had been a longtime popular establishment at the west end of Bradford Street for decades.

It was feasible, if not highly likely, that Hadden Clark was in the area during the time that the Lady of the Dunes would have been in Provincetown. Did they cross paths? Theodore could not give any insight into that. However he did know someone who just might have the answer: Hadden Clark himself.

Victor was taken aback when Theodore recommended writing a letter to Hadden Clark at the Eastern Correctional Institute. Theodore simply asked him what did he have to lose? Clark was sitting behind bars more than four hundred miles away, likely never to see freedom again for the rest of his life.

At best Clark might have information about the Lady of the Dunes. He might also give up information on one of his other purported victims that had yet to be found. At worst Victor could receive no reply. Theodore believed that it was worth a shot. Victor said he would think it over.

After thinking it over for a few days Victor decided he would send a simple letter to Hadden Clark. He did not want to waste too much of his time putting it together just in case Clark did not bother to respond. Victor sat at his desk and crafted a short and concise introduction between himself and the convicted serial killer.

Dear Hadden Clark,

My name is Victor Franko. I am a filmmaker from Massachusetts. I am writing to you as my latest project might be of some interest to you. I am currently working on a documentary about the Lady of the Dunes case from Provincetown in 1974.

My intention with this project is trying to find the name of the girl and to give some closure to her family and the people who knew her.

I have some questions I would like to ask you about the case and what you might know about it. If you are willing to answer them I will gladly sent these questions along in a future letter.

Thank you for your time.

- Victor

Once Victor mailed the letter off to the Eastern Correctional Institute he didn't give it a second thought. The likelihood of a convicted serial killer reading and responding to Victor's letter was slim to none. Knowing that, he moved on to beginning to get ready for his next project.

The film dealing with Rip van Winkle would be shot in the Catskills of New York. Victor had already set up much of the crew and made the reservations for the accommodations. He and his crew would set up shop at Riedlbauer's Resort in Round Top, New York. In a way Victor was looking forward to a project that was slightly mundane.

However that filming was not taking place until mid-May which was a few weeks off. Before that time Victor tried to maintain his focus on continuing the Lady of the Dunes film. He had his second phone conversation with Christopher Setterlund as he tried to nail him down to be the author of the Lady of the Dunes book.

Again it was a cordial, if not one-sided conversation. Victor shared some intimate details of what he had learned during his months of research and interviews. At times he thought he might be sharing too much with the documentary not even being officially finished. This stranger had the ability to throw spoilers out there yet Victor knew he had to give true facts if he wanted Christopher to potentially write the book. It was agreed upon that there would be a face-to-face meeting with the time and place to be determined later.

Victor went back over some of his notes from the previous months to see if there might be a lead he had not properly checked out. He found one in Liza Rodman.

It had been nearly two months since Victor had picked up copies of Leo Damore's *In His Garden* and Liza Rodman's *The Babysitter*. He had read both, Damore's twice, trying to learn of Tony Costa's connection to the grand stage that was Provincetown. After reading both books Victor had been sidetracked by the Sydney Monzon story as well as Peter Manso. Victor had never thought to try to follow up with the authors of those books.

Leo Damore sadly had passed away. He died in October 1995 of a purported self-inflicted gunshot wound. Liza Rodman though was alive and well. Victor decided to reach out and see if she would have some time to talk. Before doing so though he decided to do a quick refresh and read *The Babysitter* again.

It took him a week to finish the book with all of the other distractions of life but finally Victor was able to reach out to Liza. What he found was that her experiences in writing and researching her Tony Costa-centric book somewhat mirrored Victor's with the Lady of the Dunes.

Rodman was more than happy to share her own experiences with the strange stage that was Provincetown. She was not surprised to hear of Victor's difficulty in procuring much information from the locals about the Lady of the Dunes. Rodman had as much, if not more, difficulty in getting people to speak about Tony Costa. To her it had been an uphill battle and what she did get for information she was very grateful for. Rodman's words really drove home how lucky Victor had been in earning the trust of the Meads Family. He could only imagine what his project would have looked like if they had not been on board.

Victor told Liza about some of his discoveries during his research for the film. He specifically spoke of the potential mysteries that could lie in the South Truro woods. The actual murders committed by Tony Costa and Hadden Clark, and the potential murder site of the Lady of the Dunes, had Victor wondering what else could be out there. Not surprisingly Liza felt the same way.

Rodman told Victor of her reaching out to the Cape Cod National Seashore during and after her book. She in fact did ask them about doing some reconnaissance in the South Truro woods. They were not receptive.

As the conversation with Liza Rodman wound down she reiterated the fact that Tony Costa was living with Staniford Sorrentino, with Sydney Monzon there as well. The vision of Provincetown and Cape Cod in the 1960s and 70s as a large intertwined spider web again became front and center in Victor's mind.

All in all it was a good talk between Victor and Liza. She was very forthcoming with knowledge that helped add more detail and color to the world of Provincetown during the 60s and 70s. She left the door open for Victor to call again if he felt the urge to.

He knew there was much more to be done on the Lady of the Dunes project. Despite it technically being in post-production it seemed to Victor that new leads kept popping up. It would all need to be shelved, at least temporarily, as it was time for a new project to start. It had been a month since he returned from the Provincetown shoot. Now it was the Catskill Mountains that awaited Victor.

Chapter 14, Why Didn't You Get A P.O. Box?

Victor said goodbye to Maura and their son. It was a week shoot coming up, far longer than his three days in Provincetown. It was also roughly 200 miles to get to Riedlbauer's Resort in Round Top, New York. Yet despite it being longer in distance and time away Victor felt that the Rip Van Winkle horror project was to be far more banal than the dark and sinister Lady of the Dunes shoot.

It was nearly a straight shot west for Victor to get from Norton to Round Top. Along the way he passed the beautiful scenery of The Berkshire Mountains. Spring was in full bloom in New England. Although it would temporarily pop up in his head from time to time during the drive Victor did his best to leave the Lady of the Dunes project back home.

Once across the border into New York it became easier to focus. Round Top was a quaint mountain town with a population of just over 1,100. Riedlbauer's Resort had the look and feel of classic German architecture. It had sprawling grounds and ample flower beds that truly gave it the look of a mountain oasis.

It was a fun project to work on. Victor was excited to get to work with noted director and editor Mark Polonia on the Rip Van Winkle project. Mark had worked with his twin brother John directing films beginning in 1987. After John's untimely death Mark continued on. Their most well known film was Feeders. Shot in 1996 on a budget of only $500 it garnered a cult-following as it came out during the Independence Day movie craze. Feeders had been picked up by Blockbuster Video and became their top independent-film rental of 1996.

Much to Victor's delight the horror movie shoot in the Catskills was mundane in the most delightful way. Since the beginning of the year Victor had been enveloped in a sense of dread and sadness when it came to the Lady of the Dunes case. It felt good to be away from that for a while.

The weather and the colorful sprawling scenery gave the cast and crew a feeling of summer. However the calendar did not reflect that. It was still before Memorial Day. It was late in the afternoon of the fourth day of shooting. Victor had just wrapped on a bowling alley scene with the ghost of Henry Hudson. It was time for a fun dinner with the crew as had become the norm.

The onsite restaurant at Riedlbauer's Resort was not open for the season yet. Victor would have liked to stay at the resort and have the chance to sample some of the wares of Nussy's Bier Garten but time did not allow it.

Several local restaurants were visited by Victor and his crew during the first few days of the shoot. With closer locations exhausted by the fourth day of the week-long shoot Victor ventured off to neighboring Cairo. There he ordered Chinese food for the cast and crew, bringing his lead actress, Leira Turner, along for the ride. It was only a ten minute drive yet on the way back it felt like hours due to an unexpected turn of events.

The delectable aroma of Chinese food filled Victor's car when his phone began to ring. It was Maura which was not surprising as she routinely checked in to see how the shoot was going and to catch Victor up on how things were at home. He answered with a joyous bounce to his voice.

"Hey hun, how's everything back home?"

"Why did we get a letter from the Eastern Correctional Institute in Westover, Maryland?" Maura asked sounding more curious than anything.

"Oh wow, he responded?"

"Who responded?"

"Does the envelope have a name with the address?"

"Yes, Hadden J. Clark. Who is that?"

"He's a convicted serial killer I sent a letter to about the Lady of the Dunes." Victor's flippant response to a serial killer writing to their home did not sit well with Maura. He could feel the heat of her anger coming through the phone.

"A convicted serial killer is sending letters to our home?" Sensing her anger Victor tried to defuse the situation.

"He's in jail for life, he'll never get out."

"That's not the point! Why didn't you just get a P.O. Box?" Victor hadn't thought of that and was at a loss for a response. He struggled to apologize as Leira looked on in horror at the conversation unfolding in front of her.

"I didn't think of that, I'm sorry, but I promise he's safely locked behind bars hundreds of miles away." Maura finished off the conversation and hung up in such a huff that Victor didn't have a chance to ask her to read what the letter said. He realized that it was probably for the best.

Victor and Leira carried in the Chinese food from the car. Victor tried to put the conversation with Maura out of his head and hoped that Leira wouldn't bring it up. She didn't. By the end of the meal Victor's mind had ventured back to continuing the Rip Van Winkle horror movie.

The remaining three days in Round Top were a return to the sense of normalcy before Maura had revealed Hadden Clark's letter had arrived. Victor was pleased with this project and, as was his way, he was already looking toward what would be next on his itinerary. This was to be a documentary about iconic 20th century American writer Kurt Vonnegut.

Dennis Minsky had told Victor an interesting tidbit about Vonnegut. During the height of the mania surrounding Tony Costa Vonnegut randomly showed up at Costa's 'garden' to do a story for *Life* magazine while excavation was going on. Victor took it as a sign. It also fulfilled his desire to do a film a year centered around Cape Cod.

He parted ways with his cast and crew, leaving the beautiful landscape of Riedlbauer's Resort behind. Victor made a note to make a return there at some point just for fun with the family at some point. As he drove the Mass Pike back through the Berkshires his mind drifted back to the Lady of the Dunes. It was unlike any other project he had ever worked on. Victor could only find temporary distractions before the Lady and the circumstances surrounding the stage of Provincetown came rolling back to the forefront.

The passing of each of the roughly 200 miles to get him home got Victor more excited to see Maura and their son again. He had only briefly thought about the fight over Hadden Clark's letter. Victor hoped that he could plead his case to Maura that Hadden was securely behind bars until his dying day.

Victor turned off the car after pulling into the driveway and sat for a moment. He wanted to find the right thing to say to Maura as he was definitely sorry that she was upset about Hadden Clark's letter. On the other hand he was a little excited to read what it said.

When Victor walked into the house Maura was in the kitchen. He was not sure how she was feeling in regards to the Hadden Clark letter but he quickly found out. The hellos between the couple were quick before Maura picked up the conversation where they left off in the car.

"What is going on? Why do we have a letter from a convicted serial killer in our house?"

"Hadden Clark is a major person of interest when it comes to the Lady of the Dunes and I had a few people in law enforcement suggesting that I write to him." Maura barely looked up from the dishes she was washing.

"Victor, do you think it was wise of you to give your home address to a serial killer with your child in the house?" There was a pause as Victor hung his head.

"I had honestly never thought of that."

"You asshole."

"I swear though I have no reason to believe that he will ever get out of prison." Victor knew that his defense of sending the letter was not coming off well. He decided to simply apologize and leave it at that.

"Why the fuck did you not get a P.O. Box Victor!" He had no reply, at least none that would diffuse the situation. Victor let Maura tear into him as he knew she was justified.

After a few minutes of shouting her anger boiled over. She grabbed one of the dishes she had washed and flung it like a Frisbee toward Victor. Lucky for him he dodged the projectile but it crashed against the wall making a terrible sound. Suddenly the kitchen was intensely quiet.

"Clean that up!" Maura yelled at Victor as she dried her hands and stormed out of the kitchen. He did just that. The pieces of the dish were wrapped in paper towels and put in the trash. The house was still quiet and Victor dared not go and try to make amends with Maura so soon. He went through the mail and found the letter from Hadden Clark and opened it.
The letter, on a single sheet of white-lined paper, was quick and to the point and ultimately quite disappointing.

Dear Victor,

Before I answer all of your questions and tell you what the police don't know about the Lady in the Dunes in 1974 I would like you to get me these: 2 8x10 Authentic Autographs of these 2 Athletes.

New England Patriots Quarter Back Cam Newton
Tampa Bay Buccaneer Quarter Back Tom Brady

You Have a nice day, Sincerely Yours
Hadden J. Clark 233-181

Victor could feel the character of Hadden Clark seeping out of the ink in the letter. The man seemed petty and child-like to Victor. However, he did respond and seemed to be at least semi-interested in corresponding. That was as long as Victor played ball. He had a lot on his plate, most pressing being his angry wife in the other room. Victor slid the letter back into its envelope and decided that he would sleep on it before deciding just how much ball he would play with Hadden Clark.

Before entertaining the demands of Hadden Clark in his brief introductory letter Victor decided to reach out to the man who knew him best, former detective Theodore. First and foremost he was somewhat surprised that Hadden did indeed respond to Victor. After hearing the letter word for word Theodore was also surprised by how lucid Hadden seemed. After working with him for twenty years he was used to rambling pointless rants from Clark while the first letter was shockingly direct. He sounded more human. Victor and Theodore agreed that perhaps Hadden was on different medications that evened out his paranoid schizophrenia.

Victor asked how he should proceed. Theodore told Victor not to bullshit Hadden but also to not simply give him everything he was asking for. It was wise to give Hadden something while also slowly pulling information from him. Theodore suggested asking a few softball questions. Then he could gauge whether Hadden was being truthful by his response to those questions. Theodore gave one final word of advice and that was to not go back on his word. If he said he was going to send Hadden something in exchange for information Victor had to follow through.

After speaking with Theodore Victor made a call to his co-producer John Duke Logan. He was an important potential connection due to his status as a magician who worked for the New England Patriots. Even though Tom Brady no longer played for them Victor thought Logan might be able to pull some strings to get Brady's autograph for Hadden Clark. Otherwise Victor was looking at potentially spending upwards of $2,000 for such an autograph. Logan said he would look into what he could do.

Thinking back to what Theodore had said Victor decided to meet Hadden halfway. He would purchase a Cam Newton autograph to show Clark that he had good intentions. After all, the Newton autograph only cost $30. It seemed like a worthwhile investment especially if Hadden Clark revealed some insider information about the Lady of the Dunes in his second letter.

Victor sent Hadden Clark a followup letter. In it he asked a few softball questions that he could then share with Theodore. Naturally Victor asked Hadden for the name of the Lady of the Dunes. He knew this would not be answered. In addition he asked a simple open-ended question of Clark's connection to Cape Cod and Provincetown in particular.

Victor also gave his word that he was going to purchase a Cam Newton autograph to send him and to give him a week on that. It was a long shot. For all Victor knew Hadden Clark could receive the letter with a promise of an autograph but no autograph and completely revert to the crazed ramblings that Theodore had been used to. Whatever the result it was still worth a shot. The second letter to Hadden Clark was sent away with the Cam Newton autograph soon to follow.

Victor's next move was to contact the Cape Cod National Seashore. He wanted badly to be able to excavate the area at Lombard Hollow Road. If a tooth belonging to the Lady of the Dunes was there it would blow the case wide open. The more he thought about the scenario the more it seemed feasible. However, convincing the higher-ups at the Seashore to let him do so was likely a daunting task.

The person Victor contacted was named Howard. He was an historian of the Cape Cod National Seashore. Having been in charge of the historical landscapes, structures and archaeological sites among other things since joining the National Seashore made Howard the right person to speak with. It also helped that he had previously worked with Howard during the Thoreau documentary so that was the man Victor planned to call. Before doing so though he got the rest of his ducks in a row.

The mere notion that a tooth belonging to the Lady of the Dunes might be located along Lombard Hollow Road was enough for Victor to reach out to four different contacts. He wanted to build up a case for being allowed to dig out there. It was important for Victor to have all of the necessary people and equipment ready to go if he was indeed given the green light.

Before even reaching out to Howard Victor had already acquired the services of those four contacts. They were willing to come to South Truro to aid in reconnaissance. This would be more than just a walk through in the Lombard Hollow area. It would also include metal detectors, K9 dogs, and deep-penetrating radar. The only thing that was needed was permission.

Howard was cordial when Victor called. He was not very familiar with the Lady of the Dunes story and Victor's documentary. That being said due to the fact that he had previously worked with Victor, Howard was receptive to a meeting about a potential reconnaissance. Once Victor began mentioning a search crew, K9 dogs, and the lot he could tell that Howard was reconsidering. Despite the bad feeling a meeting was set for June 4th at 2pm.

Although the meeting at the National Seashore was set Victor was not feeling overly confident that he would get permission to dig at Lombard Hollow. He figured that it might be wise to make the most of the trip to Cape Cod. First off Victor would pay a visit to the Cape Cod Media Center in Dennis. It was there that a pair of interns were to be putting together a short behind the scenes piece to go along with the Lady of the Dunes documentary.

The second thing Victor added to his June 4th itinerary was officially meeting his potential author Christopher Setterlund. He needed to be certain of Setterlund's interest in writing the companion book before it got too close to the premiere date of the film. A series of emails and phone calls solidified a meeting between the two. Victor and Christopher planned on meeting at the Hot Chocolate Sparrow coffee shop in Orleans in the mid-afternoon of that day. Victor had little hope that the meeting with Howard would take that long.

His June 4th got a whole lot busier when a Cape Cod based reporter contacted him about doing a potential interview about the Lady of the Dunes project. Victor was thrilled as he had been waiting for one of the three newspapers to get back to him. He had wondered why the Lady of the Dunes and the mystery surrounding her murder had been such a tough sell to these local newspapers. At least with one reaching out and wanting to meet Victor would have a chance to get some needed publicity for his hard work.

The plan was for Victor to meet with the female reporter earlier in the day on June 4th. He chose the Pine Grove Cemetery in Truro as the meeting spot. It was partially to add atmosphere to the words Victor would share with the reporter. However it was also partially for himself. Victor planned on bringing his copy of Leo Damore's In His Garden book and taking a walk to try to find Tony Costa's garden.

The plans for the big day of June 4th were all set. Victor felt like he had a little time to relax and reinvigorate himself. He pushed away from the Rip Van Winkle table. He pushed away from the Lady of the Dunes. Memorial Day Weekend was fast approaching and Victor wanted to take some time to reconnect with Maura and their son without any sort of projects hanging over his head. It was at the dawning of this reinvigoration that the feelings began to happen.

He could not pin point the exact date or any circumstances surrounding it but Victor was unable to push away from the table when it came to the Lady of the Dunes. Since the beginning of the project Victor had been amerced in the case and the project surrounding it. Whether intentional or not the Lady of the Dunes, not the project, but the woman at the epicenter of the mystery, had seeped into his subconscious. She consumed him at times. Her identity, her fate, the stage of Provincetown upon which she was a major player, these things danced around Victor's mind almost incessantly.

However constantly thinking about the Lady of the Dunes and the project surrounding it was only part of the issue. One night it escalated. Victor woke up and had to use the bathroom. Not wanting to wake Maura he did his best to leave the lights off in the bedroom and hallway leading to the bathroom. He quietly tiptoed out into the hallway. It was there that he froze. Victor was overcome with the feeling that he was being watched. His mind and his heart raced. The sense of unease caused him to turn the hallway light on. There was darkness and shadows everywhere. A cold chill went up his spine and he quickly entered the bathroom and closed the door. Victor even locked the door behind him.

He stared at his face in the mirror, never breaking eye contact with himself. Victor had this unshakable feeling that if he looked around too much he would eventually see her. All of the work on the film, seeing the horrific case file photos, the contact made by the mediums, it all made Victor feel close to the Lady of the Dunes. It was as if she was right beside him all of the time, watching him, not malevolently but intently.

Victor washed his hands after using the bathroom. His head was down looking at the rushing water from the sink. He did not look into the mirror again. It was in his mind an irrational fear yet one that he completely bought into. Victor grasped the bathroom doorknob and slowly unlocked it.

'Please don't be there, please don't be there.' Victor rambled in his mind. He opened the door, clicked off the lights and scurried quickly back into the bedroom. So worried was Victor about the potential sight of a ghostly vision of the Lady of the Dunes that he barely felt the pain as he stubbed his toe on the door frame upon entering the room.

He lay on his back in bed closing his eyes with tremendous force. Victor then turned over to sleep on his stomach, something he never did. He did not see any sort of apparition that night. However, these late-night trips to the bathroom filled with the fear of the unknown became far too regular for Victor's liking. It became routine through the summer. Victor began making it a point to not have anything to drink after dinner. This curbed most nightly bathroom trips. However it left the bathroom and the hallway. There were nights that he curled with his face buried in his pillow, positive that if he looked up the Lady of the Dunes would be standing above him. He knew he could not simply push away from the table even for a little while.

Friday June 4th was an early riser for Victor. He needed to be at the Pine Grove Cemetery in Truro to meet with the reporter by 11am. His plan was to get there early to explore the cemetery and the surrounding grounds on his own. Being a day trip Victor packed a small bag, making sure he had anything he might need.

He pulled out of his driveway just after 7am heading back to the Outer Cape. Luckily the traffic going to Cape Cod was light even though it was now after Memorial Day. This day could prove to be a game changer for the right or wrong reasons. Victor had three separate meetings to attend and was hoping that at least one would pan out for the positive.

Pine Grove Cemetery was located in an extremely remote area. Old County Road itself was fairly rural. It was winding, hilly, and sparsely dotted with homes. In that area, one was more apt to see mountain bikers than vehicles. It was another half-mile down a bumpy, dirt road that led to the cemetery itself. When driving that road to the cemetery Victor was amazed by its sheer isolation. In 2021 Pine Grove Cemetery was in the middle of nowhere, Victor could only imagine just how devoid of civilization the area was when Tony Costa was committing his crimes a half-century earlier.

Just when it felt like the dirt road would never end a cemetery appeared like a morbid oasis among the forest. Despite seeming tiny among the sprawling trees the cemetery was home to more than 800 graves. Victor slowly drove around the outside border of the cemetery. He parked far in the back, facing one of several fire roads that crisscrossed the Truro woods. Pine Grove Cemetery was one of very few signs of human civilization in an area of over 1,800 acres that included the potential tooth site at Lombard Hollow Road. For all intents and purposes Victor was alone in a sea of death and wilderness.

Victor knew he had about two hours to play with before the reporter showed up and he planned to take advantage of it. The area he chose to park at was no accident. It was only a few steps from an ominous brick crypt. The half-circle shaped structure, built partially into the hillside, had an eerie story behind it. It was inside the crypt that legend had it that Tony Costa dismembered one or more of his victims. Victor stared at the crypt but did not get closer. He had another plan.

The fire road that Victor had parked in front of was the pathway to Costa's garden. There was a map of the area in Leo

Damore's In His Garden book. Victor rifled through his bag looking for the book.

"Ah shit," he exclaimed, tossing his bag onto the passenger side floor. The book was not there. Victor slammed his door. It echoed loudly in the overwhelming silence of the cemetery. He wagered that he could scream as loud as he wanted and nobody would hear it. That was a freeing and at the same time unsettling realization. Despite not having the book with the map Victor was in the mood for an adventure. He locked up his car and headed down the fire road.

One marker that Victor needed to look out for was a makeshift telephone attached to a tree. The story he had been told was that it say 'Tony Chop Chop's Phone' on it. How far was it? That he did not know. Victor kept walking. His head was on a swivel. Being deep in the empty woods of Truro was unnerving. He could feel the spirit of the woods around him. Victor could close his eyes and imagine Tony Costa prowling the area, working in his garden.

Twenty minutes and several winding turns later Victor had not found the phone or the garden. Dejected he turned around and headed back to the cemetery. It was empty and quiet much the way he had left it. Victor took his time walking around the grounds, checking out as many of the tombstones as he could. In his opinion Pine Grove was in a league of its own as far as creepiness, although it did not match St. Peter's cemetery.

While studying one grave in particular Victor heard a sound. A minute later he saw a car coming down the road. It was the first sign of life since he had arrived at Pine Grove Cemetery nearly two hours earlier. He waved at the woman driving. She parked and exited with a notepad in hand. It was the reporter he had been waiting for.

The two exchanged pleasantries. Victor gave her a quick crash course in what he had been doing in regards to the Lady of the Dunes. Delving into the morbid details behind the case seemed appropriate as the pair stood among the headstones. It was a fairly paint-by-numbers interview until Victor began to connect the Lady of the Dunes to the other legends of the South Truro woods.

At this point, the reporter seemed to get a bit antsy. She did not appear to be as shocked at the revelations as Victor had thought she'd be. He figured it was not the first time that she had heard the potential connection of Hadden Clark, Tony Costa, and others, to the Truro woods. Twenty minutes of talking went by and the interview ended. It was a little shorter than he had expected. Still, Victor thanked the reporter and told her that if she had any additional questions she could email or call him. He watched her car slowly vanish down the dirt road. Again Victor was alone with the Pine Grove residents. The interview had not been a failure, but it was not exactly a rousing success as Victor had hoped.

Before heading back down Cape to meet with Howard at the National Seashore Victor made a pit stop. It was not far from Pine Grove Cemetery to the site at Lombard Hollow Road where the Lady of the Dunes' potential tooth could be. Victor parked hidden slightly from Route 6. He walked the few hundred feet to where his GPS pin was on his phone. It was calm and quiet where he stood except for the muted hum of cars passing by. Victor wondered aloud how long it would take him to walk back to Pine Grove Cemetery through the web of connected fire roads. Once he realized that his staring into the labyrinth of trees was not going to make the tooth magically appear Victor returned to his car.

Victor had higher hopes for his meeting with Howard. If nothing else, they had previously worked together and knew each other a little. Victor thought he would at least be heard out about the potential of the tooth site.

The meeting was cordial. Howard reiterated that he was not very familiar with the Lady of the Dunes and the mysteries of the South Truro woods. Victor had counted on Howard's curiosity about the case. Unfortunately, he was more disturbed by the notion of digging, using metal detectors, and cadaver dogs. As each moment passed Victor could sense that the meeting was doomed. Howard did not come out and refuse to allow Victor to perform his reconnaissance at Lombard Hollow Road. However, when he ended the meeting by telling Victor that he would look into everything and get back to him it was as good as a 'no.'

The Salt Pond Visitors Center parking lot was buzzing with people looking to walk the grounds and take advantage of the bike trail that led to nearby Coast Guard Beach. Victor took a moment to collect himself as he stood next to his car. He was fairly certain that nothing would come from the meeting with Howard but he could not let that cast a cloud over the rest of his day.

Before leaving the parking lot Victor made sure to send a text to Christopher Setterlund. The plan now was to meet at a Dunkin' located just off the highway in South Yarmouth. At first, they had intended to meet at the Hot Chocolate Sparrow in Orleans but Victor was getting tired and wanted to start heading home. He would have hurried off Cape if not for this meeting with his potential book writer.

Since it was so close to the Salt Pond Visitors Center Victor made it a point to visit Evergreen Cemetery and the grave of Sydney Monzon. He explained his progress with the Lady of the Dunes project and how it concerned her and her fate as well.

Victor felt a deep connection to Sydney. There was something in her face, the black and white yearbook photo so readily available to view online, that resonated with Victor. She had become every bit as important to him as the Lady of the Dunes herself.

This minor sidetrack led to Victor getting stuck behind a slow-moving camper as he entered the dangerous two-lane highway known affectionately as 'Suicide Alley' due to its high-rate of accidents in the preceding decades.

The day had mostly been a bust. Driving slowly on the highway Victor had a sense that for better or worse the finish line was near. Then his phone rang and a sense of uncertainty came over him. It was Christopher. He said that because of ongoing pandemic protocols customers weren't being allowed inside Dunkin.' He suggested a parking lot located nearby where the Cape Cod Rail Trail passed. The nice morning had turned to a foggy and drizzly afternoon. Victor began to wonder if this was a setup. He had given Setterlund a lot of information about his film.

Victor momentarily debated scrapping the meeting but got off the highway. He laughed out loud about his paranoia. Setterlund had six books, he had a website, and a large social media presence. It was highly unlikely that he was some sort of psychotic looking to take Victor out. He was just tired and his experiences when filming in Provincetown in April had clouded his judgment.

When Victor pulled into the parking lot it was empty except for one car. Outside of it stood a short, stocky man with a shaved head. Victor parked a few spots away to keep a respectable distance at first.

Once they shook hands and got to talking all of his fears were allayed. Setterlund was all-in on writing the book and a verbal agreement was made. No timetable was set, it was just understood that Setterlund would begin to work on the book and keep in direct contact with Victor to make sure the details were as accurate as possible.

Despite being tired and wanting to get off Cape before the rush of weekend travelers arrived Victor found himself feeling quite chatty. This meeting had gone far better than the one with Howard.

The weekend saw a slight lull in the nonstop work on the Lady of the Dunes film. Victor should have known better. When Monday arrived so did a second letter from the Eastern Correctional Institution. Hadden Clark had responded. Luckily Maura was not home to receive the letter and Victor was able to hide it away and avoid another dish being thrown at him.

He sat in a chair as if getting ready to read some sort of literary classic and not look over a letter from a convicted serial killer. Thankfully the authentic autograph from Cam Newton had arrived on time. Hadden Clark was satisfied enough to give Victor some of what he was looking for.

Dear Victor,

Thank you for the autograph photo of New England Quarterback Cam Newton.
Now to answer some of your Questions.
1. It is well documented that I was not working on Cape Cod when the police discovered this girls body.
2. Yes I do know this girls name.
3. Yes I did keep some trophies.
4. I made it easy for someone to discover her body, or an animal.
5. Yes I had grandparents who lived in Wellfleet on Pamet Point Road.

6. I did not know Tony Costa, but I did know his brother who I worked for, Mylan Costa.

7. I have no bodies buried in the dunes or in the woods of Cape Cod. There is a lot of false stuff in books, TV, and internet about me. Example: Book "Born Evil" by Adrian Havill. 85 percent of that book are lies and false information.

A. In that book he mentions he visited me several times while I was in prison at the Western Correctional Inst. That is a lie; He has never visit me in prison. He visit another inmate, but he has never visit me.

B. He has me working on Cape Cod in 1974 that's a lie. I didn't start working on Cape Cod until the Summer of 1975. But I was on Cape Cod many times that summer.

8. In my next letter I'll tell you where you can find some jewelry of hers, and I'll answer the other ½ of your questions, and tell you more of what happened that night in 1974.

Hope you had a good Memorial Day Weekend. God bless you always.

Sincerely Yours

Hadden J. Clark 233-181

Victor found himself slightly unsettled from the way Hadden wished him well and blessed him. Yes he had answered some of his questions but the details were slim. In fact, it seemed that Clark was more interested in discrediting the Born Evil book rather than giving information about the Lady of the Dunes.

The letter was folded up and put back in its envelope. Victor planned to revisit it later. He began milling around some random items from over the last year or so. These went back even into his Thoreau documentary. That's when he saw something that startled him. It was a postcard. A woman was standing in it. Was she the Lady of the Dunes?

At first Victor could not even remember where the oddly placed postcard had come from. The slightly faded photograph postcard looked east down Commercial Street in Provincetown. It faced the iconic Lobster Pot restaurant. At first glance it was a quite unassuming snapshot of 1970's life in Provincetown.

He had to think back to the days before the Lady of the Dunes dominated his every waking hour. Back to when Victor's exposure to Cape Cod was a peaceful meditative walk along its great outer beach. It came back like a flash of lightning. During their last interaction after the Thoreau documentary had been filmed Victor had given Susanna Deiss a postcard of Thoreau's Oysterman House that she owned from the 1930's.

In return, Susanna gave Victor a postcard of Provincetown from the 1970s. A street scene that had no real meaning to him at the time. Victor even ended up placing it in the closing credits collage for the Thoreau documentary.

Now as Victor gazed at it he could not take his eyes off of a woman in the foreground of the shot on the right side. She was dressed all in blue. Jeans, short-sleeved Polo shirt, bandana, all were blue with the exception of her large round sunglasses that were red. Despite the photo being slightly faded and grainy the young woman jumped off the paper at him.

Briefly Victor thought back to the theory about the Lady of the Dunes being an extra in the movie Jaws. Then he remembered Art debunking it by saying that the woman was a Martha's Vineyard resident and still very much alive and well.

There was no getting around the fact that the woman in the postcard bore a resemblance to the most recent composite of the Lady of the Dunes from 2010. What made it seem more than a simple coincidence was the fact that the postcard appeared to be from the early 1970s. It was entirely plausible that the Lady of the Dunes was a summer resident of Provincetown who happened to be caught on film.

The only way to be sure of the woman in the postcard would be to find her today, or someone who knew her, and Victor had no idea of where to start. The bottom line was that to him the postcard was a great find. Whether it was her or not it was a sign that she wanted to be found.

His excitement was buoyed by a message he received from a big local newspaper. They were looking to speak with him about his film. Victor felt ready to share some details of what he was doing. The only press he had received was a Provincetown Magazine piece from May that had barely included any mention of Victor and his documentary. With these two bits of news Victor sent a quick message to Christopher Setterlund. The pair had been regularly conversing as Setterlund began peppering Victor with questions about the documentary process for the book.

Victor sent along a photo of the postcard. In another piece of fun coincidence Setterlund responded with a photo of his own. It turned out that he had recently been in Provincetown himself shooting photos for an upcoming book. The photo he sent Victor was from virtually the same spot as the 1970's postcard. It even had a white vehicle coming down Commercial Street and a person standing in almost the exact same spot as the mystery woman. It made Victor feel that he was on the right path and had chosen the right author.

Setterlund began sending along lists of questions pertaining to the Lady of the Dunes project via email. For Victor it was an odd feeling to be speaking of the film in the past tense while it was still going on. It left Victor with one foot in the past and one still moving toward the future. He had high hopes for the book bringing publicity to the project. However there was no timetable on it and as the June days ticked by Victor was looking for something to break in the present to get the word out. It was after all coming up on the anniversary of the murder of the Lady of the Dunes and it seemed like a perfect tie in to the film.

The interview with the reporter at the Pine Grove Cemetery had gone well. However there had been three newspapers that had shown initial interest in writing about the project. Victor was growing concerned by the fact that the two larger ones had been nonchalant in their communication. One of the larger papers had cut off all ties. Victor attempts to connect were unsuccessful. The other paper did respond.

Entering mid-June Victor was able to finagle a telephone chat. He laid it all out on the table. Victor was willing to share any and all information he had gathered over the previous five to six months. The talks with the DNA Doe Project, the less than stellar conversations with the District Attorney's Office, there was a story there and Victor was offering it up.

The conversation did not end well. Victor was told by this larger newspaper that they would not be running any sort of story about the Lady of the Dunes at that time. When Victor pressed them for a reason he was told it was an editorial decision. They could not be swayed.

Days later it only got worse as the other large newspaper gave a similar response. The editor did not want to run any sort of Lady of the Dunes story. Dejected Victor could only think to himself as to why two major newspapers both declined to run a story about his project. There was so much meat on the bone to the story and barely a nibble of coverage from the press. It upset him but also made him think there must be something to what he was doing.

It was after this bit of bad news in terms of media coverage of the Lady of the Dunes project that Victor decided to go back to the postcard. He wanted badly for the woman walking along Commercial Street to be the one he was looking for. There didn't seem to be a clear-cut way to pinpoint the time period when the photograph was taken. Clothing styles, vehicles in the shot, these could provide generalities but nothing concrete.

The best lead Victor came up with had to do with The Lobster Pot restaurant that was predominantly featured in the postcard. He visited the establishment's website and sent a quick email. The owner of The Lobster Pot responded quickly. This allowed Victor to send an image of the postcard for the owner to see.

Victor did get an answer as to the time period of the postcard. However it was not what he had been hoping for. The owner of the restaurant confirmed that the image could have been taken no earlier than 1979. This was a full five years after the Lady of the Dunes had been murdered. The reasoning was the fact that his family, the McNulty Family, had purchased the venerable seafood spot in 1979. Upon purchasing it the family had painted the exterior sign, changing the color from brown to white. In the postcard The Lobster Pot sign was indeed white.

Victor thanked the owner for his time. Inside though he was crushed. It was always a long shot, however Victor had held out hope that the random postcard would prove to be a valuable piece of the puzzle. Instead it went back to being a nice gift given to him by Susanna Deiss after the Thoreau documentary had wrapped up. Victor continued to hold out hope that he would find something that nobody else had found pertaining to the case. There had to be an avenue nobody else had traveled.

Coming off the back of the newspaper and postcard disappointments Victor became hyper-focused on Hadden Clark and their correspondence. He had two people in mind when it came to prime suspects in the Lady of the Dunes murder from the get-go. They were always Clark and Whitey Bulger. Clark because he was in the area and had previously claimed to have killed her. Now with a window into Hadden's world Victor wanted to pry deeper into Bulger. The famed mobster also had been in the area at the time of the murder. It had occurred to Victor that he had never asked local law enforcement if they had questioned Bulger or anyone connected with him.

Needing a palate cleanser after the pair of disappointments Victor decided to reach out. Having previously spoken with Jeff Jaran Victor sent the former Provincetown Chief of Police an email. He was straight to the point, asking Jaran if anyone had contacted someone associated with Bulger.

Jaran informed Victor that indeed they had reached out to sources about Bulger's potential involvement in the Lady of the Dunes murder. Throughout the process Jaran himself reached out to Whitey Bulger's attorneys fourteen times. When Bulger was asked point blank if he had anything to do with the murder itself he never said yes or no.

Victor wanted to hear it for himself. Jaran gave him the contact information for both of Bulger's attorneys and wished Victor good luck in finding the information he sought.
No time was wasted in reaching out to the attorneys. Victor's message was simple. He explained who he was and what he was doing. The segued into him asking what Bulger's relationship to the Lady of the Dunes case was. It was quick and to the point.

The response was nearly verbatim what Jaran had told Victor about Bulger's statement about the case.

Bulger's attorneys gave Victor the following statement via email. "I once asked Whitey if he had any knowledge of the LOTD. He scoffed, adding that 'Are they looking to blame me for all unsolved murders so that they can close the files?'"

It was not enough. Victor reached out again this time asking for a telephone call. They agreed and a time was set up.

When the three reconvened a few days later Victor finally got what he had been looking for. Bulger's attorneys were pleasant and professional which led to Victor responding in kind very respectfully with his line of questioning. The attorneys, one older and one a junior lawyer, maintained their stance that Bulger had never admitted to having anything to do with the murder.

Victor reiterated that he was not looking to sensationalize the Lady of the Dunes case. He was trying to give the victim back her name. The attorneys found this commendable. Victor was honest when he said that he had thought that either Bulger or Hadden Clark were responsible for the murder. He asked the attorneys if it was all right to mention that he thought Bulger was a suspect in the film.

They asked Victor if he had any hard evidence to back up that Bulger was involved. When he said he did not the attorneys told Victor that it was well within his First Amendment rights to mention his thoughts on Bulger. Victor breathed a sigh of relief. However the attorneys ended the conversation with a little bit of a warning. They told Victor that if he did try to pin the murder on Whitey Bulger than they would be seeing Victor in court.

Victor felt safe as far as how Whitey Bulger was to be portrayed in the film. He returned to Hadden Clark's second letter. After reading it again Victor reached out to Theodore to give him the details. Again Theodore marveled at the coherence of

Hadden's words. His backhanded compliment was that Clark sounded 'less crazy' than usual.

He told Victor about the 2000 trip to Cape Cod with Hadden Clark. It was interesting to hear it from someone who was there and not a newspaper story. He had already known about Hadden dressing in drag, the walk around his grandfather's property in Wellfleet, and finding his 'trophies.' What Victor had never heard was Theodore's recounting of Hadden's intention to kill him while out in those woods. It turned out that Hadden had a razor blade hidden in a crucifix that was meant to be the murder weapon. Luckily it never had a chance to be used. This was a sobering reminder that Victor was corresponding with a dangerous serial killer, he was not a pen pal.

Theodore and Victor discussed what questions Victor should ask in a third letter. The former detective fell back on asking him some softball questions with trick questions peppered in. Knowing him for decades Theodore explained to Victor that if Hadden answered certain questions truthfully than he'd feel that he was answering all of them that way. It was a team effort. Victor was grateful to have someone with the connection to Hadden Clark like Theodore. It gave him the best chance of getting the unabashed truth about Clark's connection to the Lady of the Dunes.

In addition to the questions a replica Tom Brady autographed 8x10 photo as well as several Cape Cod postcards were included. The postcards were a sign of good faith, while the autograph Victor hoped would pass as the real thing. The third letter was mailed away and all Victor could do was wait.

Victor spent some time in silence. He tried to clear his mind. Not having a logical next step at the moment he wanted to see what entered his thoughts. Sydney Monzon and her sad plight came back to the forefront. Much like with the Lady of the Dunes

Victor's mind drifted to how the family of Sydney Monzon must have dealt with her death.

Victor put his internet detective hat on and searched her parents to find if perhaps Sydney had any siblings. Through their obituaries he found children's names. Victor was in luck. There was indeed a living sibling, a brother living in Brookline, Massachusetts. He was eighty-three. Having gone this far Victor got the man's number and decided to give him a call. After three rings he picked up.

"Hello?"

"I'm sorry to bother you, but my name is Victor Franko. I was calling to ask you if you by chance were any relation to Sydney Monzon of Eastham?" The line was silent. Victor was not sure if the man had hung up on him.

"She was my sister," the man said barely above a whisper. Then the line went silent again. Victor wasn't sure if he should say something. "You're the first person to say her name out loud in three years. That was at a funeral and her name came up."

Victor explained why he had called. He explained about the Lady of the Dunes and reading In His Garden. Sydney's brother cried while talking about his sister. It was as if the wounds were still fresh more than fifty years later.

During the twenty minute conversation Sydney's brother spoke of his desire to kill Tony Costa when he was attending his mother's funeral at St. Peter's Church in Provincetown. The man stated with pride that he was a trained marksman and had fully intended to pull a sniper hit on Costa. The only thing that stopped him was his own mother asking him not to.

"So you're the one that's mentioned in the book? The assassination attempt?" Victor was amazed that this part of the In His Garden book was factual.

"Yes, that is me."

The man continued by saying that he believed that if Costa had not gotten into drugs the murders would not have happened and that his sister would still be alive. He wanted to kill the man who had supplied Costa with the drugs. When Victor pressed him for the supplier's name Sydney Monzon's brother would not reveal it. Victor believed that the person who supplied the drugs to Tony Costa was Sorrentino, he had heard rumors and innuendo. It would have been nice to get another person to confirm it however Victor did not want to press the man who was so clearly still angry and distraught over the murder of his sister.

"I appreciate your time," Victor began, "and I wanted to let you know that my plan is to dedicate the film to the memory of your sister." There was a muted gasp and the slight sound of weeping.

"Thank you," the man replied clearly choked up at the gesture, "she would appreciate that."

In the end Victor wrapped up the call by asking Sydney's brother if he would be open to being interviewed for the project. The man was not sure, but he said he'd think about it.

Victor had not been sure as to whom the project would be dedicated to or anything like that. While speaking with Sydney's brother it became apparent to Victor that she deserved that honor. Victor believed that Sydney Monzon tied all of it together.

June was coming to a close. Victor had gone back and forth with Christopher Setterlund four times with various questions about the project. He appreciated Setterlund's enthusiasm for the film. The entire process had been such a roller-coaster ride up to that point and answering the author's questions helped bring things back into focus. For Victor it was all about giving the Lady of the Dunes her name. Hadden Clark did just that.

Hadden's third letter arrived in the mail on Monday June 28th. Each response gave Victor a little more in the way of optimism. This was based mainly around Theodore's assurance that Hadden sounded different in these letters. Victor tore open the envelope eagerly. A piece of yellow-lined paper greeted him. It was not what he expected.

In this letter, dated June 22nd, Hadden ranted about the Tom Brady autograph not being authentic unlike the Cam Newton autograph. He demanded an authentic autograph of the Tampa Bay quarterback or he would not answer any of Victor's questions. Clark pondered whether Victor had been 'played for a fool' by the person he bought the autograph from.

Victor shook his head knowing that his replica autograph had been caught. What he couldn't explain was why Clark said he didn't get any of the postcards that Victor had included. Those were real.

Hadden ended the combative third letter by promising that if Victor sent him what he asked for he would tell him everything he wanted to know. It ended with Clark wishing Victor a Happy Fourth of July and blessing him.

It was a disappointing response. Victor had hoped for something to sink his teeth into and yet all he got was a letter of complaining. He would not bend when it came to spending potentially thousands of dollars for an authentic Tom Brady autograph. All Victor could do was hope the postcards got to Hadden to give him some inclination to write a fourth letter. Two days later another letter arrived.

Dear Victor,

I just received 7 postcards from you. Thank you very much. E.C.I. loves to fuck with my mail, pardon my language.

E.C.I. held on to one piece of mail of mine for 9 weeks before giving it to me.

E.C.I. let me receive an autographed photo of Demi Moore in a plastic case.

E.C.I. lets other inmates at E.C.I. receive photos of naked women, but not me. I tell all my pen pals when I explain them the rules in Maryland I am not allowed to receive naked photos of females at E.C.I. E.C.I. discriminates against me due to my crimes.

Other inmates are allowed to have an alarm clock but not me.

Other inmates are allowed civilian blue jeans with pockets in them, but not me.

I do not get caught up in all this bullshit.

I'm allowed to receive postcards in the mail in a letter. I receive them all the other times, even from pen pals in Europe, South America, Australia, Japan, etc.

Here's the crazy thing. If I'm not allowed to receive them, he E.C.I. mail room should of issue me a written notice of what they remove from my mail and return to sender. That's a Department of Correction rule.

Now to answer some of your questions.

You ask what this girls name? What's crazy, her first name was Laura.

The police no longer have Laura's jewelry, but I can tell you who has it now.

I have Laura's drivers license which is still in storage.

What most people don't know, Laura was a college girl who had gotten a summer job on Cape Cod.

Please send me Tom Brady authentic autograph in a Tampa Bay uniform. Not a copy of his autograph which you sent me. And I'll tell you more. You also can send me more postcards if you want to. I'm allowed to receive postcards in the mail.

    Laura. Her name was Laura. Victor's eyes kept scanning over the black ink scribble. Could it be true? Was the Lady of the Dunes a college student named Laura? Theodore had said Hadden seemed more lucid than normal. Would the convicted serial killer really blurt out the name just like that? It was a name, but was it the name?

    Then Victor thought back to April at the Meads house. Chief Meads called the Lady of the Dunes by the nickname 'Lulu.' It could be possible that Lulu was a nickname for someone named Laura as well.

    For the first time since initially hearing about the Lady of the Dunes murder there was a name to go with the legend. Victor was cautiously optimistic. How could he prove that 'Laura' was the Lady of the Dunes? After all one of Hadden's proven victims was Laura Houghteling. Was she the Laura that Hadden was thinking of? The drivers license Hadden claimed to have would clinch it. A last name would do even more.

    At least there was a starting point. Victor knew enough people that perhaps simply plugging the name Laura into missing persons databases from the early to mid 1970's could give some clues. A few more postcards might gain some more information. The Tom Brady autograph? Still no chance on that.

    Victor also could not help but find it a little off-putting that Hadden Clark thought of him as one of his pen pals. In between the excitement over possibly finding the name of the

Lady of the Dunes Victor came back to the fact that the man on the other end of these letters was a convicted serial killer. Hadden was not someone to be glorified.

Victor was going to these ends to solve the mystery of the Lady of the Dunes, period.

Victor had a lot to digest when it came to Hadden Clark's most recent letter. His first inclination was to contact Theodore. As was the case with all of Clark's letters the pair dissected them with a fine-toothed comb. Not wanting to lose his attention Victor cut right to the chase. Theodore was shocked by the revelation that Hadden mentioned that the name of the Lady of the Dunes was Laura.

He did his best to focus on what Victor was saying about Hadden revealing Laura as the potential name of the Lady of the Dunes. That being said the beautiful scenery where Theodore was, coupled with a cold beer, proved to be more appealing than a serial killer's letter.

Both Theodore and Victor felt that there was some meat on the bone when it came to Hadden Clark's claims. Yet neither knew exactly what the next step was to be. The former detective maintained that Hadden sounded different than he was used to, chalking it up to potentially being on better medication. Theodore asked Victor to keep him up to date on what was going on with Hadden and his letters before returning to fishing.

Feeling the need for more information and opinion on Hadden's revelation Victor called Agent X to share what he had found out. They had not been in contact since the end of April, approximately two months earlier. This was when Agent X had directed Victor toward a contact that led to Theodore.

Agent X for their part was surprised that Victor had not only spoken with Whitey Bulger's attorneys but had also received several letters from Hadden Clark. When it came to Clark and his potential revelation of the Lady of the Dunes' name Agent X laughed. They were not putting much stock in the convicted serial killer's word. Victor was slightly disappointed as he had hoped

Agent X might have so pearls of wisdom concerning where to look as far as finding 'Laura.'

Interestingly Agent X was more forthcoming when it came to their thoughts on Whitey Bulger. They told Victor straight out that they never really considered Bulger a suspect. Bulger was more of a go-to for suspicious crimes in Massachusetts. It lined up with what Bulger's attorneys had said to Victor, how the famed mobster had once claimed that the state was trying to pin every unsolved murder on him.

In the end Agent X wished Victor good luck with his correspondence with Hadden Clark. They were not very confident that there was any truth in what Clark was saying, yet it made for good theater in the grand scheme of the film. Victor would not end up hearing from Agent X again until October.

After the less-than-fulfilling conversation, Victor was left to ponder the name Laura on his own. Before he could figure out how to proceed though he was slapped in the face with a possibly catastrophic situation.

Since returning from the shoot in Provincetown in April there had been a pair of interns helping Victor's editor in the process of cutting the more than fifty-two hours of footage down to a reasonable film length. The interns had been working off and on at the Cape Cod Media Center in Dennis. Victor had even stopped by during his most recent trip to the Cape when he met with Howard from the Seashore and Christopher Setterlund.

Typically when Victor spoke with his interns it was business as usual. They would ask if he minded if certain bits of footage were scrapped and things of the like. This time though it was a different tone to the call. The intern on the phone sounded panicked.

It took a few moments of Victor asking what the problem was before the intern caught his breath. He informed Victor that there had been a major hard drive crash. When pressed as to what that meant the intern told Victor that there was a very real possibility that all of the footage might be lost, all fifty-two hours. What made matters worse was that there were no backups of the files.

Victor's heart was in his throat. All of his hard work might have just gone up in smoke before even having the chance to see the light of day. He thought of all of the interviews during that weekend in Provincetown. There was no way he could recapture the raw visceral emotion from those takes.

The intern was shaken by the events. Being a veteran of twenty years making films Victor was able to compose himself rather quickly. He asked the intern if there was anything that could be done. He responded that he had gotten the fifty-two hours of footage down to two hours. However when he went to transfer the data the connector to the cord of the hard drive had snapped.

The best chance to save the film was to send the entire hard drive out to a lab and keep their fingers crossed that the connection could be saved. With no other option Victor paid to have the hard drive shipped out and could only anxiously await word on whether his Lady of the Dunes project would be recovered.

July was beginning to feel like the most stress-filled time yet working on the Lady of the Dunes project. Everything hinged on whether the hard drive containing all of the project's footage could be saved. Victor had to soldier on and think positive. He did so by continuing to correspond with Christopher Setterlund. The questions the author asked began to put into perspective the road Victor had been on throughout the process of creating the film.

Time was running out to get some sort of article written in time for the anniversary of the Lady of the Dunes murder. The two major newspapers had both pulled out of any pieces citing their editors refusing to run any such articles for the anniversary. Although not imperative to the film being finished Victor thought it would be helpful to get some publicity for the project through the local newspapers.

A final blow was dealt to those hopes during the first week of July. The reporter that Victor had met with at Pine Grove Cemetery the month before called with bad news. She gave the same reasoning as the other newspapers. The reporter told Victor in no uncertain terms that she was explicitly told by her editor not to run the story because they were asked not to do a story that summer on the Lady of the Dunes murder. When Victor tried to ask who asked them not to run the story the reporter apologized and hung up.

Victor was dejected and confused. Three potential newspaper articles all canceled and all seemingly with the same directive. Victor began to wonder if the same body had contacted all three newspapers with orders not to run any Lady of the Dunes articles. It was incredibly frustrating and far more than coincidental.

Victor's mind immediately went to some sort of conspiracy theory. Someone did not want the Lady of the Dunes brought back to the surface. She needed to remain in the shadows. He thought back to Peter Manso and his work on his Lady of the Dunes themed project. Victor hadn't heard much about that since Manso's passing. However even when it was in production there hadn't been any press about it as far as he knew.

With the American Horror Story filming in Provincetown in the earlier part of the year it only felt natural that some media outlet somewhere would have mentioned the Lady of the Dunes as it got closer to the anniversary. Outside of the Provincetown Magazine piece it was radio silence.

Disappointed yet undeterred Victor maintained his promise he had made to those that had helped him work on the project. He maintained his promise he had made to the Lady of the Dunes herself at St. Peter's. No matter the roadblocks Victor would do his best to make sure his film put her, and the search for her identity, in the front of a lot of people's minds.

The Lady of the Dunes, whether her name was Laura or not, never strayed far from the front of Victor's mind. It was made easier by the recurring feeling of being watched during those late night trips to the bathroom. The feeling of eyes being fixed on him as he walked the hallway, or lay in bed, never felt threatening yet never felt comforting either.

There were times that Victor thought about speaking out loud into the darkness just to see if a voice might respond. His worry that it might kept him quiet. In the end the eerie feeling of being watched lasted throughout the summer. Victor chalked it up to his own conscience keeping him focused on why he was doing what he was doing.

One such way that Victor was able to remain focused on the Lady of the Dunes centered around Hadden Clark's most recent letter. The fact that Clark had revealed what he claimed to be the first name of the Lady of the Dunes was startling. However there were likely many potential Laura's that could have been reported missing in the time leading up to July 1974. Victor needed more.

In his reply to the fourth Hadden Clark letter Victor did not mince words. He believed Hadden that her first name was Laura, but he also wanted a last name. Could the convicted killer produce this request? If Theodore was right, and in some way Hadden was more lucid than he had been in prior years, then Victor had a least a fighting chance of getting the information he desired.

Victor did not include any sort of trinkets with the response. He hoped that Hadden might be feeling charitable and give the last name up in good faith. All he could do was wait and see.

One evening in early-July, right around the anniversary of the murder and the body of the Lady of the Dunes being found Victor and Maura sat on the couch. The television was on but low. It was background noise to an impactful conversation between the spouses.

"I was just thinking," Maura said. "Over these last few months there have been letters to our house from serial killers. There have been late-night hangup phone calls. There have been times that we have gone days without speaking more than a few words despite being in the same house."

"I know," Victor replied, "I am sorry for all of the trauma that this project has caused you." Maura put up her hand gently.

"I just wanted to say that if you do end up finding her name, finding her identity. If you end up giving her that closure, even in the afterlife, it will all have been worth it."

"That's what the point of all of this is."

"She has been suffering in anonymity for decades, my 'suffering' over the last few months is nothing compared to what she went through."

Victor felt more at peace with his compulsion over the Lady of the Dunes project after what Maura had said. There had been times where he had wondered if his wife was on board with all he was doing, or if Victor was going overboard. It was a turning point in what had been a stress-filled time in July.

For two weeks from late-June into early-July Victor and his team had been holding their collective breath. They had been awaiting word from the computer lab in regards to saving the

Lady of the Dunes film footage from the damaged hard drive. It was an understandably worrying time. However with twenty years of film-making under his belt Victor was used to unforeseen circumstances and remained relatively calm.

Word came that approximately ninety percent of the footage had been recovered. It was as close to a miracle as Victor could have hoped for. Everyone associated with the project was overwhelmed with relief. Victor felt a connection to this project unlike anything before and, despite his outward calm, would have been devastated if something had derailed it.

That being said Victor decided to play it safe. He soon after hired two full-time editors as well as nine assistant editors to make sure that no other slip ups happened during the Lady of the Dunes film production.

Once the film footage was safe and sound Victor was looking forward to a quiet summer. The months of researching, interviewing, traveling, and editing had worn him out. Victor had been bolstered by the potential of the Lady of the Dunes being identified as 'Laura' by Hadden Clark. This opened up many more paths that needed to be researched which Victor was up for, but at a far more deliberate pace. The failures of the three newspaper articles and the near-loss of the film footage pushed Victor into the idea of taking a full vacation from all of his work. That would remain only an idea.

A letter arrived at Victor's Norton home. It was adorned in the familiar scratch of Hadden Clark. This was a very fast turnaround for a response. Despite the fact that the letter was dated July 3rd Victor had gotten used to the delay. The prison held back incoming and outgoing mail for safety's sake. When Victor opened the envelope he found three yellow-lined pieces of paper neatly folded in thirds. These sheets were filled on both sides with

black ink scribbled words. This letter would reveal far more
information albeit not necessarily what Victor was looking for.

The first page was filled with stories by Hadden about
fellow inmates as well as another rant on Adrian Havill's 'Born
Evil' book. After rolling his eyes and flipping the page over
Victor suddenly found something very interesting. It began with
the mention of a fellow inmate named John Truitt.

Page 2
Yes I told the police & FBI there are bodies buried on my
grandparents property, Wellfleet, Truro and Provincetown
and even told them I killed the girl in the dunes. That's what
John Truitt told me to do. In the Bible in Matthew 7:15 John
is a wolf in sheep skin. The only thing I never did was kill a
FBI agent in 2000 which John Truitt told me to do. I could
have done it really easily. I had a shank on me.
Page 3
I have nothing buried in Massachusetts. Just because I was
working in Ohio in 1974 doesn't mean I wasn't on Cape
Cod that summer visiting my grandmother. Only 2 people
knew I was on that beach that night fishing. My
grandmother and the person who dropped Laura's body in
the dunes. I don't know why he removed her hands and

why he killed her. I'm also in prison for murdering a girl

named Laura. And Whitey Bulger had nothing to do with
this murder.
Page 4
Now you're asking yourself why didn't I go to the police
since I know who dumped this girls body.
A. Back in the 1960's I had to do some community service
on Cape Cod for a crime I never did. My grandparents were

furious when the police had found the real person who did this crime. I just happened to be in the area when this crime happened. My grandparents told me never to go to the police again. That night I also told my grandmother what I witnessed and she reminded me of what happened in the 1960's. My grandmother wasn't going to say anything to the police.

B. Do you know what double jeopardy is? That's when you're not supposed to be punished for a crime you have already been punished for. But double jeopardy doesn't apply to me in Maryland. I had to do 3 years probation, 10 years later they take me back to court and give me another 10 years in prison for a crime I never did.

Page 5

And Laura, the girl in the dunes. I'm also familiar with a few other girls that have gone missing. I just happened to be in the area when these crimes happened, doesn't mean I did them like what happened in the 1960's, and currently in Maryland, Double Jeopardy.

So yes I do know who the girl is at Race Point, but I did not kill her.

I do know who dumped her body at Race Point the summer of 1974.

Plus other information I have in my diaries in a root cellar on Cape Cod on National Park land.

Thank you for the Tom Brady & Cam Newton autographs. You have a good summer. Sincerely Yours.

Hadden J. Clark 233-181

Hadden's letter left a lot to be unpacked. He proclaimed Whitey Bulger's innocence when it came to the Lady of the

Dunes murder. Clark also claimed to have been in the area when the woman's body was dumped in the dunes. He even knew who did the drop off of said body. The big final reveal about diaries in a root cellar caught Victor's attention.

The letter was read a second time. It led Victor to several more questions. First off, having been out among the dunes and the shacks in Provincetown, Victor knew how difficult it was to get out there. Why was Hadden Clark out there at night? More so than that how did someone get the body out to the drop site? Victor started to think that perhaps Hadden was lying.

As had become the tradition after receiving a letter from Hadden Clark the next step was to contact Theodore. Victor wanted to bounce some of his ideas off of the man that knew Clark so well. He gave him a call.

"I got another letter from your boy Hadden," Victor said.

"What do you got? Anything interesting?"

"You ever hear anything about him having diaries?"

"I think so, why did he mention something about a diary?"

"Yeah, in fact more than one. At least he wrote 'diaries.' Also something about them being in a root cellar on National Park land."

"Now it's coming back. Yes Hadden in the past has mentioned the root cellar and diaries."

"What exactly is a root cellar?" Victor had never heard the term until Hadden's letter.

"It's like a dirt basement, usually not connected to a house though. You store fruits, vegetables, and the like there."

"Do you think there really are diaries and a root cellar?"

"Honestly, no, I think he's full of shit. He's full of shit about a lot of stuff. The man is so full of himself and even though he's been more lucid in the letters he's still crazy to a certain degree. He's a copycat killer at best, Hadden's no Charles Manson or John Wayne Gacy."

"Should I keep writing him? Or am I on a wild goose chase?"

"I'd respond. There's still a chance that he might slip up and give something like a name or something else pertinent to the case."

Victor went on to tell Theodore about Hadden's claims of being in the area and seeing the body being dropped off. He also mentioned how Hadden was backing off saying that he had killed the Lady of the Dunes. This had been something he had said to police back in 2000 when he had brought them to Cape Cod to search for the jewelry bucket.

The fact that Hadden was contradicting things he said to police caught Theodore's attention. He recommended that Victor send the letter, or at least a copy of it, to Hadden's handlers as it might need to be admitted as state's evidence. To Victor and Theodore, this showed that Hadden was capable of letting things slip that he shouldn't. It was enough to keep Victor on the hook as a morbid pen pal. He promised he'd reach out to Theodore again if he heard anything newsworthy.

Victor planned to make a copy of the letter to send to Hadden's handlers. Even after hanging up with Theodore he sat at his desk looking over the letter more. He was trying to figure out the connection between Hadden Clark, the Lady of the Dunes, the supposed 'real' killer, those who dropped the body off, and even the dune shacks themselves.

In Hadden's letters he says that the Lady of the Dunes was working in Provincetown in 1974. What was she doing and how did he know her? Clark had been a local hood and petty thief when growing up. He was by all accounts an odd person. Victor saw young Hadden as a loser, not a ladies man. The only way Victor saw Hadden getting a girl was by paying for her. He felt that it was possible that Clark knew of the Lady of the Dunes as a woman that frequented the bars, perhaps a sex worker.

The wheels in Victor's mind kept spinning. What exactly was the occupation held by the Lady of the Dunes? That was a big key as to perhaps how Hadden knew her. If she was a sex worker then why did she end up in the state she was in out in the Province Lands dunes?

When it came to Clark proclaiming that Whitey Bulger was not involved how could he be so sure? Hadden might not have personally known Bulger, but maybe he did indirectly. Maybe he knew some of Bulger's associates? Victor believed in the possibility that the Lady of the Dunes was murdered in the woods at Lombard Hollow Road. Why was she dropped in that location out in the dunes though?

Was it possible that the killer, Bulger or someone else, had their associates with knowledge of the area choose the drop site? Then it was the matter of how the people knew of the specific secluded area? In reality the Lady of the Dunes was not very far from the C-Scape dune shacks former location. Could there have been a connection between the dune shack and the people who dumped the body?

Victor wondered why law enforcement never questioned the C-Scape shack owners, or the owners of the neighboring shack. Not to ask if they had something to do with it, but to ask them if perhaps they had ever rented either shack out to anyone 'interesting.' The dune shack connection was intriguing to Victor. There were locations both east and west of where her body was dumped that would have been even more secluded. So why there?

Hadden did have four-wheel drive. Could he have been the driver? Victor knew Clark had been known to go night fishing, and he was in possession of knives due to his restaurant work. It was within the realm of possibility that Hadden just happened to be fishing in the area and saw the body being dropped off. It was also possible that Hadden saw the body after it was dumped. Theodore had agreed that Clark could have been involved since the panties of the murdered woman had been taken. Still, Hadden could have come upon the corpse and taken the panties off of her after.

There was so much to process with Hadden's newest letter. How much of what was in it was truth? How much of what was in it was the ramblings of a killer looking to regain relevance? The diary aspect intrigued Victor, but how far was he willing to go? Victor decided to set it down and let things settle a bit before responding. Hadden wasn't going anywhere.

Chapter 18, A Visit With Whitey

A few days passed from Victor reading and then re-reading Hadden Clark's latest letter. He remembered that he needed to send the most recent letter to Hadden's handlers. His contradictions of his previous statements made it necessary for the letter to be entered into state's evidence.

Victor made a copy of the recent letter. Then he decided to also make a copy of the previous letter where Hadden named the Lady of the Dunes as 'Laura.' Victor felt this might be a valuable piece of evidence for authorities to have.

The process of copying the previous two letters, and thereby reading them again, got Victor in the mood to respond to Hadden's latest letter. He remembered what Theodore had said about continuing the thread of asking questions as you never knew if Hadden might let something slip.

Victor decided to focus on the purported diaries and the root cellar. He offered to go out into the woods and look for Hadden's diaries. Despite not truly wanting to do so, or even believing there was anything out in the woods, Victor thought a gesture of good faith might open Hadden up to answering other questions. Sure it was a bit manipulative, but Victor was dealing with a convicted murderer. Typical rules did not apply.

What Victor could not have anticipated was the relative speed of Hadden's response. There was a lag due to the protocols of mail coming and going from a state penitentiary, usually about a week. However, it was as if Hadden was waiting, pen in hand, when Victor's latest response arrived.

Victor had been away from home for eight days for a film shoot. When he returned home on July 27th Victor found a new letter from Hadden. Maura said it had been there for five days. This letter came in a manila envelope. When Victor opened it inside were six pieces of white-lined paper filled with black ink scribbles. It was a tough read. First Victor skimmed it as he did with all of Hadden's letters. That's when he noticed it. There was an illustration and a map.

The piece of paper marked Page 7 began with the line "Whitey Bulger did not kill this girl either." Below it was a map. Pamet Point Road went horizontally across the page with Hadden marking his grandparents' house along the road. It was drawn upside-down with Route 6 heading north to Hyannis and south to Provincetown. This was the opposite of reality. Victor was able to figure it out after a minute.

What would have been north of his grandparents' house Hadden marked a dirt road with 'old foundation to house' written north of the dirt road. The map was not to scale and left few clues. The location of the diaries was identified by Clark with the description: 'Somewhere back here is the root cellar on National Park Land.' The majority of the map was colored with a green crayon and the word 'woods' was written several times. It was a very primitive treasure map. Clearly, Hadden did indeed wish for Victor to attempt to find his diaries.

The other side of the page was filled with a creepy drawing that took up half the sheet. It was a drawing of the Lady of the Dunes as Hadden had found her. She was nude and face down. He identified her clothes as being 'neatly folded and her head on top of them.' She was also described to have 'her arms in the ground as if she was doing push-ups.'

Victor decided to wait until later in the evening to read the full six-page letter. When he did pick up the pages again it was apparent that Hadden did not believe that Victor had received his previous letter. This was because Clark began his letter by saying as much. Then he proceeded to tell the tale of his Jesus-resembling inmate at Eastern Correctional named John Truitt again. Clark ranted his scathing thoughts about the book Born Evil and its author Adrian Havill which Victor had already heard. The first two pages of the letter, front, and back, were akin to a rerun of a bad television show. Luckily beginning on the third-page things got a little more interesting.

Page 5
My grandfather showed me the root cellar behind his property. I don't know how he discovered this root cellar. As a child did you ever have a secret place no one knows anything about where you can go to? I did at Cape Cod in Wellfleet. What's great about this root cellar, it's like a storage unit where you don't have to pay any rent. One thing I'm not able to do in prison is keep a diary. You can only have so much property in your cell. When I was on the street I kept a diary. But all of the diaries of all these girls or females...at least one in the root cellar in a plastic tube, ID's, license, etc. I'm glad I have all these diaries. With all the concussions I have suffered in prison where Correctional Officers have tried to use inmates to have me killed.

Page 7
I was at Race Point that night fishing when I observed that body being dumped in the dunes. I saw everything, even the license plate on his car. When I always went fishing I took a pair of binoculars with me all the time, for a few reasons. With binoculars, you can see what other people are using as bait or lure from a long distance away. Or if you want to have some privacy when you want to take a shit in the dunes. This way I can keep an eye on my fishing stuff.

Page 8
But I could see anything else at a far distance away. My binoculars work just as well at night as they did during the day.
I made sure this guy did not follow me back to my grandmother's house. I told my grandmother everything and she advised me not to say anything to Provincetown Police since they already punished me for something I never did in the late 1960s.

Finally, on Page Nine of Hadden's letter, he began to answer Victor's questions he had asked in the previous letter about Laura aka The Lady of the Dunes. In other words, he had indeed received Victor's last correspondence and chose to spend most of nearly eight pages of text rehashing previous stories and complaints about how he believed he was treated in prison.

Page 9
Question #1: What was Laura's last name? I can't remember Laura's last name, but all that information is in the root cellar.
Question #2: Did she work on Cape Cod that summer? Yes, I said she worked a summer job on Cape Cod. Cape Cod, Nantucket, Martha's Vineyard, Block Island, and parts of Long Island N.Y. like Montauk. College and high school students apply for summer jobs. All these places are very big tourist attractions in the summer time. And from what I have in the root cellar she was working on Cape Cod.
Question #3: Was she a college student? Yes she was a college student.

Question #4: What happened that night? I caught this guy dumping Laura's body at Race Point. I don't know why he removed her hands. The next morning I told my grandmother what I witnessed and she warned me not to go to the police. She didn't want to see me punished again for something I didn't do. I was at Race Point to fish that night.
Page 10
Question #5: Why was she put where she was? I don't know why. I have never spoken to this guy. I don't know why he has never done anything to me. He knew I surf cast at Race Point and also the ocean side of Truro and Wellfleet. In 1975 he also found out I was working at The Moors Restaurant.

Just recently the owner of The Moors died in June, Mylan Costa. If you come across an article of Mylan Costa in the Cape Cod newspaper can you please send it to me? Mylan was a very great person to work for. He gave me a room to sleep in. When I originally asked Mylan for this room I didn't tell him why I wanted it. I didn't want this killer to follow me back to my grandmother's house. I do not know how many other people this guy has killed. All I know is Race Point.
Page 11
Question #6: Did you ever visit St. Peter's Cemetery in Provincetown? The only cemeteries I visit are Wellfleet and Meriden Connecticut where I have family.

Question #7: Did Staniford Sorrentino have anything to do with Laura's murder? I do not know and I definitely do not recognize the name Staniford Sorrentino. Am I supposed to?

Question #8: Do you have anything belonging to Laura? I have this girl's license, ID's etc in the root cellar, but the police have all her clothes and jewelry.

Question #9: Did you see what Laura looked like after the murder? It was night time when the body was dumped in the dunes. I didn't touch the body after this guy left and she was face down so I really didn't get a good look at her face.

Question #10: Did you know James 'Whitey' Bulger? No I do not know James Whitey Bulger. I have seen him in the news I believe when they arrested him in California. He was a Boston mobster I believe.

Question #11: Did you spend a lot of time in Truro? No I did not spend a lot of time in Truro except for visiting friends or fishing on the bay side where the old railroad track bridge once stood at an inlet to the ocean on the bay side.

Question #12: So you were there the night the Lady of the Dunes was murdered? Yes I was there that night fishing at Race Point when this guy dumped the body.

Page 13

I have now answered all of your questions. When you have been rushed to the hospital 4 or 5 times in prison and suffer as many concussions as I have it's hard to remember every little detail. That's why you keep a diary. Maybe someday I'll write a book.

I probably haven't been able to answer all of your questions. I did the best I could for the situation I'm in. I drew you a map of the general area this root cellar is at. All that remains is this root cellar of this house.

You have a great July and God bless you always.

Hadden

Interesting to Victor was the fact that Hadden had answered all twelve of his questions twice. Perhaps his stories of concussion problems were true. There was not much to gleam from Clark's purported recollections of the night that the Lady of the Dunes was left on the cold sand. However, the prospect of a diary in a root cellar somewhere in the Wellfleet woods waiting to be discovered was tantalizing.

A successful treasure hunt could blow the case wide open. Again it was a chance to find something nobody else had when it came to the Lady of the Dunes. If Hadden Clark, a convicted serial killer, was telling the truth. In Victor's mind, it would be better to overturn every stone and find nothing than assume Hadden was lying and live with regret. He decided to make a rough plan for what an expedition to the area surrounding Hadden Clark's grandparents' property would look like. What he would need to bring, who he would bring along when he would plan to go, all of these questions needed to be thought out.

Naturally, before putting anything concrete together Victor needed to get his ducks in a row. He contacted Theodore. Victor explained about the diary and the root cellar. His mind was made up that he would be making a trek out into the woods near Hadden's grandparents' house at some point. Victor acted as if he was not sure though. Theodore, for his part, thought this was a wild goose chase Clark was putting Victor on out there. He felt Victor would be wasting his time.

Despite not being one hundred percent certain that a diary even existed Victor needed to at least try. Besides, Hadden had drawn the map, as primitive as it was. Victor ended up writing another letter to Clark. In it, he flat out asked the convicted killer if he wanted Victor to find the diary for him. It was phrased in the letter that way to make it appear as if Victor was doing Hadden a favor. In reality, Victor simply wanted the diary for his film. On top of that, it gave Victor another chance to ask Clark questions. There was still hope that he might share some more details about the whereabouts of the root cellar and maybe answer a few more questions.

Victor visited the Media Center in Dennis on July 30th. He had set up an impromptu meeting with Christopher Setterlund for early afternoon. Setterlund arrived as Victor was keeping cool in the shade of a few trees in the parking lot. Much like their first meeting at the bike trail parking lot theirs were the only two cars in the lot.

Victor shared as much as he could about the recent letter with Hadden. He spoke about the diary, the root cellar, and the idea of going on a hunt for it at some point. Setterlund was intrigued. Victor planned to have a small group of people meet on the rural Old County Road that ran parallel to Pamet Point Road where Hadden Clark's grandparents' house stood.

The details were few at that point. However, Victor thought a late-October attempt to find the diary would work best. At that point, Cape Cod would be in its off-season. This meant that a few cars could park on Old County Road and be seen by very few people. Victor invited Setterlund along and he was on board.

The pair had exchanged countless texts, emails, and phone calls in the past two months. Victor felt he could trust that Setterlund was all in on the book version of the Lady of the Dunes project. He offered up all of the Hadden Clark letters to be used in the book. They were all in their envelopes and left inside the large manila envelope that had held the most recent letter with the map.

Setterlund promised to be careful with the letters. He told Victor he knew what an important piece they were to the film.

Before parting ways, Victor asked Setterlund to keep the email questions coming. It helped keep the details of the Lady of the Dunes project fresh in his mind.

All of the focus throughout much of June and July had been on Hadden Clark and his series of letters. August brought another name to the forefront, Whitey Bulger.

The first week of August saw Amanda the medium give Victor a call. He hadn't heard from her in a while. She had an odd request of Victor.

"Do you want to visit Whitey Bulger's grave?" At this point in the project, there was nothing that occurred that felt out of the ordinary anymore to Victor.

"Sure, why not? Is there any reason why this is coming up now?"

"I've been there twice and have gotten some interesting insight from him. I figured it might be good for you to come along and maybe ask some questions that I'm not thinking of."

Victor met Amanda at St. Joseph Cemetery in West Roxbury a few days later. The sheer scope of the cemetery caught him off guard. At approximately two hundred acres in size, it was one of the largest cemeteries in all of New England. Victor followed Amanda as she drove her way down a couple of narrow side roads of the cemetery grounds. Luckily for them, Bulger's grave was not far from the road.

Victor and Amanda chatted a little before they entered the grounds. She mentioned how she liked Bulger. Amanda thought he was a nice guy, charming, and a bit sexy in a way. Victor thought about rolling his eyes at the over-the-top praise for the convicted killer. Then again he had brought an official Boston Red Sox baseball as a sort of present for the deceased mobster. The grave itself was only two rows deep into the sea of granite stones. It was engraved with a simple cross and the name 'Bulger' on it. This was the place.

There were a few moments of silence. This silence was broken by a few cemetery employees in the distance. They argued about where a new tombstone marker was to go. Amanda appeared to be trying to establish a connection with Bulger despite the obvious distraction. She began speaking out loud toward the stone. Amanda then looked at Victor.

"He says he likes what we're doing," the medium said, the 'he' was Bulger.

"Thank you," Victor replied to Amanda. He handed her the baseball and she placed it next to the grave. The medium was now the conduit between Victor and Whitey Bulger.

"What would you like to ask?" Victor cut right to the chase.

"What was her name?"

"Why does it matter?" Amanda replied channeling Bulger.

"We want to be able to put her name on her grave."

"Who cares? I don't have my name on my grave."

"Okay, did she know Hadden Clark?"

"He knew her, but she didn't know him." There was silence for a minute while Amanda bowed her head. It appeared she was listening. She began to walk away from the grave.

"Where are you going?" Victor wasn't sure if he should follow Amanda.

"He's leading me to another grave." Amanda began to walk off through the maze of headstones.

Victor took a moment to stop and just feel the warm summer air on his face. He looked around at where he was standing and gave a wry smile to himself. So many things had happened in the span of only a few months. His brief daydream was stopped after catching a glimpse of Amanda staring back his way. She began walking toward him.

"What is it?" Victor asked.

"He led me to a purplish stone with the name Ann on it. He says he knew her as Ann, but also showed me a grave with the name Helen. I feel like one name was a stage name, if you will, and the other was her given name."

"So you think maybe Helen was her real name?"

"That's what I am feeling." Victor shook his head in slight disappointment. The reason being that if the Lady of the Dunes was truly named Helen that meant that Hadden Clark had been lying much like Theodore had warned. It threw much of the diary treasure hunt into question. Before Victor could stew too much about Hadden's possibly false statement Amanda piped up with another juicy bit of information from beyond the grave.

"I'm feeling a heavy blow, something heavy hitting the ground."

"What does that mean?" Amanda was quiet for a moment and then nodded as if receiving her answer.

"He(Bulger) is saying she was hit over the head."

"Hit over the head?" Victor asked.

"That was the blow that killed her." It was time for Victor to stop beating around the bush.

"Did he kill her?" Amanda grimaced a little knowing that this was a serious question to be asking. Still, she did ask it, albeit in a hushed tone.

"No, he wasn't the one who did it. Someone else was given that job."

It was not lost on Victor that Amanda was hearing that Bulger did not do the actual deed of murdering the Lady of the Dunes but that he did appear to have been involved in her death. Naturally, there was nothing Victor could do. He had no evidence.

After all, his goal had always been what he had said and that was to give the Lady of the Dunes her name. For that part, he had several leads. In addition to Hadden Clark's name of Laura, there were now two more names, Ann and Helen.

There was a lot for Victor to think about after the interesting visit with Whitey Bulger from beyond the grave. He was unsure what to believe at that point. The Lady of the Dunes was the proverbial riddle, wrapped in a mystery, inside an enigma. Before heading back to their respective cars Amanda stopped and appeared to be listening again next to Bulger's grave. Victor waited.

"Someone threw away the Irish flag sticker that was placed at his grave." Victor saw a trash can nearby and walked over to it. Sure enough, inside was an Irish flag sticker. He fished it out of the garbage. Victor walked back to Bulger's grave and placed the sticker next to the Red Sox baseball.

"He thanks you," Amanda said. Victor smiled and nodded. Strangely, Victor was looking for respect and approval from Bulger even from beyond the grave. He felt that even as he stood over the man's final resting place that Bulger was in control of the situation.

Fortunately, or unfortunately, there was plenty of time to think while still at the cemetery. A nearby funeral had clogged up the routes in and out of St. Joseph. It would be a while before Victor and Amanda were able to leave the cemetery grounds. Rather than stew about being stuck Victor decided to make the most of it.

'Chatting' with Bulger brought Boston's Combat Zone back to the forefront of his mind. Victor sat and thought of who he could potentially speak with that could give him a more intimate view of what life was like there back when it was jumping. The only name he could think of was Chesty Morgan.

She was nicknamed 'Chesty' for her seventy-three-inch bust. Victor began searching on his phone and found her IMDb page with her real name. Morgan had not only been an exotic dancer in the Combat Zone but had also starred in a pair of sexploitation films directed by Doris Wishman in 1974: Deadly Weapons and Double Agent 73.

Victor found a woman with the same name living in Florida and decided to take a chance and call the number. After a few rings, a woman answered.

Politely Victor asked if this woman used to be known as Chesty Morgan. She said she was. He explained the project he was working on and the potential connection between the Lady of the Dunes and the Combat Zone. Victor asked if she could share any of her knowledge and experiences of that place and time.

"I'm sorry Mr. Franko," she began, "I don't remember much about that time. What I do recall was not positive for me."

"I hope I didn't stir up bad memories for you, I apologize."

"Oh no, it's a part of my life. I had promises made while I was there. A tour, co-ownership of a cinema. All of that went up in smoke."

"Do you remember any of the other girls from when you were there?"

"All of the girls I knew from that time period either died penniless, or worse. That's all I really want to say. I wish you good luck on your project though Mr. Franko, godspeed." The former Chesty Morgan hung up leaving Victor sitting in his car and staring out at a sea of granite markers on a sunny summer afternoon. The words 'died penniless or worse' rattled around his head. Victor felt that finding someone else from the Combat Zone to talk to might be next to impossible.

The remainder of August was quiet. Victor enjoyed the opportunity to breathe a little. Though he did remain busy with the Lady of the Dunes film, as well as various other projects, Victor was able to step back and enjoy family life during the dog days of summer. Little did he know that things were going to get a jolt come September.

Chapter 19, RAD

September began with an introduction and a reunion. Labor Day approached and Victor found an unfamiliar email in his mailbox. Once he opened it though he knew who it was. This woman, named Tiffany, was a well-known and respected psychic. Victor had thought about contacting her but with Amanda and others already on board to varying degrees he wasn't sure if there was room.

Tiffany had heard about what Victor had been doing. She had been in contact with the Lady of the Dunes and felt compelled to go out to the drop site in Provincetown. She left a phone number for Victor and even though he was not sure if he wanted to go trudging back out into the dunes he decided it would be rude to not at least call her.

The two chatted for a bit, comparing notes about the Lady of the Dunes. Tiffany was very charming and nice. Victor was easily convinced to revisit Provincetown. She mentioned that while they were speaking that the Lady of the Dunes was reaching out to her. She was telling Tiffany that she wanted her to go to Provincetown.

Victor agreed to meet Tiffany at Race Point Beach. There they would take a trip out to the drop site via Art's Dune Tours. He also agreed to meet with her at St. Peter's Cemetery as well. The meeting was set up for the weekend which was only a few days away. Before hanging up Tiffany mentioned something that seemed innocuous at the time. She told Victor that she had this feeling that she was going to meet a man with a dog at the beach. Victor barely acknowledged it before the two parted ways. He headed back to Provincetown again.

The next day Victor was pleasantly surprised by another unexpected phone call. It was his Uncle Richard who was up in Massachusetts from Florida. The youngest brother of Victor's father he had always had a close relationship with Victor. Back in April Richard had surgery and had taken a while to recover. Victor was happy to hear from him.

Richard wanted to meet up with Victor. When told about the impending trip out to the Cape, and more specifically Provincetown, he wanted in. Victor thought it would be a bit of a break from the routine to bring him along on this trip. The plan was for Richard to drop his car at Victor's house and the two would travel to Cape Cod from there. Once arriving in Provincetown they would meet up with Tiffany the psychic and begin the trip out into the dunes.

The night before the trip Tiffany and Victor chatted again. They set up the basic logistics of their time in Provincetown. Victor had set it all up with a room at the Blue Dolphin Inn in Eastham. He and Richard would spend the night there and meet Tiffany at Race Point.

While speaking on the phone Tiffany mentioned that the Lady of the Dunes was with her and imploring her to come to Provincetown. Before hanging up she again mentioned that she expected to meet a man with a dog at the beach. He smiled but did not mention Richard joining him, or the fact that he owned a little dog. That would be a bonus to the trip.

The drive from Norton to Eastham was filled with laughter and reminiscing between uncle and nephew. It was also filled with a crash course from Victor as to exactly who the Lady of the Dunes was and why he was undertaking the film.

Although he had gotten some basic information a few days earlier Richard had no idea of the case. Victor enjoyed getting the chance to brush up on his knowledge. It was a dress rehearsal for the film's premiere that would inevitably happen. Richard was intrigued, shocked, and saddened as Victor answered all of his questions. Victor knew those feelings. He had felt them, sometimes all at once, on most days since beginning the project.

Victor and Richard did not linger long at the Blue Dolphin Inn after arriving. The pair set out for some pizza and a few drinks. It was time for some more catching up. Victor broke the news to his uncle that the next morning would be an early rise. That did not deter Richard who was getting increasingly excited to be a part of his nephew's project.

The next day was perfect weather for an adventure in the dunes. Victor made a call to Art's Dune Tours, the leading company when it came to bringing people out among the beautiful sandy scenery of Provincetown. He mentioned to Rob, the owner, that there would be three of them on the tour. Victor then made sure to mention that one of the passengers was a psychic.

Rob thought it was cool. He also figured out what the underlying mission of the special trip out into the dunes was. Rob would not tell Victor where he had been told that the Lady of the Dunes drop site was. Victor laughed a little and said that he hoped Tiffany would find it anyway.

Victor gave Richard a fly-by tour of the area as they drove from Eastham to Race Point Beach. Perhaps fittingly the beach parking lot was deserted. When Victor drove in his car was the only one there. He parked in the area of the lot closest to the ORV gate. Tiffany arrived shortly thereafter.

She was happy to finally meet Victor face to face. It also was not lost on her the fact that there was Richard, a man with a dog at the beach, whom she had not expected. Despite being there as a part of the Lady of the Dunes project it was clear to Victor from the start that there was some sort of connection between Tiffany and Richard. They chatted like old friends.

Victor spotted the Art's Dune Tours SUV pulling into the parking lot. The driver pulled up and ushered the three guests and the little dog into the vehicle. Maneuvering over the rolling dunes was a slow process. It was a new experience for Victor who was used to hiking across the sand from behind the Province Lands Visitors Center.

The trip in the SUV began quietly. Victor was trying not to talk too much to give Tiffany the chance to try to connect with the Lady of the Dunes. Unfortunately, she was somewhat distracted by Richard and his fidgety dog. Several minutes passed. Victor decided to make some small talk with the driver.

He asked about the frequency of the tours. Victor also asked how many of the people that ventured out among the dunes and dune shacks ever asked about the Lady of the Dunes case. Before much could be answered Richard asked Tiffany what was wrong from the back seat.

Tiffany hung her head and began to clutch at her stomach.

"I feel sick," she said weakly.

"Was it something you ate?" Richard asked.

"No, it's this place," she replied. This caught Victor's attention.

"Are you feeling her?" Victor asked. Tiffany took a deep breath.

"Yes, she's all around here."

The next few minutes of the drive were spent staring at Tiffany. The driver wondered if he needed to stop the vehicle to let her out if she was going to throw up. Tiffany leaned against the door with a pained look on her face. Victor knew they were getting closer to where the drop site had been.

"Can you stop here, please?" Tiffany asked from the back seat. The driver stopped almost immediately. The psychic nearly fell out of the vehicle. Richard rushed around to help her.

"Are you all right?" Richard asked. Victor thought about getting out to join them but he stayed put, surveying the scene from the front seat. He saw Tiffany bend over and assumed she was about to get sick.

"Look here, Richie," she said, sounding reinvigorated. Tiffany stood back up holding a single purple flower petal in between her thumb and forefinger.

"What does it mean?" Richard asked.

"She's with us." Tiffany needed Richard's help to get back into the vehicle for the last leg of the journey. She went from feeling at peace that the Lady of the Dunes was chaperoning them, to feeling sick as the vehicle drew within sight of the C-Scape dune shack.

It was at this point that the vehicle stopped. There was a policy to not let people get out and walk among the dunes. However, this was a special case. Victor stepped out of the front seat while Richard helped a struggling Tiffany out of the back. Nothing was said.

Tiffany began to move. She needed Richard as a crutch to walk over the soft sand. However, she began moving in the direction of where Victor remembered Amanda leading him during the previous walks out to the drop site.

Though she was leading the group southeast Tiffany kept staring off to the northwest. The C-Scape shack was looming on the horizon behind them. What Tiffany was looking toward was the second-most western shack. Located less than five hundred yards east of C-Scape was a shack called Leo's Place. Tiffany kept stopping and staring at it.

"What are you feeling?" Victor asked. Tiffany did not break eye contact with the shack in the distance.

"There's something about that one," she said pointing. "I feel like it has something to do with where her body was found." Tiffany could not pinpoint exactly what the connection was though. She continued her uneasy walk until she hit the spot. There Tiffany sighed and doubled over. Victor knew she was at the drop site. This made the second medium who had found where the Lady of the Dunes had been left without any clues. Victor looked over at the driver who nodded his head, admitting this was the place he had always heard she was found.

The three men stood silently by while Tiffany bowed her head. She did not speak out loud, however it seemed apparent she was listening to something, or someone. Once she had heard all she needed to hear she gently motioned for Richard to come back as support. The pair headed back for the ORV. Victor and the driver chatted for a moment about Tiffany's ability to find the drop site.

"I still wonder about how the hell she got out here," Victor said while looking south toward where he assumed the Province Lands Visitor's Center was.

"Back then there was an access road that came out here," the driver bluntly replied. "So I've always assumed that a car drove out here." This revelation was major news to Victor who had never heard of another over-sand road leading out toward the dune shacks.

"Wait, what? There was another road?"

"Yeah, decades ago. It led out from near the visitor's center. It was more of an enlarged path. It was used by smaller vehicles."

"So you're saying that back in '74 someone could have loaded a body in the trunk of a car and driven it out here and dumped it?"

"Absolutely."

"Are there any photographs of the road, or at least where it started from?"

"I'm sure there are somewhere, but I don't know where to look."

This was a game changer for Victor. It added a whole new dimension to the story. Now it made it feasible that the Lady of the Dunes might have been murdered at Lombard Hollow. She then could have been transported out into the remote dunes via automobile and left out there. Victor made a note to look into more details about this heretofore unknown access road later.

It also became more apparent to Victor that the spot where the body had been found was not chosen at random. Victor felt that the people involved in getting her out to that spot knew the area. He looked around the vast sandy landscape. A little further west or south of the location would have left the body too close to people in the dune shacks. Who would have intimate knowledge of places deep in the dunes where a body could be left and not found for an extended period of time?

However those who dropped the Lady of the Dunes among the patch of scrub pines knew she would be found eventually, just not within a few days. The fact that it took weeks for her body to be discovered, purely by accident, proved that those who stayed in the nearby shacks did not venture very far out into the dunes.

Victor's inner monologue and daydreaming was abruptly cut short by the sound of a plane. A small engine plane flew directly overhead. It was not dangerously low, however it was low enough that Tiffany pointed it out. The odd timing of the plane seemed normal for Victor by this point of working on the project.

Tiffany's condition improved as the vehicle departed the drop site area. By the time they had returned to the Race Point Beach parking lot she was in good spirits. Victor thanked the driver before they left in the SUV. Next up was the three-mile drive south to St. Peter's Cemetery. It was here that Tiffany would be face to face with the grave of the Lady of the Dunes.

Victor drove into the cemetery leading Tiffany in her vehicle right up to the unassuming grave of the Lady of the Dunes. She knelt over the grave with her head bowed. Victor and Richard stood on either side of her, close but not too close. The muted chatter of countless wild geese throughout the cemetery broke up the peaceful silence. A few deep sighs filled the air as Tiffany nodded. She turned her head up toward Victor, her eyes welled up with tears.

"What are you feeling?" Victor asked.

"She is here," Tiffany replied. "She is all over the place."

"You mean like with us wherever we go?"

"Yes, but more like her mind is all over the place. She's spinning. It is from the drugs she was on at the time of her murder."

"Is it gibberish?"

"No, I just have to really listen." Victor went silent. A few moments passed and Tiffany spoke up again. "She doesn't want to open her mouth still."

"How so?" Victor asked.

"She feels like if she kept her mouth shut she might still be alive and with Whitey Bulger."

"Did she say something that got her killed?"

"That's what she's saying. She spoke when she should not have. There's something about a boat."

"Boat?"

"They were on a boat, celebrating the Fourth of July holiday and a birthday at the same time."

"The Lady of the Dunes and Bulger?"

"Yes, and others. She wanted to leave. She is saying 'oh you want off the boat? Fine, take her off the boat.' It sounds very ominous."

"Was she taken off the boat and killed?" Tiffany was losing the connection. She wiped a few tears from her eyes. Richard began to turn his head side to side.

"Where is Costa's grave?" Richard asked Victor. He had wanted to see Tony Costa's resting place, although it was unmarked. Victor pointed his uncle in the direction. Tiffany stood up. They started walking but she stopped. Something had caught her attention.

"Look at all of the rose petals," Tiffany remarked. She bent down to pick up one of the purple leaves. The psychic rubbed it between her thumb and forefinger. "They're fake." They appeared almost like a trail of breadcrumbs though. Tiffany began to follow them. Victor followed a few steps behind her as she walked.

The purple petals beckoned Tiffany to a different grave. She stopped and stared at it. Victor noticed right away the pink flowers that sat in front of the stone. The name on the grave was Morgan.

Tiffany mentioned to Victor while standing in front of the grave that the name Morgan stuck with her when it came to the Lady of the Dunes. She could not be sure if it was her real name, or a stage name, but it was present in the front of her mind when it came to the slain young woman.

The threesome left the Morgan grave and walked to where Tony Costa had been buried. Victor wanted to make sure that his uncle at least got to stand where the convicted killer was. Before wrapping up the day Victor produced a the folded piece of white-lined paper that the New York psychic had scrawled during their time in Provincetown back in April.

Victor asked Tiffany if any of the writing spoke to her. Most of the words passed by uneventfully. When he mentioned the name Helen Tiffany stopped him.

"That could be her name," she said.

"Helen?" Victor asked with a little excitement in his voice. He remembered Amanda being summoned to a stone with the name Helen while visiting Whitey Bulger's grave.

"Yes, like I said before I keep feeling Morgan, Helen, the -an or -en, that sound, it is prevalent when her name comes up."

"I have to ask if you know what RAD means?" Victor hoped Tiffany could solve the mystery of RAD that had been dogging him since he first read the New York psychic's letter..

"No, I don't know what that might mean. Is it a word, or abbreviation?" Victor was disappointed. That was until Richard spoke up.

"That's me," he said sounding a little surprised. Both Tiffany and Victor looked at him with confusion. "RAD, those are my initials. Richard Anthony D'Agostino."

Victor was shocked. Tiffany smiled. Richard could not explain why he was in the psychic's letter from April. Still there he was, R.A.D. It was a perfectly surreal ending to an eventful return to Provincetown.

Tiffany said her goodbyes to Richard and Victor. The two men had a lot to talk about on the ride back to Norton. The mystery of R.A.D. had been solved, possibly. More questions remained though. Morgan, Helen, Ann, were one of, or all of, these names connected to the Lady of the Dunes? What of the former over-sand road? Could a vehicle have driven out there and dropped off the body? Victor knew there was a lot to unpack from the day in Provincetown. He would wait until a later date though. Victor wanted to spend as much time with his uncle before he went back to Florida the following week.

A few days after Richard had gone back to Florida Victor was knee deep in the Lady of the Dunes again. He had gone more than a week without having that feeling in the pit of his stomach during his late night trips to the bathroom that he was being watched. Victor felt he must be doing enough work to keep the Lady of the Dunes happy that she did not feel the need to haunt his nights.

The most important talking point coming out of the trip to Provincetown was the revelation of an old access road that crossed the dunes.

Victor reached out to Mildred Champlin. He figured if anybody would have knowledge of an old access road it would be Mildred with her sixty-plus years of owning the shack. She did indeed remember the road in question. Mildred referred to it as Race Road. This access road at one time began from near the Province Lands amphitheater and went out to the old Coast Guard Station in the dunes. That station burned in the late 1950's.

Mildred went on to tell Victor about how back in those days near the end of the access road there was a structure on top of the hill the you could climb and look around. It was called Ocean View. However when the Province Lands Visitors Center was built the access road was forgotten about and allowed to become overgrown. When Victor asked Mildred about photos of the road she directed him to a Facebook group called My Grandfather's Provincetown.

Luckily this was an open group, meaning Victor did not have to ask to join. He began searching for photos of this old access road. It was while looking at a photo of a concert from 1972, known as Cape Cod's Woodstock, that he finally saw it. Among the throngs of thousands of people was the access road stretching off into the distance toward the horizon. There was also a large parking lot near the Truro town line of the dunes. It looked capable of holding well over one hundred cars. Seeing all of this again brought to the forefront how different Provincetown was back in the 1970's. Victor kept coming back to the possibility. It was possible that the Lady of the Dunes had been murdered elsewhere and driven out to the drop site via the access road.

It was now mid-September. Victor had been working on the Lady of the Dunes project for nine months. The editing process was going smoothly at the Cape Cod Media Center in Dennis. Although there were several loose ends he wished to try to sew up Victor was overall pleased with the amount of information he had been able to find out about the case and the women at the center of it.

Victor's eyes began looking ahead to the premiere of the documentary. He had firmly believed that his work on the project was only a step in the process. Victor hoped that shining a new light on the Lady of the Dunes case might force the hands of those associated with it. He hoped that even if he could not solve the case perhaps new information would come to the forefront because of the project. Victor and Christopher Setterlund even joked at times that the book would not be done until after the film came out and that any new information would naturally find its way onto those pages.

The list of names that had helped Victor on the project seemed to be complete. Nine months into the project there were few stones that he had not looked under. At least that was the prevailing thought. Victor was wrong on that account.

When a strange number popped up on his phone Victor didn't think much of it. After all he had received random 'RESTRICTED' calls for several months leading up to and during the filming. Those calls had stopped not too long after the documentary wrapped in late-April but Victor had always figured at some point they'd begin again as long as the documentary was a thing.

Feeling adventurous Victor picked up the phone. The caller cut right to the chase and began grilling Victor about his work on the Lady of the Dunes project. It was a bit unnerving.

Victor asked how this person had gotten his number. Only after a few minutes of speaking in vagueries did it click in Victor's mind. This person was someone that the former member of the Providence, Rhode Island police department had named back when they initially spoke. Victor had not reached out simply due to time constraints and simply forgetting. It was fitting that here they were reaching out to Victor once he had thought finding new contacts was over.

For their part, the person on the phone claimed to have already known who Victor was and what he was doing. Victor was suspicious of the timing since it had been several months since he had first heard this person's name. Why were they reaching out now?

The person was not keen on staying on the phone for too long, and they did not want to exchange any emails. That in and of itself was a little odd. However they asked Victor to meet them at the Blue Hills Reservation on Canton Avenue in Milton about twenty miles north of his home in Norton. Victor agreed and hung up. There was a little regret at first about accepting such an odd invitation. He felt a little uneasy meeting in such a wide open space as Blue Hills but nonetheless thought there could be some important information coming his way. Thinking that this person was likely the last connection to come from the law enforcement field Victor decided to refer to them fittingly as Agent Z.

Victor arrived at the Canton Avenue parking lot not knowing what to expect. The Blue Hills Reservation was 7,000-acres in size. Luckily Agent Z told Victor to meet them near the pond not far from the parking area. It was a sunny and seasonably warm September day, meaning that the grounds were dotted with people. Still, Victor could not help but have this unsettled feeling as he locked his car and walked in the direction of the pond.

In the distance Victor saw a figure sitting on a bench near the water. This was Agent Z. It was a surreal setting Victor came upon. The figure, bundled up a little too much for the waning days of summer, sat on the bench with a container of clam chowder. This was not the typical picnic food. Plus they were eating with a metal spoon, likely brought from home. They had slicked back hair, gold bracelets and a gold chain. To make things more odd was that Agent Z was wearing a set of fingerless tactical gloves akin to those worn by motorcyclists or weight-lifters.

Victor announced himself which elicited an overly toothy smile from Agent Z. The mysterious person added to Victor's unease by again claiming that they knew who Victor was and what he was doing. They began to have a rather tense conversation about the Lady of the Dunes case. All the while Agent Z never stopped smiling at Victor, even while tossing Ritz crackers to an otter swimming near the shore of the pond. A smirk crossed Victor's face briefly as he gazed at the nearby sign warning visitors explicitly to not feed the otters.

Agent Z immediately differed themselves from Agents X and Y. They brought up their hourly fee which nearly ended the meeting then and there. Victor's budget was tight when it came to the documentary. He had relied on a lot of help and goodwill from people who wanted to help get the Lady of the Dunes case solved. Having Agent Z prefacing the conversation with talks of money raised red flags with Victor.

Victor felt uneasy around Agent Z despite being in a relatively safe environment. They managed to stop Victor from heading back to his car briefly with a bit of proof of their credentials. Agent Z pulled from their pocket a series of photos of Whitey Bulger. These photos were ones of the mobster that Victor could not recall ever seeing. It showed that Agent Z might have some helpful connections.

As Victor began to let his guard down and ask some truly meaningful questions Agent Z brought the wall back up. They again mentioned their price although teasing some potentially impactful leads in their arsenal. The unsettling tone continued when Agent Z began to brag about people they knew from the mob, the private eye world, FBI, and Homeland Security.

Though noncommittal Victor said he'd think about it when it came to paying Agent Z for their time. He softly reiterated his budget when it came to the documentary. Agent Z seemed to ignore this while continuing to throw Ritz crackers like Frisbees to the otter.

The two parted ways with a still-smiling Agent Z promising to call Victor with information if they found any. He left the mysterious Agent Z to their chowder and otters. Once seated back in his car Victor let out a deep sigh. That was one of the oddest interactions he'd had yet. He didn't have much hope that Agent Z would give him anything pertinent to the case.

Victor barely had time to process the surreal meeting with Agent Z when another new contact came into play. It was the third week of September, fall was officially underway. When Victor's phone rang and the voice introduced himself as Thomas he could hardly keep the smile from his face.

Thomas was a retired State Police officer who had actually pulled over Tony Costa on Route 6 in 1968. He was someone who had been front and center during the wild times that surrounded the Lady of the Dunes case. This man was someone that Victor had been hoping to speak with. Agent X had brought the retired officer to Victor's attention months prior. Victor had attained his number from Agent X's Providence connection. He had forgotten even leaving the man a message.

It was a fascinating conversation. Although he had not worked on the Lady of the Dunes case Thomas said he was always hearing things. What he did have a lot of information on was Tony Costa.

He confirmed some things that Victor had assumed. After Costa's arrest a full reconnaissance of the expansive South Truro woods was never done. There was no walk around, there were no metal detectors, there were no cadaver dogs. Essentially after the four confirmed victims were found the shallow graves were filled up and everyone went home.

Thomas also confirmed the conversations that he had with Costa that were detailed in the *In His Garden* book. Without much prompting this former state trooper was tying up several loose ends for Victor. He agreed with Victor's assessment that Costa got his drugs from Staniford Sorrentino. There were also several names of other potential victims of Tony Costa that the man shared.

Eventually the conversation circled back around to the Lady of the Dunes and Victor's documentary. Thomas did not agree with current law enforcement's belief that Whitey Bulger was never a suspect in the murder back in 1974. He did not have any concrete evidence to divulge but there was too much smoke around the fire that was Bulger to not investigate him further.

The biggest surprise for Victor in the chat with Thomas came when he asked about one of Victor's highest profile sources. Thomas specifically asked if Victor had been in contact with Agent Y. When Victor stated that he had talked with them multiple times the retired officer let out a bit of a grunting sigh.

Thomas did not mince words. He told Victor to make sure to question everything that Agent Y said. Victor had always taken Agent Y's statements with a grain of salt. They were named Agent Y specifically because Victor found himself constantly asking them 'Why?' This was normally in regards to information being fed to him. However as time had gone on Victor found himself wondering why Agent Y was sharing certain information in general. They had likely given Victor access to the original police case file which was great, but they had denied it, and essentially left Victor on his own to decipher what was important and what was not.

Although it would be their only conversation during the documentary process Thomas left an impact and gave Victor a lot to process.

Jimmy Meads Jr. became front and center again just before September ended. He sent Victor a seemingly innocuous photo of a large manila envelope with some writing scribbled on it. However upon a little further questioning it ended up being a major bombshell.

Meads explained to Victor that the handwriting on the envelope was his father's. Not only that, the writing was in fact notes Chief Meads wrote while investigating the Lady of the Dunes case in 1984. Victor was stunned.

What was more stunning was the fact that the photo was three years old. Jimmy Jr. mentioned that he had given the envelope and its contents to Peter Manso and Warren Tobias three years ago, right after he took the photo. Jimmy Jr. had forgotten all about the envelope until that day.

Victor asked if Jimmy Jr. knew of where the envelope and its contents were now. He said for all he knew it was in the hands of Tobias, or in Manso's home. Victor asked if he at least remembered what was inside the envelope when he gave it away. Jimmy Jr. said it was dental records among other information.

Dejected that the full contents were not readily available Victor made due with what he had. The envelope was chock full of useful potential leads. There was a phone number with a 617 area code meaning it was Boston-based. There was the name Robert Brooks. Perhaps he was the dentist in charge of the records? The term 'Per 6' was scribbled underneath it. Most exciting to Victor though was another name. Ann Dolce.

Ann had been one of the potential names of the Lady of the Dunes mentioned by Amanda the medium while at Whitey Bulger's grave. The fact that the name Ann was written on a piece of evidence in Chief Meads' handwriting gave Victor's heart a flutter. He was practically jumping out of his skin when he realized that it was Ann Dolce's dental records that had been in the envelope.

The only nod to her dental records was that she had gold in her teeth. More important than that was the fact that there was an address for Ann Dolce which corresponded to the Combat Zone in Boston. There was also a note that Ann had an aunt living in Lawrence, or at least she was in 1984.

The envelope itself was such a potential goldmine that Victor was not even really upset that he did not have access to its contents. After speaking with Jimmy Jr. Victor was busting. He needed to find someone who could answer his questions about the information both inside and outside of the envelope. Victor sent copies of the photo of the envelope to several connections. He was looking for information about Robert Brooks, 'Per 6,' the phone number and address, and most importantly Ann Dolce.

Victor asked a Boston contact to look at criminal records from 1972-74. Little useful information came from that. When he reached out to former Provincetown Police Chief Jeff Jaran Victor learned that Jaran had never seen the envelope before. This meant that the envelope had to have disappeared before 2000 when Jaran came aboard.

Jaran's revelation brought the idea of malfeasance back to the front of Victor's mind. He needed to find out if Chief Meads had ever followed up on the name Ann Dolce. However that was a tough hill to climb. Victor imagined that there had to have been more evidence Chief Meads was working on, or working with, back in 1984. What happened to it?

The more he sat back and thought about it the more Victor came to a disappointing conclusion. Victor believed that whatever evidence Chief Meads was working on had to have been sent to Boston before his retirement in 1992. Unless these pieces of evidence were copied Victor believed that they were likely lost. Whether accidentally or purposefully was a different question. Throughout his time working on the Lady of the Dunes project Victor leaned more and more toward the malfeasance argument.

Victor got a break when he found information on the phone number scrawled on the envelope. It turned out to be the old phone number for the Cambridge Health Alliance Hospital in Everett, Massachusetts. This was significant because it was at the CHA where the Tufts University School of Medicine's teaching site was located. It was a shot in the dark but Victor reached out to the CHA asking for copies of the records that were in Meads' envelope. It proved to be a fruitless endeavor.

Despite not receiving any records from CHA the new evidence gave Victor a shot in the arm of energy. His candle was steadily fading under the pressure. Not only did he have his film to finish and release, he also felt a sense of obligation to do what he set out to do and that was to find the name of the Lady of the Dunes. Victor did not want to cut the investigation short, but deep down he knew that his time on this case was running out.

The calendar flipped to October. Victor's mind was on a self-imposed deadline for the project. He wanted October 31st to be the last day of filming, win, lose, or draw. Plans were being put into place for a day-trip back to Cape Cod. This would include a thorough search of the grounds behind Hadden Clark's grandparents house. Victor had low expectations when it came to finding any sort of diary, but he needed to tie up that loose end regardless.

Throughout the Lady of the Dunes project's duration it seemed like when things were hitting a bit of a quiet period something new and exciting would pop up. It happened with Agent Z. It happened again with the photo of the mysterious envelope that Jimmy Meads Jr. sent to him. This time it was yet another unfamiliar phone number coming across the Caller ID. It was a Montana number.

"Who do I know from Montana?" Victor asked himself before picking up.

The woman on the line introduced herself as Kimberly Dudik. She not only was an elected official in the state, but she also hosted her own true crime podcast. Victor let out a hearty 'hello!'

In doing his research Victor had come across her podcast episode she had done about the Lady of the Dunes. He had sent her an email asking if she would like to talk about the case and what she had learned. She was more than happy to chat.

They compared notes for a short time. Victor mentioned that the case was still active according to local law enforcement. He recommended she call the people currently in charge of the case to see if she could get any worthwhile information from them. She agreed and it was decided that the woman would call them and then get back in touch with Victor later.

Surprisingly it was only a matter of house before Victor's phone rang again with the Montana number. When he asked her how it went she let out a laugh. A message was left for the people in charge of the case and they did return her call. Interestingly when Kimberly began to talk to the people they stopped her mid-sentence. They asked her if she was calling them as an elected official, or for her podcast.

When she said it was for her podcast the people in charge of the Lady of the Dunes case said they had no comment to give and the phone call ended. Victor knew exactly what she was talking about. During his time in Provincetown he specifically remembered Dolly and Dicky both mentioning the people working on the case and how they weren't doing nearly enough to solve it. Victor had not bothered reaching out, figuring that his questions would be ignored. The fact that they had responded to Kimberly made him think twice.

After chatting for nearly an hour the two parted ways. Victor decided to call the phone number and leave a message for the people in charge of the Lady of the Dunes case. He was polite, almost overly-polite, as Victor explained who he was and what he was doing. Knowing how small a community Provincetown was

Victor figured whoever listened to the message would know exactly who he was.

Victor selfishly hoped for a quick response like Kimberly had received. That did not happen. In fact there was no return call. He waited forty-eight hours before calling again. Victor was polite again, saying he just wanted to talk and compare notes. He said he wanted to help solve the case. There was no response again. Dejected but not surprised Victor did not call a third time. There were plenty of other people that had been willing to help him on the Lady of the Dunes project.

Chapter 20, Judy

Agent Z gave Victor a call during the first week of October. It had been a few weeks since their odd meeting at Blue Hills. Victor had not been expecting to hear from them. Their first meeting had left Victor feeling skittish. This phone call doubled-down on that.

"I got something for you to check out," Agent Z said. There was no beating around the bush.

"Okay, what is it?" Victor was nervously curious.

"There is a movie, from 1970," they began, "it's called 'Judy.' You can find it online and watch it for free."

"Judy? What's it about?" There was a brief pause.

"Well, let's just say that it might hold some clues that might be of some interest to you. Just throw it into a search and watch it."

"All right, I'll check it out. Is there anything you can tell me? The reason why you think I need to see it?"

"It was locally filmed, and from what I've seen most of the women associated with the movie in one way or another disappeared."

"How did you find this movie?"

"I talked with an expert who wrote some articles about the red light district. He recommended I watch this for the simple fact that all of the girls in the movie worked in the Combat Zone. Plus the film's investor dated the lead."

Victor was intrigued and let Agent Z know that he would be checking into this 'Judy' movie once their conversation ended.

The search for 'Judy' got off on the wrong foot immediately. Victor typed it into a search and that's when the truth came out. The film was an old soft-core pornographic film.

Victor had no trouble finding a link to watch it, there were numerous pornographic sites that popped up.

Despite being alone in the house Victor still looked nervously around. He was not sure he wanted Maura to walk in on him watching a fifty-year old skin flick. Still, it could be pertinent to the case. Agent Z would not have alerted Victor to it if they hadn't felt it was important, right?

He did a little more poking around before watching the film. According to IMDb.com the film's synopsis was: A depraved sex killer preys on women of ill repute in the red light district area of Boston, Massachusetts. Hard-nosed maverick private detective Gunner Sloan gets hired by the wealthy Fairchild to find the psycho after the creep attacks Fairchild's daughter Regina.

The 'red light district' caught Victor's attention. It meant the film was in some way tied to Boston's Combat Zone. He took a deep breath and clicked 'Play' on the tab with 'Judy' on the screen.

"Well, this ought to be something," Victor said to himself.

Victor immediately saw the low budget quality of the film. It felt like a college course film. A few minutes into Judy's seventy-five minute runtime Victor was feeling like this was not as important as Agent Z had made it out to be. However then he saw her.

The character, named Regina Fairchild, looked out of place in the film to Victor. She was young and beautiful with long dark hair that went past her shoulders. There was a pureness and innocence to her face, as much as there could be for a young woman in an adult film. She looked and felt familiar.

The film went on as adult films do. Regina is attacked and raped with Private Detective Gunner being brought on board to solve the crime. The scene itself was what lined things up in

Victor's mind. The Regina character is attacked in a secluded, wooded area. Her face, the location, it all felt familiar. Victor's eyes grew wider as he paused the movie.

"Is that her?" As unbelievable as it seemed to him, Victor wondered if this young actress in Judy was in fact the Lady of the Dunes. The rumors of sex work, the potential ties to the Combat Zone and organized crime had been there from the start of the project. He rewound the movie, finding stills of her face, then looking at the most recent composite of the Lady of the Dunes done by the National Center for Missing and Exploited Children. The film was from 1970 and the composite was of the skull in 2010 but the hair, the face, though not an exact match it was possible.

Curious, Victor looked at the film's credits. Regina Fairchild was played by a woman named Lee Sherry. Try as he might Victor could not find any information about an actress named Lee Sherry. It was like she was a ghost, yet there she was on his computer screen in living color.

Despite the morbid, albeit campy nature of the opening attack scene, Victor got chills when he re-watched it. Looking at Lee Sherry as potentially the Lady of the Dunes as she is attacked in an area eerily similar to where her body was found was creepy.

Victor was far more interested in the film after making the Lady of the Dunes connection. He watched until the bitter end. Lee Sherry was the star and she was in several other scenes. The movie plot itself was nonsensical but that was beside the point. Who was Lee Sherry? Even if she was not the elusive Lady of the Dunes why was there no information on her anywhere he looked online?

Once the movie ended Victor felt dirty and unnerved. Did he just watch an adult film starring the Lady of the Dunes? It was set mostly in Boston's Combat Zone. That meant that some of the locations could be found doing research.

Finding no luck searching for Lee Sherry Victor worked his way down the cast list. There was little to no information about anybody. Sure it was a low budget adult film from 1970 but in the age of technology, where anything could be found online, Victor was stumped as to why this film was seemingly a dead end in all directions.

The research on Judy's two directors was even more disheartening. Both of the men were dead. To make matters worse they had both died in 2020, making it so close to when Victor began his work on the film. One of the directors had worked at MIT while the other work in a photo lab in the Combat Zone. The second one was reported to have hired many girls for these films. Did they hire the Lady of the Dunes in 1970?

The directors were both dead. Lee Sherry was seemingly a ghost. Most of the cast and crew of Judy were MIA. Victor's thoughts went to money. Who bankrolled Judy? There was no listing for that, unless it was one of the directors.

There was one person who Victor thought could help him. That was Agent X. They had not been in contact since June, but this startling discovery seemed like a perfect reason to reconnect.

Before preparing an email explaining the pornographic film he was sending to Agent X, Victor had something to do. He went back through Judy. Stopping at the scenes with Lee Sherry. Victor took several screenshots of parts of the movie. These screenshots were then uploaded to Judy's IMDb page. In particular Victor stopped at a scene of a happy, smiling Lee Sherry in a button-down navy blue coat. She was standing in the wooded area that looked eerily similar to where the Lady of the Dunes was found.

"Is that you?" Victor said aloud as he posted that screenshot to IMDb. He felt strongly that it was in fact the Lady of the Dunes. It gave Victor chills to see her hands.

He was disappointed that he could not find a definitive answer to Lee Sherry's identification. However Victor felt there was much more to this film and that it was worth a far deeper look.

The first step was reaching out to Agent X to get their thoughts on Judy. He had yet to hear back from his contact after sending them a photo of the Chief Meads envelope so it couldn't hurt to reach out again. Victor's second step was to send a message to Vinegar Syndrome. They were the film restoration and distribution company that owned the rights to Judy. A short message was sent to Vinegar Syndrome. However the note to Agent X was forgotten about as Victor went back down the rabbit hole of trying to find Lee Sherry.

Within an hour Victor had likely watched Judy more than anybody ever. Something struck him as odd. There was a name in the opening credits that Victor could not find on IMDb. There was an Executive Producer named Salvatore Sezar. In his experience with film Victor knew that the Executive Producer was the one that would get the money for the film. So who was he, and why was he not listed on IMDb? Was Sezar the investor who dated the film's lead, Lee Sherry?

It was possible that since the movie was so unknown and low budget that nobody cared to update the IMDb page to put Salvatore Sezar in it. However the many months of odd occurrences in working on the Lady of the Dunes project made Victor more skeptical. There had to be more to it.

When it came to new leads and information nothing could have prepared Victor for what he received on October 18th.

Amanda and Tiffany got together via Zoom to compare their psychic notes from the investigation. They then spent nearly four hours performing a spiritual table tipping. After they finished they called Victor to reveal what they had learned.

According to Amanda and Tiffany the woman known as the Lady of the Dunes was born in New York, near the borders with Massachusetts and Connecticut. Her birthday was September 6, 1948. This would have put her at two months shy of her twenty-sixth birthday when she was murdered on July 9, 1974. Her legal name was Helen Dennison and she was of Jewish faith. However she went by several nicknames including Lauren and Anna among others. During the table tipping two words kept coming up. These were 'love' and 'paid.' Victor's mind immediately went to sex work, as in getting paid for love/sex. Ann Dolce was purported to be Helen's stage name.

These revelations got Victor excited. Helen had been the name that had been floating around the Lady of the Dunes since he and Amanda had visited Whitey Bulger's grave. Although not an exact match the 'Anna' nickname could easily have been 'Ann' like at Whitey's grave as well. This matched up with the name Ann Dolce on Chief Meads' envelope. It also was not lost on Victor that Hadden Clark's 'Laura' could be 'Lauren.' Two important names on Provincetown's stage came forth. Amanda and Tiffany were told that Hadden Clark did in fact know the Lady of the Dunes. However she did not know him. In addition Helen did frequent the Crown and Anchor. She said she was nervous around Staniford Sorrentino though.

There was much more that came through to Amanda and Tiffany. Helen's father was purportedly named Ricky. There was no mention of a mother. At the time of her murder Helen was in school taking paralegal courses. Helen was seen as a chameleon who changed her appearance as the situation dictated.

Several other names that could be potential leads came forth. Two of the names were mentioned as friends of Helen Dennison, Sandy whom she knew from the Combat Zone, and Catherine. The shocking revelation was that one or both of these other women could be dead in the dunes as well with their bodies having never been found.

The name Joyce came through. She was mentioned as a Madam, a friend, and a mother figure to Helen. A woman named Jessica was said to be the money girl when it came to the affairs Helen was involved in. Amanda and Tiffany told Victor that this information was corroborated by Chief Meads who came through to them, saying 'that makes sense.'

Jessica's connection to the Lady of the Dunes deepened when Amanda and Tiffany found that the reason she was even in Provincetown on that fateful day was perhaps to celebrate Jessica's birthday. The pair of mediums asked Helen to expand on her relationship with Jessica, however she did not wish to speak about her. She also did not want to go into any detail about her father.

Helen herself, according to Amanda and Tiffany, was all talk. She was an actress by nature and was not used to being honest with people. It leaned into her chameleon persona. When questioned at the table tipping by Amanda and Tiffany Helen was open about finding sex work to be fun. She enjoyed her time at the Crown and Anchor, playing darts, drinking, and of course the men. Helen got lots of attention from men.

When it came to her last night on Earth Helen shared some sad details with Amanda and Tiffany. Her murderer was 'baby-faced,' perhaps no more than twenty-three years old. He tied her hands together. The name Joe kept coming forward as the name of Helen's actual murderer. As to the reason why she was murdered and left in the Provincetown dunes? Helen might have been a police informant. She could have been working with law enforcement as she was purported to have connections to sex work and potentially sex trafficking. Helen's eyes were taken out after her death. She doubled down on the fact that there could be more bodies buried somewhere in the dunes or in the woods out in Truro and Provincetown.

Once Amanda and Tiffany were finished sharing all of the information they had gathered through the table tipping Victor had to sit back and take a moment. There were so many potential avenues to go down with these names and birth dates. Victor needed help though. He had repeatedly reached out to Agent X and was awaiting a call-back. While waiting Victor decided to send a quick email to Agent Y giving them an update on what had been found.

The email was to the point. Victor mentioned the Meads envelope with the name Ann Dolce specifically. He clicked 'send' and waited. Hours passed. Eventually after not hearing anything from Agent Y Victor decided to send them a text. He knew the Meads envelope and the potential leads were important and Agent Y might be able to help.

Victor's text read: 'Are you free this week to talk about what I found with the Ann Dolce leads from Jimmy Jr?' Surprisingly Agent Y responded almost immediately.

'I got my bowling league this week, not really a good time to talk.' Victor had already been sort of phasing Agent Y out of the Lady of the Dunes project due to being inconsistent with his stories. This blatant brushing off of something highly important to the case enraged Victor. There was no text back, Victor gave Agent Y a call.

"What the fuck?!" Victor angrily asked when Agent Y picked up.

"What are you talking about?"

"What are you doing? You don't have five minutes to talk?"

"I'm really busy," Agent Y replied sounding as if they wanted to end the conversation quickly.

"Don't tell me that you're busy. What's your deal? What horse do you have in this race?" Victor needed to know if Agent Y really wanted to help solve the Lady of the Dunes case or not.

"I don't have any clue what you're talking about and really am busy."

"You don't think this envelope, Ann Dolce, the address, none of it is worth your time?"

"It's all dead ends, I saw it a few years ago and there's nothing worth digging into." Victor's eyes grew wide.

"What do you mean you've seen it?"

"I was shown it by Jimmy Jr. and found nothing worth pursuing." Victor was shocked that Agent Y had access to the Meads envelope but had not shared any of that info with him.

"Okay, I've gotta go," Victor said.

"Fine, me too." The two mutually hung up the phone.

The brief but exacerbating phone call left Victor with more questions. He hadn't even thought to probe Agent Y about the case file. In his heart Victor believed that Agent Y wanted him to succeed but at the same time there were so many inconsistencies. It came back to the Why's of Agent Y. Why did they downplay the Meads envelope? What if anything had they looked into from that envelope? What did they find, good or bad?

One thing was for sure, Victor was going to have to move forward without any additional help from Agent Y. It was a shame as Agent Y knew the lay of the land and the personal side of Provincetown. They also knew the roadblocks. Ironically Agent Y ended up becoming a roadblock themselves. Victor hoped that

Agent X, or even Agent Z, might be able to help some of these puzzle pieces together because he was burning out.

After not hearing from them for much of the summer Victor was happy to finally get a call back from Agent X a few days later. It was a little over a week before Halloween. The trip out to the Cape Cod woods was set for October 30th and there was so much that needed to be discussed. First and foremost Victor wanted Agent X's opinion about Judy. There was a bit of a laugh as Agent X admitted that they hadn't expected Victor to be sending porn to their computer. That being said they found it intriguing much like Victor had. Agent X was drawn to Lee Sherry much like Victor had been. They could also see where Lee Sherry could be the Lady of the Dunes. More proof would be needed obviously.

There were two bits of information from Agent X that Victor took notice of. First off Agent X told Victor he needed to find the house that is used in the opening scenes of the movie. It would be possible to find names associated with the house if an address could be found. Agent X remarked about the Combat Zone connection. They reminded Victor of what they had said months before. It was important to learn what Boston was like in the 1960's and 1970's. It was a different location but a similar stage as Provincetown was in the same time period.

The second interesting tidbit came when Victor asked Agent X about a financier for the film. They thought that the person who fronted the money for Judy could have been the sugar daddy of the Lady of the Dunes/Lee Sherry. Both Victor and Agent X agreed that the financier of the film likely had a goal of making Lee Sherry famous, or at least give her the feeling of being famous.

Agent X was curious how Victor found Judy. He explained about Agent Z and their odd interactions. Agent X was quick to make known that they were not a fan of Agent Z. Victor was told in no uncertain terms to steer clear of Agent Z. Agent X warned that Agent Z was pretending to act on good faith. In reality they were looking to get paid because, according to Agent X, they owed a lot of people money. Victor was already skeptical of Agent Z after they had mentioned money during their first interaction. He also put stock in Agent X's words. He would keep his guard up even more when it came to Agent Z.

Judy was an interesting new development and one that Victor would be making more time for in October. However there was a lot of new information to share. Although he had mentioned Hadden Clark to Agent X when they last spoke in June Victor jumped into the more recent letters. Specifically Victor wanted Agent X's opinion of the purported diary and the primitive map Clark drew.

Agent X, much like in June, was not interested in Hadden Clark. They felt as though Clark was likely lying to see how far Victor would go. In his mind Victor agreed that it was possibly a dead end but he still had that shred of hope that Clark was being truthful.

The lack of interest in Hadden Clark's part in the project from Agent X was quickly forgotten when Victor asked them about Meads' manila envelope. They were intrigued by the plethora of potential leads. Victor mentioned that he had been working on some of them but likely needed help above his pay grade to make any headway. He mentioned Ann Dolce which naturally didn't ring a bell to Agent X.

Victor saved the most intriguing information until the end. He explained to Agent X about the table tipping event with Amanda and Tiffany. Victor shared the name Helen Dennison. He tried to quickly sum up why the Helen and Ann names were relevant to the case. Victor mentioned the words 'love' and 'paid' which came up during the table tipping. When he mentioned September 6th, Helen Dennison's purported birthday, Agent X chimed in.

"She has the same birthday as me," they said. Agent X finished up by agreeing to touch base with Victor after the trip out to search for Hadden Clark's diary was over. Victor said he would send much of the information he just shared in an email to make it easier on Agent X to remember.

As the hours and minutes ticked closer to the excursion back to Cape Cod it became a race for Victor. It was a race between wrapping up the filming of the documentary and complete burnout. In all of his years in the film business Victor had always been able to compartmentalize each project. It was this sort of mild detachment that made it easy for him to dive into deep subjects. This same detachment also made it easier for him to close the book on an old project and move onto the next one with little issue.

The Lady of the Dunes was different. Victor felt a sense of obligation. He felt as though he and the crew helping on the film were the only ones who cared about the young woman who had lost her life in such a cold and gruesome way. Victor had become attached.

Each potential piece of the story revealed by his mediums Victor became more attached. Was she Helen? Was she Ann? Was she a college student who was pushed into sex work to help make ends meet? Was she someone who had been young and naive and got in with the wrong crowd and was in far too deep before she realized?

Victor had become attached to the Lady of the Dunes. However his attachment and dedication to finding her name and revealing her story could only take him so far. Victor had spent months and months, hundreds and hundreds of hours working diligently. He had found dozens of amazing people to interview, some of them had found him. Victor was very proud of the work he had done. In the end, though, he would feel a little hollow if nothing came of the work. If after the film was done and had premiered the Lady of the Dunes remained a nameless unsolved Jane Doe Victor would feel as though he had failed.

Feeling that the trip out to Cape Cod to search for Hadden Clark's diary was the final act of this play Victor decided to send the incarcerated killer another letter. He hoped that perhaps Hadden would give more in the way of clues as to the purported diary's location. Victor hated playing nice but there was a method to his madness. It could lead to an easier path to a potentially huge piece of evidence, or it could just be another chance for Clark to rant. Either way it was worth the time it took to write and mail the letter.

After mailing the latest letter to Hadden Clark Victor jumped back into his research into the Judy movie. Not being sure where to take his research Victor began reaching out to everyone. This included all of his mediums. Much like with Agent X they made jokes about Victor sending them links to adult films.

There was a consensus among them as they all felt a strong connection between the actress known as Lee Sherry and the Lady of the Dunes. The two mediums that watched the entire movie flat out said that it was in fact the same person. There were the sad eyes she has in the film, her hairstyle, the fact that she looks Jewish, and the fact that she is beautiful compared to the rest of the girls in the film.

One scene in particular seemed to seal the deal for the two mediums. It was the same one that Victor had been drawn to. When Lee Sherry is found nude and raped in the woods there was a similar feel to how the Lady of the Dunes was found after her murder. The two mediums who watched the movie remarked how Lee Sherry's face looked strikingly similar to the 2010 3D composite of the Lady of the Dunes. They also noted the filling in one of her teeth.

It made Victor wish he had access to the dental records that had been in the Chief Meads envelope. All of these things gave the mediums reason to believe that there was at the very least a strong possibility that Lee Sherry was the Lady of the Dunes.

Tiffany the psychic reached out to Victor with some helpful information. She had a contact in Boston who had owned nightclubs where Whitey Bulger had been a regular client. Through this contact Tiffany was able to get Victor another connection. The man was a retired Boston cab driver.

Victor immediately sent an email to the man. There was a brief introduction of who he was and how he got his information. With the email was a few screenshots of the house at the beginning of Judy. The man responded rather quickly. He stated that the home was located in the Chestnut Hill area of Boston. It was an interesting revelation.

Chestnut Hill itself was located six miles west of Boston proper. It was approximately nine miles from the Combat Zone area of Washington Street. However Chestnut Hill was also the area where Boston College was located. Could Lee Sherry have been another stage name for Helen Dennison who could have been a student at Boston College doing paralegal studies? The only way to know for sure was to either find the home in Chestnut

Hill and get as much information as possible about it, or to find Lee Sherry's whereabouts today.

It was yet another breadcrumb. There were hundreds of houses in Chestnut Hill. Taking the time to look through each and every one was not possible at that moment. Victor began checking with historians and locals alike to see if any could identify the house. He did not even get a single useful lead.

The Judy movie mystery deepened further. Victor continued to research any and all names associated with the film. The more he dug the more he found an eerie reality. Most of the people associated with Judy were either dead or had disappeared. Granted it was a fifty-year old movie but it was an odd coincidence that many of the people in the film were ghosts. This included Executive Producer Salvatore Sezar, and worst of all it included Lee Sherry. There was just nothing there to be found.

It took a great deal of restraint to let go of the research on Judy. Victor was up against his own deadline for the end of filming. He had to finalize the plans for the trip out to Cape Cod to search for Hadden Clark's diary.

The crew was to be a small contingent. Victor and his cameraman Rich, Christopher Setterlund, and a pair of metal detector enthusiasts. Victor had put out a blast on several social media metal detecting pages to see if he could find anyone willing to come out on the adventure.

Scouring internet search engines Victor came across a man named Brian based out of Wareham, Massachusetts. He gave Brian a call. Initially Brian was hesitant to join the group. He stated that although he enjoyed metal detector work that was not really something he did anymore. Victor explained exactly what the purpose was of the trip out to the woods in Wellfleet. Within minutes not only was Brian onboard but he also had a friend named Jason who was another metal detector enthusiast that would likely come along. That made it a party of five.

A final bit of appropriate irony came the day before the trip to Cape Cod. Scheduling conflicts arose. This led to the trip being pushed back to the following day which was Halloween. Victor and the other four members of the treasure hunt crew felt it was fitting to end the production of the project on Halloween. Did it mean anything? Good luck? Victor hoped so. Whether he found something in the woods on Halloween or not Victor knew that the Lady of the Dunes project was coming to an end on Halloween. Maybe.

Before Victor took that final drive across the Sagamore Bridge onto Cape Cod he received a response from Hadden Clark. Only a few hours after having to delay the trip until Halloween the latest letter from the serial killer hit Victor's mailbox.

28 October 2021

Dear Victor,

I guess you're not familiar with root cellars from houses from the 1700's or 1800's. All that remains from this house from the 1800's was the root cellar. This root cellar was made with stones and cement. I had to make a top door out of plywood and put 4 or 5 coats of plastic sealer on the plywood so no water could get in this root cellar. I put this waterproof sealer also on the walls and floor of this root cellar.
The only thing in this root cellar is plastic or paper. There is No metal and no metal hinges on the door. So no metal detector is going to find this root cellar. Before I came to

prison I put a couple layers of plastic sheets over the door and covered it with 6 inches of dirt. No water is going to get into this root cellar. And all the plastic & paper ID's etc are in plastic buckets from the food business. You could walk right over the root cellar and never know you were standing on it. That's exactly what I had the police & FBI do in 2000 when I knew they were going to play me for a fool.

I have no bodies buried in Wellfleet or Cape Cod. I did tell the police I did in 2000 because an inmate told me to. He told me he was going to help me get into a hospital. This inmate lied to me. This inmate is mentioned in the book 'Born Evil' by Adrian Havill.

Page 2

In the book he is mentioned as Jesus. His real name is John Truitt.

Let me tell you something about cadaver dogs. If it's not a shallow grave and it's deeper than 3 feet no cadaver dog is going to find any body that is bury. No cadaver dog has ever found anything I bury.

In your last letter you mention you could contact Tom Brady's agent and get his autographed photo for 500.00, now you say it cost 1,500.00 dollars. I knew you weren't going to send me Tom Brady's real autograph, that's why I didn't give you this serial killer name who has been killing all these college girls in Connecticut, Rhode Island, and Massachusetts.

A friend introduced me to another serial killer at one time. At the time he introduced me to Michael Ross. I didn't know he was a serial killer, either did my friend. I wrote my friend about Michael Ross about 10 or 20 years ago while I was in prison. And my friend told me all Michael's murders were in Connecticut, New York, and New Jersey. To bad you can't speak to Michael Ross, he is now dead. I once had the article of where he asked the state of Connecticut to put him to death.

Your not going to find anything I bury. Unless I go show you where it is. And I'm tired of people playing me for a fool, or trying to play me for a fool.

Page 3

Soon as this Covid-19 thing is over I plan on doing a documentary too. And talk about all the things people have promised me and how my Constitutional and Miranda rights have been violated and also double jeopardy. See I have kept all your letters.

And I'm definitely not going into anymore woods where a sniper can shoot me. Someday someone might find that root cellar, but I know no construction, houses, shopping centers will be on it since it National Seashore park land.

I even have stuff hidden in cemetery's in Wellfleet and Hyde Park NY.

Back in 1973 I was working at Camp Welmet part time in New York where I met Bonnie Bickwit when she and her boyfriend Mitch Weiser went to a concert and never

returned. I probably was one of the last people to see

Bonnie before she disappeared. Her girl friends used to write me at one time.

Thanks for the phony money and postcard. And thanks for all the other postcards as well.

God bless you in 2022.

Sincerely Yours,

Hadden J. Clark

Hadden's claims that Victor would not find anything with metal detectors meant little to him. Throughout their correspondence Victor knew to take most things with a grain of salt thanks to Theodore's advice. It was not going to stop Victor from heading down to Cape Cod.

Victor did take a moment to do a quick search for the two unfamiliar names Hadden mentioned near the end of the letter. Bonnie Bickwit and Mitchel Weiser were high school sweethearts with Bonnie indeed working at the Camp Wel-Met in Narrowsburg, New York that Clark claimed to have also worked at. The pair disappeared on July 27, 1973. Reports stated the pair could have been hitchhiking to the Summer Jam concert in Watkins Glen, New York that featured The Allman Brothers and Grateful Dead. The pair was last seen hitchhiking along State Route 97 and have never been found. Victor made a note to come back to that case once he was finished with the Lady of the Dunes,

Regardless of Hadden's belief that Victor and his crew had no chance to find his diary out in the woods behind his grandparents house the trip was on for Halloween. Victor was ready for the adventure, and ready for the adventure to be over.

Chapter 21, Happy Halloween

This was it. Victor had wanted the process to be over for a while as he had become overwhelmed and a bit burned out from all of the telephone calls, leads, and wild gooses chases that the project had entailed. This was it. One more trip to Cape Cod with two leads. The two final leads. Win, lose, or draw Victor was leaving the Cape at the end of the day and he would not be back until the film premiered in April. Despite that fact he wanted to finish strong.

The morning was a mix of clouds and sun and seasonably warm for the end of October. Victor had left home just after sunrise with a Dunkin' restaurant in Wellfleet as the first destination. It was there that he planned to meet cameraman Rich and author Chris. From there it was a short trip to Pamet Point Road and a treasure hunt for a serial killer's diary.

Victor bought a dozen donuts and a box of coffee to share with his crew. He had a little time for himself as he awaited Rich and Chris' arrival. Although he was ready to begin work on the Kurt Vonnegut project Victor was a little wistful thinking of how much had happened concerning the Lady of the Dunes film.

He thought of the kindness of the Meads Family and how they had given him a credibility that had opened many locked doors. There were his interactions with Peter Manso and his likening the scene in Provincetown in the 1970's to one giant stage. Victor thought back to all of those in the Provincetown community who had donated money or services to help him in his quest to give the Lady of the Dunes the closure she deserved. Victor was proud of the work he had done but unless something new came up during that day's excursion, or from one of the calls he hoped would be returned in the next week, it was time to put a wrap on the filming portion of the documentary.

Chris was the first to show up, exactly at 9am. Victor had grabbed his phone to call Rich and check in but he pulled into the Dunkin' parking lot at 9:01.

"You're late!" Victor yelled with a laugh.

"Eh, so fire me," Rich retorted.

"Fine, you're fired!" A few laughs and cups of coffee were shared before Victor suggested they make the drive to Pamet Point Road. The caravan of three mid-sized sedans rolled out of the parking lot and down Route 6.

Pamet Point Road was winding and quiet. A recent storm had done major tree damage to Cape Cod and left branches scattered on the road like an obstacle course. The road ended and connected with Old County Road. It was here that the treasure hunt would begin. According to Hadden Clark's rudimentary map the old root cellar was located along an overgrown fire road known as Paradise Hollow.

The best Victor could surmise was that it was located in an area nearly straight north from Clark's grandfather's property that resided on Pamet Point Road. Not wanting to arouse any suspicion Victor and Christopher both agreed to visit the former Clark family home on Pamet Point Road. They wanted to at the very least alert the current owners as to what they were doing despite the fact that the crew would be several hundred yards north of the home. It was a courtesy.

Victor drove his car from the Paradise Hollow fire road to the former Clark family home. A newspaper lay wrapped at the end of the driveway.

"A peace offering," Victor said as he scooped it up while Setterlund raised an eyebrow.

They drove to the end of the long driveway and spotted a vehicle parked off to the side. Victor stopped the car and got out holding the newspaper. He wasn't sure how far he wanted to go to let the current owners know that they were up to.

"Hello? Is anybody home?" Victor took a few steps out in front of his car and waved the newspaper around. "I brought you your paper." There were no lights on inside and no movement or sound from inside the house. He called out again and waited for a minute.

"What are you thinking?" Setterlund asked popping his head out of the passenger side window. Victor shrugged.

"Either nobody is home, or they really don't want to talk to us."

"Would you come outside if you saw two guys like us pulling up unannounced?" Victor smiled.

"Yeah, plus I'm sure they are leery of strangers since they have to know the history of the property." Victor took a few steps and dropped the paper on the ground. At least they had tried.

"How did it go? Rich asked upon the pair's return.

"Nobody was home," Victor said. Brian and Jason were on their way to the location with their metal detecting equipment. Not wanting to stand around waiting Victor asked Rich to wait by the three cars parked on the shoulder of Old County Road. In the meantime he and Chris would walk down the Paradise Hollow fire road for ten minutes to see if they could find anything.

The dirt road was uneven and sparsely populated with puddles after the week's storms. Both Victor and Chris were unsure of exactly what they were looking for. Chris insisted it would likely be a hole in the ground that doesn't look like a natural hole. Victor was focused on finding the old house foundation as scrawled on Hadden Clark's map.

Knowing that they had a short time to walk before they needed to turn back Victor took an offshoot path that led him up a hillside. Chris continued down the main fire road. It was at this point that Victor's phone began to ring. He figured it was Rich to tell him that Brian and Jason had arrived. It was a surprise to see that it was Tiffany the psychic.

She was on vacation in Maine yet had began receiving communication from the Lady of the Dunes. Tiffany wanted to let Victor know that although the Lady of the Dunes was with him that she was telling Tiffany that he was not going to find what he was looking for. She insisted that the root cellar Hadden mentioned was not something that could be seen with the naked eye and that it was essentially a fruitless endeavor.

Victor was undeterred and slightly stubborn. He had come this far and would see this final chapter through to the bitter end. Rich sent a text saying Brian and Jason had arrived so Victor caught up with Chris and the pair headed back down the fire road. They had yet to find anything of note but hoped metal detectors would change the game.

Acquaintances were made among the group of five men who stood together on the rural stretch of South Truro road. Now with four cars parked along the shoulder the first car to pass by curiously slowed down to see if there was an issue. The young women in her SUV rolled her window down to ask if the men needed any help.

Victor being a natural salesman immediately began to explain the documentary and the search for the diary. The women had never heard of Hadden Clark but did bring up the name of Tony Costa. Victor said Costa was involved in the bigger picture but not this particular quest.

"A lot of strange stuff has happened in this area for it being such a small community," the woman said. Victor nodded.

"You're telling me," he replied. "Hadden Clark, Tony Costa, the Lady of the Dunes."

"And Christa Worthington," she added.

"Oh yeah, you're right. That was not that long ago."

"I was a kid then, I didn't know her, or her daughter, but I know people who did. Such a horrible thing." Victor thanked her for stopping and joked that his crew needed to get moving just in case anyone started getting suspicious of the four vehicles parked along the roadside.
She went on her way and the men laid out their next steps.

Rich, Brian, and Jason planned on walking out on the Paradise Hollow fire road much in the same way Victor and Chris had. However a check on Google Maps showed that there was in fact a second fire road only a few hundred yards north of where they were. Hadden Clark had not been specific about the fire road, insisting that it was behind his grandfather's property. Could he have meant this second road?

Victor decided to split the team up. He and Chris would drive down to the other fire road and walk out to a pronounced fork in the road. It lined up roughly with Hadden's grandparents' house. Despite it being a relatively long shot Victor knew this was the last day for filming. He did not want to leave a stone unturned and have regrets after the documentary had premiered.

It also helped that Victor had another engagement a few hours later. A very reputable cadaver dog trainer named Deb was driving down all the way from Concord, New Hampshire. The plan was for her to meet the crew at Lombard Hollow Road to see if her canines might be able to pick up a scent of a tooth somewhere in the area that had been pointed out back in April. Victor had some time to kill, but not too much.

Pulling his Nissan up into the beginning of the second fire road Victor and Chris began walking and scanning the edges of the road. It was a bit intimidating to Victor just how isolated the South Truro woods were.

"You know," Victor began, "if you had been planning on killing me this would be the perfect place. Nobody would find the body for a long time." He turned his head with a wry smile as Setterlund shook his head. It was a morbid statement yet was also truthful. The further the two walked along the overgrown fire road the more that cell phone reception faded. It was just the two of them and a seemingly agitated group of blue jays circling the nearby trees.

Victor and Chris walked a little over half a mile. Three different times the pair had to remove a fallen tree from the pathway. Victor grew weary of the chore but Chris cracked that the film gods were 'making him work for it.' The fork in the fire road grew closer according to the spotty Wifi on Chris' phone. Victor hoped they'd find some sort of root cellar to at least give them a sliver of hope.

No more than fifty feet from the fork the pair spotted something. It must much like Chris had said, a hole that didn't look like a natural hole. Victor was not overly enthused but at least it was something. With Deb and the cadaver dogs not arriving from Concord until well after 2pm the group certainly had the time to make a second trek out to that point to do some metal detecting.

As if right on cue Victor's phone went off, catching a little blip of service in the deep woods. It was Rich with a strange comment. Apparently a man who lived in the house directly next to the Paradise Hollow fire road had come out to see what Rich, Brian, and Jason were up to. When Rich explained it the man said he and his son knew of an area where a home once stood out along the fire road. He said he would lead them all out to it.

Victor and Chris headed back to the car and drove back to Paradise Hollow road. Both were hopeful that the man leading the rest of the crew out there had some real information. About a quarter-mile down the fire road Victor and Chris caught up with the rest of the group. Brian and Jason were in among a mass of branches and thorns a few yards off of the road. One of them had numerous nasty-looking cuts from thorns crisscrossing his forearms. Rich was standing in the road thanking the man and his son before they left.

Once sufficiently out of sight Rich asked Victor if he knew who that guy was. Victor of course had no idea and thought he was simply the man who lived in the nearest house.

"No, that's the whale guy!" Rich exclaimed. Victor gave a cockeyed glance.

"Whale guy?"

"Yeah, he's the one a few months ago that said that he was swallowed by a humpback whale." Brian and Jason chimed in about the story, telling Victor that it had been in all of the newspapers locally and on TV.

"I can't make this stuff up," Victor replied. He looked at Chris who had been used to hearing the unbelievable stories of the Lady of the Dunes film second-hand. Now he had just seen it up close and in person.

"It really is like being a part of a movie," Chris said with a wry smile.

The questions turned to what exactly the group was doing at this location. Brian and Jason were getting lots of hits on their metal detectors in the surrounding area. Jason had found a belt buckle and a few Pilgrim nails. Not wanting to get sliced up like them Victor asked Chris and Rich to go back to the cars and retrieve some gloves.

Upon their return a few minutes later Chris pointed out a slightly obscured pipe partially spray-painted red. He called the rest over to check it out. Victor then spotted a large, flat stone a few feet from the pipe.

"This looks like part of a house foundation," Victor said, "like it could have been the front step." The pipe was determined to likely be a former well as water could be seen inside of it. Chris scanned the immediate area around the pipe and stone.

"Hey, did you notice that this tree is also spray-painted red?" Sure enough, a small tree only a few steps from the large, flat stone also had an odd red paint on its trunk. Taking this as a sign Victor asked for Rich's shovel and began to dig under the tree. He struck something hard and was intrigued. Could it be Hadden Clark's diary inside the sealed container as he had mentioned in his most recent letter?

Victor clawed at the ground. It ended up being broken pieces of bricks. Slightly disappointed the group continued searching the area for a little while longer before deciding to pack up and try the other fire road Victor and Chris had scoped out.

Victor and the rest of the crew began walking out to Old County Road. The faint sound of a dirt bike grew closer. The man referred to as the 'whale man' by Rich, Brian, and Jason had returned. When he was told that they had not found anything specific to Hadden Clark in the area he showed them the man was disappointed. He had hoped they'd find something. Jason showed him the Pilgrim nails but that was it. The group continued on their way leaving the whale man trailing behind on his son's dirt bike.

All four cars were able to be fit up in the fire road, or at least on the shoulder so as not to be in the way of any oncoming vehicles. Victor was less optimistic about this route but he kept coming back to the fact that this was the last day of filming. He needed to turn over every potential stone before calling it a wrap.

Although Victor and Chris had just walked the same road less than an hour earlier it somehow felt and looked different. Chris found it odd but Victor blamed it on the several cups of coffee they had ingested up to that point. The walk out there was dotted with several interlacing conversations about where they all had grown up, stories of local true crime, and other random topics that helped the walk go by a little quicker.

Once at the fork in the road, Victor pointed out the two potential root cellars and let Brian and Jason do their thing. He then tried his best to get a cell phone signal so he could check in with Deb on her arrival from New Hampshire. She was set to arrive nearly an hour ahead of schedule which suited Victor just fine. His mind was drifting toward the Kurt Vonnegut project and away from the Lady of the Dunes.

Perhaps feeling a bit skittish after being shredded by thorns at the first site Brian and Jason scanned around the area of the two potential cellar holes but did not go down inside them. It was a quick five-minute scan of the area with nothing of consequence being found. The group was in agreement that the Paradise Hollow site was the more likely spot to find the diary. Yet even that had come up as inconclusive at best.

Victor was nonplussed by the lack of a diary from either site. In his mind, it was a wild goose chase from the mind of a convicted serial killer. He had had low expectations about finding the diary from the beginning. The potential of finding a tooth from the Lady of the Dunes at the Lombard Hollow Road site was something of far more importance to him. It would quite literally solve the case.

Back at the vehicles on Old County Road Victor thanked Brian and Jason for their hard work on the day. He asked them if they wished to join the rest of them at the potential murder site. The two politely declined and headed home. There was one last stop for the Lady of the Dunes project.

The caravan of three vehicles, led by Victor, made its way through the back roads of Truro back to Route 6. Lombard Hollow Road was a road in name only. Victor slowed down when he got close to the turnoff. Luckily both he and Rich had been in the area back in April and were at least slightly familiar with the area.

Victor remembered the last time there when a panicked medium had insisted that the Lady of the Dunes had been murdered there. A five-by-five-foot area of ground, that purportedly held a tooth extracted from the Lady of the Dunes, was the place where Deb and her cadaver dogs would focus their search.

Victor pulled into Lombard Hollow Road. His Nissan made it safely in about fifty feet as that was roughly the extent of the asphalt bit of the road. Chris and Rich followed in close behind, making sure to leave room for Deb's vehicle. Victor wondered what people driving by on the highway thought of the site of the cars pulled into this semi-secret roadway. He was slightly worried about attracting unnecessary attention, especially at that point so close to the end of the filming.

In the minutes before Deb arrived Victor led Chris to the area to be searched as he had never been on Lombard Hollow Road. He painted the picture of what the medium had described. The area around the purported murder site was littered with beer cans. Victor noted that the area was frequented by people looking for a secluded place to drink, do drugs, and have sex. He stood with Chris and Rich soaking in the eerie isolation that permeated the woods.

An SUV slowly pulled into the road, splashing through a pulled left over from the recent storm. Victor went down to meet Deb and her pair of cadaver dogs. She had come from Concord, New Hampshire, a three-hour drive, and Victor was highly appreciative. He handed her a small wad of dollar bills as a 'donation.' The pair then walked back to the purported murder site. Victor explained what he was looking to have done. Chris and Rich stood quietly and observed.

Deb was quite blunt when explaining the situation. She could tell this area was frequented by humans regularly. The dogs for their part would sniff out human remains as well as bodily fluids. This meant that while there could be a tooth left from the Lady of the Dunes there was also a likelihood that it might be overwhelmed by more recent human activity there. Victor was still hopeful. Deb returned to her SUV to retrieve the first cadaver dog, a 2 ½-year-old named Sellea.

She came bounding up the road with Deb having to reign in her youthful exuberance. Once in the area in question, the all-black German Shepard was turned loose. She began sniffing in a particular area around a mound of dirt and rock. Deb directed traffic while the three men watched in amazement. Rich filmed the scene just in case something was found.

Sellea honed in on a particular tree several times with Deb pulling her away. She explained that it was likely a favorite spot for visitors to the woods to relieve themselves. It went back to what she had mentioned about the site being contaminated and thus difficult for a cadaver dog to find legit human remains.

Undeterred by the younger dog's lack of findings Victor was on board when Deb said she could go and get her other dog to give it a go. This dog, a 10-year old named Eisen, was far more seasoned and would give them their best chance of finding something.

It was a similar process where Eisen sniffed and dug at the same areas as Sellea had minutes before. Each time the veteran cadaver dog thought he found something and lay down Deb would ask him to keep searching. The five by five square-foot area that was of the greatest interest had gotten a few extra sniffs from the pair of dogs but it was nothing to sound the alarm bells over.

When it became apparent that the searching was over Deb shared her impressions of the area. Again she was blunt. Deb said that the grounds were highly contaminated by more recent human activity. Although she could not say for sure that a tooth wasn't there, she also could not say there was. Victor listened intently all the while seeing another potential chapter to the project that he was not sure he wanted to pursue. Deb recommended looking for a nearby college that featured archaeology. There Victor could find students that could come out to the area and dig the grounds.

Victor took the recommendation under advisement, although in his mind when he left Lombard Hollow Road he was closing the door on the Lady of the Dunes project. He, Chris, and Rich each thanked Deb for coming all that way. They prepared to leave the area when Deb asked if any of them knew a good area to run the dogs since they had been cooped up in the car for three hours.

Victor put Chris on the spot as he was the resident Cape Cod tourism expert. He was stumped. Deb asked how far Lombard Hollow Road went into the secluded South Truro woods. Figuring it was at least a mile and a half Victor told Deb that she could simply run the dogs there and likely not find another soul. She liked the idea.

Deb backed her car out onto the shoulder of Route 6 allowing Victor, Chris, and Rich to leave, each beeping their horn and waving in appreciation. Victor took one last look at Lombard

Hollow Road and took off for home. Nearly the entirety of his 2021 had been spent working on the Lady of the Dunes project. Although he was ready to start a new assignment Victor knew this was not truly the end.

As he drove Route 6 through Orleans, Brewster, Dennis, and beyond he thought back to how it all started. Victor thought back to his intentions for the project, the intentions that never wavered. He wanted to give the Lady of the Dunes her name back. That was still the hope. There were still many months between Halloween and the film's premiere in April. Who knew what information could come to light in that time?

Before Victor caught sight of the Sagamore Bridge to carry him over the Cape Cod Canal he gave Chris a call. He thanked him for his help on the book side of the project as well as for walking seven miles around the woods searching for Hadden Clark's diary and the Lady of the Dunes' tooth.

The two agreed that what Victor had been doing was incredibly important. At the very least it shone new light on a case that deserved a new look. Victor reiterated that he felt burned out and that he was done 'chasing ghosts' as Agent X had repeatedly said. Chris reminded him that he was still working on the book and that if anything new came to light it would go inside those pages.

Victor needed a little while to be just a father and husband again. He again thanked Chris for his help. Before hanging up he made sure to wish Chris a 'Happy Halloween.'

With the click of the phone Victor also closed the door on the Lady of the Dunes, at least for a while. There would still be drips and drabs of information and editing on the film, but all in all the project was finished. All that was left was getting set for the premiere.

Victor watched the Sagamore Bridge fade into the background. He said a quiet goodbye to Cape Cod, to Provincetown, and the Lady of the Dunes. He would not be returning to Cape Cod until the spring, unless of course something major came up. Victor got into the slow lane of Route 3 heading north. He turned the radio on and got lost in the music. It would be so good to be fully home again.

Chapter 22, The Premiere

Five Months Later.

Victor stood on the steps outside of the Cape Cinema in Dennis. Much like the project's last filming day being Halloween it was almost too fitting that the initial premiere of the Lady of the Dunes documentary was on April Fool's Day.

Although he had sworn up and down that October 31st was the end of his work on the project that proved to be easier said than done. Victor felt it was symbolic to formally end the project on November 1st. The idea of the three number ones had a deep meaning of new beginnings or a new cycle. It also was a sign of angelic guidance. Victor had learned much from the four mediums that had helped so much in the film.

Victor had a final conversation with Agent X on November 1st. The conversation was brief. Agent X told Victor that they had taken all of the information Victor had shared, specifically the name Helen Dennison and the September 6, 1948 birth date, onto the State Department. They then told Victor that they would be in touch again if they could. That was the last Victor heard from Agent X.

Agent Z was a different story. Victor had more to ask them when it came to the Judy movie and those contacts who helped to find the movie. Agent Z pushed the compensation side of things. They were angry that Victor was not paying them for their time. They continued by stating if Victor wanted any more information it would cost him. In the middle of Victor explaining the low budget of the production Agent Z hung up the phone. Moments later Victor received a text from Agent Z.

It read: Sorry to do this, but I can't help you. I recommend, you bag this baby soon and end your investigation. Best of luck.

It seemed as though Agent X had been right about being wary of Agent Z's intentions. The abrupt exit from the project though got Victor's antennae up. It was so sudden that he wondered if Agent Z had been spoken to. It only added to the thought that someone did not want the case to be solved.

Word of Victor's project seemed to be getting out. November 10th saw a surprising phone call out of the blue. It was from a Cape Cod-based Democrat who was focused on the 2022 elections. Victor thought it a bit early to be speaking about potential elections a year out but this person was highly interested in his Lady of the Dunes film. It seemed as though the issue of the case might be going public. This political candidate was looking for a statement from Victor as well as more information about the documentary.

Despite the urge to delve back into the investigation part of the Lady of the Dunes project, Victor held his ground. He focused on the post-production of the documentary. Besides, he knew that the companion book was still in the process of being written by Christopher Setterlund. This meant that if anything newsworthy should come up it would end up in the book.

In the process of the film itself, Victor made a big change by bringing in a new editor. Her name was Connie Yip. She had been an intern at Shotgun media and liked the concept of Victor's documentary. Over the next few weeks, she and Victor watched nearly all of the footage that had been recorded over the preceding year. For the most part, it was a fun, yet mundane, look back at all Victor had seen and done when it came to the Lady of the Dunes. However, an interesting development happened when watching the April meeting at the Meads home in Provincetown.

He had not been sure if he had ever watched the complete meeting that took place between the Meads Family and the New

York psychic. As Victor and Connie watched the footage he was shocked to hear Chief Meads asking the psychic to ask his sons about something. The psychic mentioned the Chief asking about a piece of paper, a letter, or a card. At the time Jimmy Jr. and Michael were not sure what was meant by some piece of paper. This must have been the envelope that Jimmy Jr. sent a photo of to Victor all of those months later.

Vinegar Syndrome, the owners of the Judy movie that might have held some connections to the Lady of the Dunes, finally got back to Victor later in December. Their response was paint-by-numbers. It said they would look into any contact information that came with the movie from when they took ownership. There would be no follow-up from Vinegar Syndrome. In fact, despite sending numerous emails to local historical groups there was not a soul who could identify the house seen at the beginning of Judy. It appeared as though the movie, as tantalizing as some of the leads were, was destined to be a dead end.

Near the end of January Victor had another long-shot idea. He decided to take a chance and contact local law enforcement directly and ask if there was anything from the Lady of the Dunes case file that they would share with him. Victor had never simply asked about the case file, although he had previously seen the original thanks to the mysterious person who dropped it off in April.

It took several weeks but finally, a four-page typed letter arrived. There was a lot of legal jargon mixed in. The main gist of it as far as Victor was concerned was that the police department was open to looking through their archives for documents and photos about the Lady of the Dunes case. They were initially denying the request though.

Any hope was somewhat quelled by the catches that followed. First off the police stated that the case was still open they mentioned working on the investigation of the Lady of the Dunes case as recently as December 2021. Part of the reason for denying the request was the notion that releasing information and photographs to the public might alert the murderer, if still alive, to police activity on the case. Victor laughed out loud at much of what he was reading.

On the third page of the letter, it was stated that the department would be willing to see if there was a limited amount of documentation that could be released. However, that came with a huge monetary catch. The process of having someone search through the records would cost $25 an hour and the necessary searches would take approximately twenty-five hours. The documents likely were not digitized, meaning that photocopies would need to be made, adding to the fee. In all Victor looked at it as costing at least $650 just for the police department to look. This did not mean that they would find anything to share. Victor would need to pay the money upfront as well.

After receiving the letter Victor sent photos of it to Christopher Setterlund and Kimberly Dudik. He was on the fence about dropping so much money with no promises of getting anything out of it. Setterlund felt it sounded fishy. He told Victor it was unlikely the police would find anything and would end up with a charitable donation from Victor for his troubles.
Victor took some time to think about his next step. He had been so keen on exploring every avenue when it came to the Lady of the Dunes. It would go against what he had been doing if he simply refused to pay the police's price. However, it was a big risk with no guarantees.

A couple of weeks later a plan of action was put into place. Victor and Kimberly decided to put in much of the money

for the archives search by local law enforcement. Setterlund
agreed to cover the rest of the cost. They all agreed to get some
sort of confirmation before simply forking over hundreds of
dollars.

Victor wanted to know beforehand what the odds were of
the police finding something they were allowed to share. He also
wanted to know if there was a guarantee that they could do their
search for the amount of money the three of them planned on
paying. Finally, Setterlund told Victor to find out if anything the
police shared would be allowed legally to be used in the book he
was writing.

It turned out the answer to all of the questions was no. The
police could not guarantee the price. They could not guarantee
finding anything they'd be willing to share, and if they did they
could not guarantee it would be legal to share them under the
Freedom of Information Act. This left Victor open to potential
liability. In the end, all three decided not to waste their money.

Disappointed but not surprised Victor moved on. He was
in the final stages of the film's premiere. There was a little editing
to be done as February ended. It was at this time that he nailed
down the when's and where's of the debut of the Lady of the
Dunes documentary.

Of course, he wanted the film to have a showing in
Provincetown. The entire project would not have been possible
without so many from the town, especially the Meads Family. It
was decided to show the film on April 2nd at the Provincetown
Theater at 7:30 pm. Though the theater was relatively small,
seating somewhere around seventy people, it would be a fitting
bit of full-circle irony that the room where so many important
interviews were done would now be showing the finished project.

However, Victor thought it would be wise to have another show somewhere else on Cape Cod. While working on the editing process at Cape Media in Dennis he had kept in the back of his mind having the film on the big screen at Cape Cinema. Located in the heart of Dennis Village on historic Route 6A Cape Cinema was a century-old theater. It came complete with a beautifully colorful mural across the ceiling that would fit well with the beautifully tragic story that was the Lady of the Dunes.

The decision was made to host the first screening of the documentary at Cape Cinema on April 1st. It was a good choice since the theater could seat upwards of three hundred people. Victor was conflicted though as the show time was at 12:30 pm on a Friday. He hoped people would show up.

Above all else Victor wanted the screenings to be free of charge. He had never been about exploitation. He had never been about making money from his efforts. Victor had said from the start that the purpose of the film was to give the Lady of the Dunes her name, not to make a profit. Victor would keep his word.

A few days after the dates of the premieres had been solidified Victor was surprised by an email from Christopher Setterlund. He was finishing up transcribing the last of Hadden Clark's letters into the book when he noticed something that stopped him cold.

Setterlund mentioned Hadden's final paragraph. It was in it that he casually mentioned working with Bonnie Bickwit at Cape Wel-Met in Narrowsburg, New York July 1973. Clark also dropped the notion that he might have been one of the last people to see her alive before she and her boyfriend Mitchel Weiser went missing.

The high school sweethearts had been on their way to a concert called Summer Jam headlined by the Allman Brothers and Grateful Dead. The show was located in Watkins Glen, about seventy-five miles from Narrowsburg. Bonnie and Mitchel were last seen hitchhiking along State Route 97. Neither has ever been seen since.

Victor only faintly remembered Hadden mentioning Bonnie Bickwit. His mind was in an advanced state of burnout by this time. Setterlund thought this was too much of a coincidence that Hadden just tossed out the names of two more missing people.

Setterlund asked Victor if it was all right to reach out to the Sullivan County Sheriff's Department in Monticello, New York. Before emailing Victor, Setterlund had done some quick research on the Bonnie Bickwit/Mitchel Weiser case. He came across a website run by the families of the victims. Setterlund had already contacted them with this potential new lead, also including a photo of the section of Hadden's handwritten letter.

Victor asked why Setterlund thought it necessary to get his permission to contact law enforcement. The writer responded that if by chance the authorities did contact Hadden Clark to question him about the disappearances of Bonnie and Mitchel, Clark might recall sharing his little tidbit of information in a letter to Victor. Even though he was likely to be locked behind bars for the rest of his life Setterlund knew that Clark had Victor's home address and did not want to put him or his family at risk.

In the end, Victor gave his blessing. He even told Setterlund that he could give his email to whoever might need it so that they could contact him directly. Victor and Christopher found it to be a potentially ironic twist to the Lady of the Dunes film. It would be fitting if the creation of the documentary ended up helping to solve another cold case. Both Victor and

Christopher had agreed during the process that the stage that was Provincetown in the late 1960s and early 1970s was a spiderweb. The Lady of the Dunes was at the center, at least for Victor's film, yet the further from the center he got the more things seemed to get caught in the web. The Lady of the Dunes, Hadden Clark, Whitey Bulger, Tony Costa, Staniford Sorrentino, Sydney Monzon, the Crown & Anchor, the Combat Zone, and now potentially Bonnie Bickwit and Mitchel Weiser, all were a part of the spiderweb now.

Later in March, with only two weeks to go until the premieres, Victor decided to take one last trip to the Outer Cape. The Provincetown Theater showing of the Lady of the Dunes film had just sold out. The Cape Cinema show was moving far slower which concerned Victor, but he could not dwell on that.

This last trip was two-pronged. He went on March 19th to St. Peter's Cemetery and then to Pine Grove Cemetery. Victor brought Christopher Setterlund along. On the drive up to Provincetown Christopher interviewed Victor for his In My Footsteps Podcast.

Setterlund knew the right questions to ask to get Victor thinking. He reiterated his desire to give the Lady of the Dunes her name while also not exploiting the case in any way. Victor was realistic though. He hoped that if he could not be the one to solve the mystery that perhaps the film or the book could be the catalyst for someone else to do so.

On the drive up they passed Sydney Monzon's grave, Lombard Hollow Road, Pamet Point Road, and eventually the towering dunes themselves as they entered Provincetown. These places were ingrained in Victor now, whether he liked it or not. This film had been unlike any other he had ever done. The Lady of the Dunes had seeped into Victor's soul.

Victor and Christopher arrived early and parked next to the grave of the Lady of the Dunes. The pair was soon to be joined by the psychic making a return trip from Upstate New York. It was a cool and misty day with the threat of rain looming. They had initially planned on traversing the Province Lands dunes to the site where the Lady of the Dunes had been found. However getting caught in the cold rain was not appealing to Victor, especially at this stage of the game.

Upon arriving at St. Peter's Victor made it a point to stop at the grave of Chief Meads. He said a quick hello and gave a heartfelt thank you. He brought Christopher over to the unmarked plot of land where Tony Costa was buried. This brought an idea to Victor's mind.

He knew in a touch of cruel irony that one of Costa's victims, Susan Perry, was also buried in St. Peter's. Victor wanted to pay his respects. The cemetery was enormous though, and with no map showing where Perry's final resting place was, it was a daunting task trying to find her grave.

For fifteen minutes, Victor and Christopher wandered the grounds of St. Peter's without luck. They decided to head back to the car. The road that led back to the Lady's grave was lined with small rectangular markers. Setterlund was focused straight ahead. Victor just happened to turn his head to the left and to his shock there she was. Susan Perry's grave, nearly fully overgrown by grass, was staring Victor in the face. He knelt in front of the stone and pulled the grass and dirt away, revealing her name and dates of birth and death. Sadly Susan Perry's final resting place was only a few hundred feet from where her killer was buried.

The New York psychic arrived and was introduced to Christopher. He was planning on shooting some videos to help promote the Lady of the Dunes documentary. The cemetery was silent but for one squawking bird located across the street. The psychic bowed their head beside the Lady's grave and began to communicate.

The Lady, through the psychic, thanked Victor for creating the documentary. She thanked Christopher for working on the book. When he asked her forgiveness for not bringing coins to place on her grave as he always did she said his work on the book was worth more than coins.

The three of them found it fascinating as the Lady revealed that she did not spend a lot of time at her gravesite. She said she enjoyed checking in to see what had been left on her marker. It was like going to check the mail. The rest of her time in their world was spent at places she remembered and loved from her living years. She did mention the name 'Marie' and the word rose repeatedly came up. Nobody could seem to pinpoint what those words meant at the time.

Before wrapping, Victor asked the psychic if they could communicate with one other person. He led them over to the grave of Susan Perry. Whereas the Lady of the Dunes was more than happy to communicate from the beyond, Susan Perry was far different. The psychic noted her as shy and reserved and not wanting to speak much.

Setterlund had the camera rolling as the psychic slowly got Susan to open up. It was mid-sentence when they stopped and looked around.

"Did you hear that?" They asked while looking directly into the camera. The only sound echoing throughout the cemetery had been the squawking bird. The psychic though mentioned a sound akin to a buzzing wind. When asked what it meant by Victor they said that it was as if sensing that Susan was uncomfortable communicating other spirits from the cemetery had come to give her support. Though nobody else could say for sure if they heard anything, Setterlund promised to go through the footage to search for the 'buzzing wind.'

Before leaving Victor asked the psychic if they would go over to another grave. This was a man long suspected of being involved in the murder of the Lady of the Dunes as the potential driver of the vehicle that brought her body out to the drop site. Victor hoped that the psychic might be able to get him to admit from beyond the grave his involvement. They looked over in the direction of the man's grave and flat out refused. The psychic said they could sense the bad vibes coming from that direction and would rather leave St. Peter's with the positive communication they'd had with the Lady of the Dunes and Susan Perry.

The three of them went their separate ways from St. Peter's. The New York psychic went off to explore Provincetown again, while Victor and Christopher had another interesting meeting ahead of them.

Several miles south in Truro Victor and Christopher planned on meeting Tiffany the psychic. The plan was to take a walk around the woods behind the Pine Grove Cemetery. Liza Rodman had given Victor a copy of a map of the sites pertinent to Tony Costa's murders. He wanted to bring Tiffany to these areas to see if she felt anything. He had no intention of telling her where to go, instead as he had done before Victor would let Tiffany lead the way.

The meeting at Pine Grove was far different from St. Peter's. Before entering the woods behind the cemetery via one of many rustic fire roads Victor asked Tiffany to approach the brick half-circle crypt at the back left corner of the cemetery. Legend had it that Tony Costa had done some bad things to at least one of his victims inside there. For her part, Tiffany felt nothing. No connection to any victim or Costa himself was felt around the crypt.

"I'm being pulled toward the woods," Tiffany said while pointing east. Victor and Christopher followed her as she began to walk down the fire road. At some point many years earlier there had been a mangled piece of metal apparatus nailed to a tree down one of the fire roads. It had been engraved with the words 'Tony Chop Chop's Phone.'

Setterlund had found it a decade earlier. He even had sent Victor a low-quality photo taken with an old flip phone. Was it a real phone? No. Was it placed there by Tony Costa? Unlikely. Was it left in an area that designated where bodies had been found, or where Tony's 'garden' had been? That was the hope.

The story was that the 'phone' had been removed a few years earlier to keep people from wandering the woods there, or worse doing drugs, having sex, or potentially performing occult rituals around the phone. Victor hoped to find markings on the tree where it was left. However, after wandering up and down the main fire road nothing had been found.

It was at this point that Tiffany began to feel faint. She asked Victor if any of Costa's victims had been drugged. When he said yes she knew that she was connected to one of them. Setterlund filmed while Tiffany suddenly grabbed the back of her head.

"I've been hit, they've been hit," she said frantically. Tiffany stepped off the fire road and began walking unsteadily straight east through the overgrown brush.

"Look up, I need you to look up," she pleaded as Victor and Christopher followed her. Tiffany revealed that she was seeing the last moments through the eyes of one of Tony Costa's victims. She had been drugged, then struck in the head. This poor victim was scrambling to get away through the overgrown brush. She had no sense of where she was or what she could do. All the while a maniacal serial killer loomed over her.

Tiffany pleaded with her to look up so she could get a sense of where she was at that point in time. Her steps were labored and meandering as Tiffany traced the horrifying last moments of a young girl in the presence of evil. All at once, the steps stopped. Tiffany stood still, looking at the ground.

"This is it, this is the end." The psychic took several deep breaths as she slowly regained her faculties. She had relived something terrible and was standing where someone had met their demise. Victor and Christopher could only stare in silence as Tiffany took a few steps forward and began to feel like herself again. In the pit of his stomach Victor felt a pang of sadness wondering if it was Sydney Monzon whose last moments Tiffany had been witnessing.

The next step in the journey was trying to find Costa's garden and where he had buried three of his four known victims. At this point, Tony Costa himself began to come through. Tiffany was taken aback when Costa mentioned to her about a tree. He was very proud of something beneath a tree.

Victor remembered in Liza Rodman's book *The Babysitter* that Tony had a few favorite trees in the area of his garden. Where the three of them stood, a few hundred feet deep in the woods, two trees did not match the rest. The woods were filled with relatively unassuming pine trees. Then there was a pair on opposite ends of a green clearing. They resembled bony hands reaching up from the ground. Could they be standing amid Costa's infamous garden? Victor was certain that at least one of these trees was the one Costa was communicating about.

When trying to get Tiffany to press Costa for what exactly it was that he was proud of she replied that his communication was in bits and pieces. She likened it to receiving a text message as opposed to an actual telephone call.

Victor's mind began to race. When on trial Costa had been asked if he had anything else to say. His response was to 'keep digging.' Although convicted of four murders rumors persisted that he could have killed as many as eight. If Tiffany had led them into Tony's garden was the thing that he was 'proud of' another victim yet to be found?

Retired state trooper Thomas had told Victor that a full reconnaissance had not been done in the woods after the initial four bodies had been found. Could Tiffany have led them to another burial site? Not having any sort of digging tool Victor began using his hands and feet to pull the grass and moss away from around one of the tree's bases. He had no idea what he'd hoped to find. A murder weapon? Some piece of jewelry belonging to another victim? Or perhaps Costa was enjoying messing with them, much like it seemed at the time that Hadden Clark had done in his letters.

In the end, Victor gave up, at least for that day. He hatched a plan. He had faith in Tiffany and her abilities. Victor decided to return in two weeks, on the day of the Provincetown premiere of the film. On that day he would bring mediums, metal detectors, and if possible ground-penetrating radar. If there was something related to Tony Costa in those woods Victor was going to do his best to find it. He also decided it would be kept quiet as digging in that area could get him in trouble.

Before exiting Cape Cod again Victor asked Tiffany if she could make one more stop. This was in Eastham, the Evergreen Cemetery, and the grave of Sydney Monzon. Victor was dedicating the Lady of the Dunes film to Sydney's memory and he wanted to make one last stop there.

The rain began to fall as the two cars pulled into the cemetery. Christopher filmed as Tiffany began to communicate with Sydney. Tiffany turned to Victor and said that Sydney was telling her that she was not at the cemetery. She did not spend her time around her grave, instead, she was at the places she loved going to when she was growing up in Eastham and Orleans. Sydney was not interested in communicating at the Evergreen Cemetery.

"If we guess where you are and go there will you talk to us?" Christopher asked. Victor wanted to let Sydney rest. He politely refused to go on any other searches. For a few minutes Victor, Christopher, and Tiffany sat in Victor's car reflecting on their experiences. Once the rain let up a bit the psychic thanked both men for their work on the film and book and exited.

Victor was full of excitement about the potential return to the Truro woods to look for connections to Tony Costa. For a few moments, it overtook the Lady of the Dunes in his mind. Christopher would not be going back to Truro with Victor, but he would be front and center at the premiere in Provincetown. They sat in a rainy parking lot in Dennis chatting before going their separate ways.

"I'm going to call you out at the premiere," Victor said with a laugh.

"That's fine with me," Setterlund replied.

"Then I'm going to get the hell out of there."

"You're not going to watch it?"

"I've lived it for over a year, besides I'll see the opening at Cape Cinema. I need a break, this project has taken a lot out of me."

Christopher said he understood, although he admitted that he was ready to keep up the search for the Lady of the Dunes even after Victor had recused himself from the project. Victor said that was exactly what he had hoped he would say.

A few days passed and it was time for Victor and Christopher to record an episode of the REFORM Podcast with Kimberly Dudik. She had been a fabulous connection for Victor and their times bouncing theories off of each other had been eye-opening for Victor.

The episode was another chance for Victor to reflect on his last year-plus. Throughout the entire process, he had remained steadfast in his desire to give the Lady of the Dunes her name back. Still, he was burning out. There were nearly fifty years of history, questions, and roadblocks that he had stared down. Not to mention the grander stage of Provincetown that Victor could not ignore. When the premieres ended he knew he would feel relieved that he could put this project to bed.

It was opening day for the Lady of the Dunes. Ticket sales had been slow at Cape Cinema. Victor chalked it up to the time of day. He knew his film had been done to the best of his abilities and he hoped word of mouth would spread and bring more eyes to it. Only about a third of the seats had been reserved. Victor paced the lobby of the theater as the minutes ticked down toward the first premiere. Vehicles began to arrive. Some familiar faces greeted Victor as they entered the theater. He smiled a weary smile.

Then something wonderful happened. Vehicles, more and more of them, kept pulling into the parking lot. It was filling up. The number of walk-up ticket buyers was astounding. It included members of law enforcement, members of the media, and strangers who were interested in the Lady of the Dunes story.

The hum of the chatting crowd was music to Victor's ears. He looked up at the beautifully painted mural on the ceiling of the theater and then looked down at the audience. Every seat was full.

There appeared to be a few standing-room people as well. This was the culmination of all of the hard work.

The house lights dimmed and Victor stood in the front under a bright spotlight. He said a few words chronicling why he had undertaken this project and what he hoped would come of it now that it was finished. Victor stepped out of the spotlight and the Lady of the Dunes stepped in. The film opened with sweeping views of the Province Lands dunes and a haunting poem by Robert Frost read by Jessica Harper.

Ninety-two minutes later a loud standing ovation greeted Victor as the credits rolled and the lights slowly brightened. He felt a huge sense of relief that he had done right by the Lady of the Dunes. If even one of the sell-out crowd began to question why the case was not yet solved after almost fifty years then Victor had done his job.

Saturday, April 2nd dawned with Victor having four things on his plate. First was a visit back to Tony Costa's woods. He was equipped with Jason and Brian and their metal detectors. Amanda the medium was also along as a part of what Victor stated would be his last ever trip to those woods.

The crew ventured out to the Costa-related spots which were creepy. The metal detecting seemed to provide little. There was a coffee container top, but no bottom. Next was a piece on an old Volkswagen Beetle. There was a thought among them that it could be from the original crime scene but nobody could say for sure.

Victor and Amanda left the area with Brian and Jason remaining behind. When all seemed to be for naught they found something. It was a bullet fragment determined to be from a .22-caliber pistol. This was the same type of gun owned by Tony Costa. Ironically Liza Rodman had once mentioned to Victor that investigators had not accounted for all of the bullets Costa had used to murder his victims out there. It was thrilling to come away with something tangible and potentially important.

Although a sunny morning, Victor could not wait to get out of the woods and leave Pine Grove Cemetery behind. As he drove down the desolate pothole-filled road, and the cemetery faded away, Victor knew in his mind he'd likely never gaze upon it again. That chapter was over. In a sense, April 2nd was to be the ending of several chapters.

Next up was a return to St. Peter's Cemetery. Amanda the medium had come along as she was more than willing to communicate with the man that the New York psychic did not want to communicate with when he had been there a few weeks earlier.

Peter Manso had told Victor early on in the production of the documentary that all of the answers he was looking for were buried at St. Peter's. Score had repeated that same statement when Victor had talked with him. He had disregarded it for a long time as Victor was not looking at the dead, but was focused on the living. Now as the end of the journey was near Victor realized that it had been an important bit of advice. He had been chasing ghosts all along.

Amanda stood before the man's grave. It looked unkempt and more decayed than many of the surrounding stones. It was Joe just like had come up during the table-tipping with Tiffany back in the fall. This was the same Joe that Score had called a 'crazy fuck' and had believed was involved in the murder of the Lady of the Dunes. Now here they were standing before his grave. Amanda got right to the point and asked him if he had been involved in the murder of the Lady of the Dunes. Amanda nodded and looked over at Victor.

"He says yes." Victor's eyes grew wide.

"Was he the killer, or the driver?"

"The driver. Hold on."

"What's he saying?"

"It's his mother. She's telling him to get it all of his chest."

"What else does he have to say?"

"He's saying he was just a kid. Just a scared kid. He didn't kill her but he is saying that he did agree to drive them out into the dunes to drop her body off."

"He didn't think of saying no?"

"He says he was scared shitless of what might happen to him or his family and he did what he had to do."

"Yeah, okay," Victor understood but was lacking in empathy for Joe. All of the terrible things he had heard about this man, drug smuggling and connections to organized crime among them, made him believe he was full of it, even from beyond the grave.

"There's something he wants to say to you Victor."

"What is it."

"It's time to let this go," she said, "let it go." Victor closed his eyes and let out a sigh. He and Amanda walked back to the car. Once inside the medium said she agreed with Joe. This was the end of their journey. Another chapter was ending.

Slowly Victor drove out of St. Peter's. He said goodbye to the Lady of the Dunes, he said goodbye to Susan Perry, and finally, he said goodbye to Chief Meads. Victor knew as he exited back onto Route 6 that he was likely to never return to St. Peter's.

Before he left Provincetown later that night Victor made it a point to visit the police department. He planned to leave them all of his notes from the production of the film. Even if Victor could not solve the murder via his film he hoped that the police might find some interesting new leads from his notes.

He walked in and found an older woman sitting behind a desk. She was the dispatcher and the only person Victor saw. He stated who he was and that he was looking to leave his Lady of the Dunes notes at the station. The dispatcher told Victor he could not leave anything there. She said it was best to email the detective working on the case.

Victor tried to remain cordial. He told the dispatcher that the detective had never returned any of his phone calls. She said there was nothing she could do. That was it. His visit to the police had been a bust. Victor knew he had done all he could to involve law enforcement in the process of the film as a courtesy.

Exiting the station Victor knew for certain he would not be returning. It was another chapter ending. All that was left was the Provincetown premiere of the film and Victor was throwing in the towel.

The late afternoon sky began to cast a golden shadow across Provincetown. The water in the harbor was still as glass. Victor soaked in the scenery and cracked a weary smile. Provincetown really was a beautifully unique place. He got to the Provincetown Theater an hour and a half early to make sure he had a parking spot in the back. The plan was to give his speech and fade into the sunset.

So much had happened in the last year-plus. After parking Victor stood by the side of Bradford Street looking from one end to the other. He thought about all of the people that had been a part of his life during that time. Victor thought back to those who recommended he work on a Lady of the Dunes project. There were the initial few that gave him the financial support to get the film off the ground.

Victor could not help but get a little misty-eyed as he thought about how Nancy Meads and the Meads Family had vouched for him and opened so many doors. They didn't have to do that. Their belief in his work helped him when he felt like he was hitting roadblocks.

Then of course there was Maura who had been there through thick and thin. From the 'restricted' phone calls to letters from serial killers, she had supported Victor on his journey. It would be good for him to step back from being a film producer for a bit to just be a husband and a father.

People began arriving. Victor grabbed a drink from the bar and made the rounds. Dennis Minsky, the New York psychic, Tiffany the spychic, and a good portion of the Meads Family, all came out to see the fruits of Victor's labor.

Christopher Setterlund arrived. He said he had parked a mile away which didn't bode well for a long dark walk back later on. Victor introduced him to some of the people there. Setterlund said he was happy to put faces with the names of people in the book.

Victor led Christopher into the theater and introduced him to Liza Rodman and her husband. He then retreated to the lobby. Victor was ready to go. This was the final chapter that needed to end.

It was a few minutes after seven when Victor was introduced onto the stage. Victor spoke about the reasons he had created the film. He mentioned going from not having a clue what a 'lady in the dunes' was, to gaining the proper perspective on the person behind the case. Victor said he did his best to honor the Lady of the Dunes and to validate the faith put in him by so many, specifically the Meads Family.

True to his word Victor then called out Christopher Setterlund. He asked him to stand and mentioned the book he was writing. Victor joked that the premiere was the last chapter so if anybody spoke to him they'd likely be in the book. Next to Christopher a young man named Josh, the boyfriend of Chief

Meads' granddaughter Emily, perked up and leaned over to introduce himself. This got a laugh from the sold-out crowd.

Victor as he had done the previous afternoon left the spotlight and the Lady of the Dunes stepped into it. However, this time was different. As the lights dimmed and the Robert Frost poem began to be read Victor made his escape. The sound of his film faded as he exited the front door into the chilly dusk air. This was the last chapter that was ending. He had done all he could to bring the Lady of the Dunes and her case back to the forefront of people's minds.

There was no reason for the case not to be solved. That being said, Victor had carried the baton as far as he wanted to. It was time for someone else to pick it up.

Still, before rounding the corner to find his car Victor paused for a moment and looked back at the theater. What was next for the Lady of the Dunes? He took a deep breath and let out a sigh.

"Goodbye for now dear Lady."

"They're having a press conference," a familiar voice excitedly shouted. It was the New York psychic sounding out of breath.

"What do you mean a press conference?" Victor asked with confusion.

"Something about details pertaining to the oldest unsolved murder in Massachusetts. It has to be the Lady of the Dunes!"

It was early on Halloween, a Monday, and Victor was blindsided by this breaking news. Months had passed since the documentary had premiered and although Victor had moved on to other projects the Lady of the Dunes still had a spot in his soul.

Once he did his research on social media Victor saw the press conference news was true. State law enforcement, the FBI, and the District Attorney's Office were holding an 11 am press conference where they would indeed share the identity of the Lady of the Dunes.

Victor's phone began ringing repeatedly, as would be the case for the next week or so. He answered a few calls but mostly let voicemail do the heavy lifting. A call to Christopher was placed.

The author was in the town of Orleans getting two new tires for his car. He was in shock at the upcoming announcement. Though nobody was able to make it to Boston in time for the press conference they all did their best to watch it. Christopher later told Victor that he fittingly watched the press conference on his phone at the beach surrounded by dunes.

Victor stared in stunned silence as the press conference began and the camera zoomed in on a collage of photos. None of the four photos shown looked familiar. Although each had a slightly different appearance it was obvious it was the same woman. Then he saw the name.

"Ruth Marie Terry," Victor whispered. It wasn't Ann Dolce. It wasn't Lee Sherry. It wasn't a Morgan, Helen, anything with the - en. The press conference consisted of four members of law enforcement and they did indeed announce that Ruth Marie Terry was the famed Lady of the Dunes. She finally had her name back.

How did she get her name back? Forensic genealogy, or as they referred to it, forensic genetic genealogy. Victor gave a half smirk as he heard the law enforcement admit to using the methods he and many others had been begging for. This fact was validation for the DNA Doe Project and Dr. Glynn who had been a part of the documentary.

He was torn. Seeing the Lady of the Dunes as a real flesh and blood person was shocking. However not having the name match something Victor had researched was slightly disappointing.

Perhaps the greatest shock came not from the name but the backstory. Ruth Marie Terry was not young and single in her early twenties as had been thought by Victor and many who worked on the documentary. She was older, in her late thirties, and to top it off was a wife and mother to a son. The death of the Lady of the Dunes was sad and tragic when she was a young, single woman. The death of Ruth Marie Terry was all the more heartbreaking knowing she had left behind a child.

In the hours that followed the press conference, Victor's life was a whirlwind. The spark had been reignited with the news of the identification of the Lady of the Dunes. It was as if he was back shooting the documentary all over again. Through all of the phone calls that came pouring in one stood out. It was from Agent Z.

Victor had not heard from them since they abruptly cut off communication a year earlier. The conversation was brief but poignant. Agent Z had called Victor to offer congratulations. They said in no uncertain terms that Victor's Lady of the Dunes project had influenced the identification of Ruth Marie Terry.

He was unsure how to react to Agent Z's statement. They continued by adding that they didn't know if it was the film itself, or the various cages Victor had rattled during production, but the small-time filmmaker had made serious waves that necessitated action from law enforcement.

Agent Z would not be the only person to insist that Victor had contributed to helping identify the Lady of the Dunes. They were, however, the one with the deepest connections to law enforcement. Agent Z's phone call gave Victor some validation for his work. He knew that those working on the case would never give him any credit and he was fine with it.

In the days that followed the press conference, Victor began rearranging everything he had thought he knew as more information began coming out. Ruth Marie Terry had been born in Whitwell, Tennessee. She had a son and had been married at least twice that were known. She also had connections to Michigan, California, and naturally Massachusetts. It was a connection to Nevada though that seemed to have the greatest impact on the murder case.

In February 1974 Ruth Marie married a man named Guy Muldavin in Reno, Nevada. Muldavin quickly became a person of interest in Ruth Marie's murder. The man, described as an antique dealer, had previous brushes with the law including suspicions of murder. Muldavin's second wife Manzanita Mearns and her daughter Dolores Ann had both been murdered in 1960.

Despite bits of human tissue being found in a septic tank at Muldavin's then-home, he was never charged with the two murders. Muldavin had several aliases including Raoul Guy Rockwell and Guy Muldavin Rockwell. He died in 2002.

Victor wondered how Ruth Marie ended up in the dunes of Provincetown. What was her connection to Cape Cod? The answer could have been through Guy Muldavin's father, Albert. In the 1940s and 1950s, Albert Muldavin owned a large amount of real estate in Provincetown, specifically around Bradford Street. It was not enough to definitively connect Guy to Provincetown, however, it was not out of the realm of possibility that Albert Muldavin had some contacts in the area that his son could have taken advantage of.

As had occurred many times over the life of the Lady of the Dunes project Victor found himself fully engrossed in the case after believing he had closed that door. He, along with Christopher, did a bit of detective work as they tried to piece together Ruth Marie's life.

Days passed and the initial national coverage of the identification of the Lady of the Dunes began to quiet down. Victor felt that there would likely not be any more new information being shared with the public, at least not until other potential suspects were named.

One thing that piqued Victor's interest was the fact that there was a roughly ten-year gap in Ruth Marie's life where nothing was known of her or her whereabouts. This, combined with the fact that she had used many aliases, brought some information from the documentary process back to light.

Ruth Marie had gone by the names: Teri Marie Vizina, Terry M. Vizina, and Teri Shannon. Could she have also been Ann Dolce or Helen Dennison? Could she have been known as Lauren or Anna as Tiffany and Amanda had mentioned in their table-tipping? What other potential leads that the documentary dug up could end up being true? What did she do for work during those ten years? Could she have visited Massachusetts during that time? The Combat Zone? Although she had been identified there was still so much about Ruth Marie that was unknown.

Victor and Christopher had their detective hats on. They wondered about the last name Vizina. Was Ruth Marie married a third time to a man with the last name Vizina? Victor began searching social media and found a thread featuring people who had known Ruth Marie, family and friends.

He was startled to see a particular comment mentioning seeing Ruth Marie and Guy Muldavin in Provincetown shortly before she would have been murdered. They were seen driving in an over-sand vehicle, either a Jeepster or Volkswagen Thing. Those vehicles had the ability to traverse the access roads to the dune shacks and the capacity to haul a body out there without difficulty.

Despite the inability to interrogate Guy Muldavin it became more apparent to Victor, and naturally law enforcement, that Muldavin was the prime suspect. He either murdered Ruth Marie, or had someone else do it for him. The fact that in the years after she disappeared Muldavin's story was that Ruth Marie had run away with the Jim Jones cult and died in the Jonestown Massacre in 1978 only cemented the opinion. However there was not much more that Victor could do.

It was at this time that Victor began to think about the final closure. He needed to go back out to the dunes, to the spot where Ruth Marie was found, with all of this new information. Victor needed to say goodbye to the Lady of the Dunes, goodbye to Ruth Marie Terry. Christopher was on board to go visit the drop site in the Provincetown dunes. He had never been to the spot.

The walk into the dunes took place close to Thanksgiving. Victor and Christopher spent the drive to Provincetown discussing the case and what other revelations they thought could end up coming out. By this point, Victor had successfully contacted Ruth Marie's son and they had made plans to meet in person come spring. Victor had even sent him a copy of the documentary to show all of the care and respect that had been shown to their mother. Christopher sent an unfinished copy of the book manuscript to him as well.

The morning was bright and sunny. Victor led the way as he had made the trek through the remote sands several times. Christopher lagged behind snapping photos and shooting videos. Victor made him promise to not detail where the drop site was. He remained true to his word to not exploit the Lady of the Dunes.

Forty-five minutes of walking down access roads, over rolling dunes, past the venerable C-Scape dune shack, and through scrub pine forest, led the pair to one of the most infamous spots in all of New England. There they stood where the Lady of the Dunes, Ruth Marie Terry, had been left back in July 1974.

Christopher remarked that it was so close to a pair of dune shacks, yet so far away from them as well. The patch of scrub pines was sheltered just enough that it was plain to see how a body could be placed there and not found for weeks. Christopher said it was both horrifying and humbling to be standing in that spot.

From his jacket pocket, Victor produced a blue bandana much like had been found with Ruth Marie on that hot July afternoon. The filmmaker in him was big on symbolism so Victor tied the bandana to a tree as a way to mark the importance of that patch of ground.

"Do you think anyone will know what it means?" Christopher asked. Victor shrugged.

"So few people visit this spot, and even fewer likely know about its significance." The majority of the walk out to the drop site had been eerily quiet. Now as they stood where the Lady of the Dunes had been found the air was filled with the somber squeak of a pair of weathered tree branches rubbing against each other in the breeze.

Before heading back to the car Victor produced a metal canister from another pocket. He then scooped some sand from the area. He had a reason for doing so.

The final stop was to St. Peter's Cemetery to pay their respects to Ruth Marie Terry. This time felt different. Victor made the rounds to several graves important to the Lady of the Dunes story as well as the stage that was Provincetown in the late 1960s and early 1970s. He paid respects to Susan Perry, Leslie Metcalfe who had found Ruth Marie on that July afternoon, and of course Chief James Meads who worked so hard for so long trying to find the resolution that had finally arrived in 2022.

The most pleasant surprise awaiting Victor and Christopher at St. Peter's was the addition of an engraved stone at the grave of the Lady of the Dunes. Resting on top of the original marker was a stone roughly a foot in diameter. Engraved into it were the three most satisfying words Victor could have seen: Ruth Marie Terry.

A stone with her real name on it was what Victor had wanted for her and that was what he got. At that moment it mattered less about how it happened and more that it had happened. Victor pulled the canister of sand from his jacket and poured about half onto the marker beside the new stone.

"Symbolism," Victor said with a smile. The rest of the sand he said he was going to save in case Ruth Marie's son wanted it. A rush of emotion mixed with nostalgia washed over Victor as he stared at the grave he had visited so many times over the previous nearly two years.

He had met so many people that had become important to him. He hadn't been 'chasing ghosts' as some had suggested and he certainly didn't just forget about it and walk away. Victor had stuck it out until the bitter end and fought the good fight. At that moment as he stared at the grave he knew that what he had done had been important and that he had made an impact.

"Ruth Marie Terry," Victor said as he ran his gloved fingers over the engraved stone, "she finally has her name back."

Epilogue, Victor/Frank's Letter to Ruth Marie Terry(Lady of the Dunes)

To my Lady,

I visited the dunes last Saturday to say goodbye. I hiked out to where you were found, left something behind to know I was there, and took some sand to give to your Son.

For the last 2 years, I have invested myself in your story. I gave what I could so one day your name would be returned.

With all the names that we found, I for one was shocked to find out your name was Ruth. Part of me was hoping that you were named Lauren or Morgan to give the documentary more merit for hitting the nail on the head. That we did not.

Another part of me wanted you to be Ann Dolce. Whether it be a nickname or even a stage name, I saw you center stage in your youth as the object of affection and desire. This too, as far as I know, was not your name.

For almost half a century you had the title of Lady. Throughout the years you have earned the title as you became a legend, a mystery, and folklore as the years rolled by.

Now, you have been given your name, and from what I have been told you will be finally leaving Provincetown to be relocated to your childhood home in Tennessee to be laid to rest next to your mother and father.

To remind you, and to state to the reader, you were loved by many in the Provincetown community who kept your story alive. They gave you a place to rest until your Family could be found. For decades many in this community kept your story going. Local journalists, authors, law enforcement, and others who would leave flowers at your grave. You were the most visited grave at St Peter's. Many have read your story and have waited for this day to come.

Now, I will say goodbye to you and thank you for being a footnote in your story. Your journey is coming to a close as I move on to the next.

No longer lost to the world and no longer a nameless victim, you are still present in the dunes that gave you your name. With every gust of sea breeze that is sensed, every ocean wave that can be heard, and with every grain of sand that is felt, the Lady will be present.

Sincerely,
Your storyteller
Victor/Frank

Final Note From the Author

I am a proud Cape Codder. My family is twelve generations deep on these shores. As a child of the 1980's I grew up with the story of the Lady of the Dunes. Over time she became less a person and more a myth or a legend.

When it comes down to it. When you strip away the mystery and the brutality of her last moments on this earth. When you strip away the questions and the decades without sufficient answers. When you remove all of the noise surrounding her it comes down to the fact that Ruth Marie Terry, for decades known as the Lady of the Dunes, was a real person.

Ruth was someone's child, she was someone's sister. Ruth was someone's mother. She had a hometown in Tennessee with family and friends from that hometown. She had a story long before her vicious end became her story. Much like Frank/Victor, my goal in writing this book was not so much to find the people responsible for the murder. It was not to point fingers and make accusations against those that could have solved this mystery since 1974. No, my goal, my hope, was to give the Lady of the Dunes her name back.

Although Ruth became somewhat of a celebrity in the afterlife, with her grave constantly overflowing with trinkets of affection, she deserved what the rest of us have: a name. The Lady of the Dunes deserved to be called what her parents named her. Ruth deserved a stone with her name marking her final resting place.

Searching For the Lady of the Dunes as a book at times felt like living in a mystery movie playing out before my eyes. However, I never lost sight of the goal begun by Frank/Victor and continued by myself, to give the Lady of the Dunes her name back. Even if this book, and the documentary that preceded it, did not achieve this on their own, I truly believe our work helped Ruth get her name back.

More so than a chance to solve Cape Cod's most enduring mystery I considered this a chance to do right by the Lady of the Dunes and her family. I thought of if she had been my child, sister, niece, or friend. I would hope someone would care enough to ask why. Why does she not have a true name?

In closing, I say this to you, Ruth Marie Terry, our dear Lady. I hope that Frank/Victor and I have done right by you. I am so proud and honored to have played even the most minute part in returning your name to you. Wherever your earthly remains end up, whether back home in Tennessee, or on the grounds of St. Peter's, you will always be a part of Provincetown, a part of Cape Cod. Goodbye Ruth Marie Terry, goodbye Lady of the Dunes.

Acknowledgments

Thank you first and foremost to Frank Durant(Victor Franko). You believed me worthy of taking your documentary, and all of the research you did on it, and crafting it into a deserving book, and for that, I am eternally grateful.

This opportunity as an author came through hard work and determination. That would not have been possible without the support and belief of those closest to me. My mother Laurie. My siblings: Katie, Matt, Lindsay, and Ashley. My nieces and nephews: Kaleigh, Emma, Liam, Landon, Lucas, and Sylvie. My aunts, uncles, cousins, and those who are like fathers: Serpa and Maui. The friends who are like family: Steve, Barry, John, Shayna, Crystal and Adam, KO, Dawn and Monique, Deanna and Michael. The great Bill DeSousa-Mauk who I owe so much in my writing career, and Wendy who started me on the journey that led to this.

This book would not be possible without those who worked with Frank or were willing to be a part of the investigation itself. It begins with Nancy Meads, James Jr., and Michael. Thank you to the five mediums who provided so much beautiful, deep spiritual knowledge and information. Thank you to those that worked on or appeared in the documentary and therefore the book including: Frank Santin and Sue Smith, Dr. Claire Glynn, Steven Desroches, Dennis Minsky, Dr. Glenn Kinahan, and Jeanette de Beauvoir.

Thank you to those I met through the work on this book like Liza Rodman, Kimberly Dudik, and others.

Thank you to those who appear in this book but have had their names changed to protect their anonymity.

Thank you to Chief James Meads Sr. who laid the groundwork for Frank's documentary and this book with his tireless work and research into the Lady of the Dunes case for years.

About the Author

Christopher Setterlund is a proud 12th-generation Cape Codder and comes from a large family. He has previously written seven books. The In My Footsteps travel trilogy through Schiffer Publishing, a Cape Cod history trilogy through Arcadia Publishing which includes Historic Restaurants, Cape Cod Nights, and Iconic Hotels and Motels, and most recently Cape Cod: The Heart and Soul Beyond the Beach through Fonthill Media. In addition he hosts the In My Footsteps Podcast. Lastly he is also a Certified Personal Trainer and Medical Fitness Specialist.

References

1. Boston Globe Online Newspaper Archives,
www.proquest.com/hnpnewyorkbostonglobe/index?
accountid=9675&groupid=107814&parentSessionId=2k
%2FCsNLasFBnTYthhWnvM0TVaCwYwqX9OQd9bDhwcmU
%3D. Accessed 20 Aug. 2022.

2. Manso, Peter. Ptown *: Art, Sex, and Money on the Outer Cape.*
New York, Scribner, 2003.

3. Damore, Leo. *In His Garden.* 1990.

4. Rodman, Liza. Jordan, Jennifer. The *BABYSITTER : My*
Summers with a Serial Killer. S.L., Atria Books, 2022.

5. Hanson, David W., et al. "Judy." *IMDb*, 1 July 1970,
www.imdb.com/title/tt0222078/. Accessed 20 Aug. 2022.

6. WRITER, KAREN JEFFREY, STAFF. "Hadden Clark
Returned to Cape to Search for Graves." *Cape Cod Times,*
www.capecodtimes.com/story/news/2000/04/10/hadden-clark-
returned-to-cape/51010606007/. Accessed 20 Aug. 2022.

7. "Interesting Photos Glimpse into Everyday Life of the Combat
Zone, Boston in the 1970s." *Thevintagenews*, 25 Dec. 2015,
www.thevintagenews.com/2015/12/25/42749/?chrome=1.
Accessed 20 Aug. 2022.

8. "Home - Provincetown History Preservation
Project." *Www.provincetownhistoryproject.com,*
www.provincetownhistoryproject.com/. Accessed 20 Aug. 2022.

9. "Building Provincetown 2020." *Building Provincetown 2020*, buildingprovincetown2020.org/. Accessed 20 Aug. 2022.

10. UPI. (n.d.). *Guy Rockwell Muldavin: FBI nabs murder suspect - UPI archives*. UPI. Retrieved January 29, 2023, from https://www.upi.com/Archives/1960/12/01/Once-wealthy-antique-dealer-sought-in-disappearance-of-wife/5491667577736/